Adonai Zeus Shekhinah Eli___ O___ ___ ___ Buddha
Wyame Hel Rama Mitra Ode___ ___ ___ ___Het
Heru Agni Cagn Thor Br___ ___ ___ ___ner
Lugaba Papang Diana Al-Rah___ ___ ___one
Yoma' Tirawa Atius Gane___ ___ ___gua
Quetzalcoatl Hamakom Ribbono shel-olam Shaddai
Atibruku Moma YH Bunjil Harahaman Watauinaiwa
Sarasw___ kaong

THE DIVINE MOSAIC

Tonan___ Head
Olodu___ Heru
Nurrundere Daramilun Adon Ca Vishnu HaYotzeir
Hecate Chi Musubi Hintubuhet Ausar Ti Ubusuna
Nanderuvucu Erishkigal Laxha Yahweh Brahman
Tsui-goab Ometeotl Osiris Aum Huitzilopochtli
Surya Elohim Nyankopon-Onyankopon Rudra Ilu
Woden Great Spirit Lesa Boyjerh El Dan Gongoro
Poseidon Chineke Nhialic Aciek Kari Auset Tcuwut
Makai Wakantanka Inari Ha-Qadosh barukh hu'
Tara Krishna Avaloket-iswara Rabb Goryo Qat Oke
Nurunderi Indra Shang-ti Amaterasu Ohmikami
Kannon Quan Yin Ise Lakshmi Awonawilona Bast
Omecihuatl Ruhanga Kosane Sophia Dionysus Ixchel
Mawu Ra Ardanariswara Oluwa Deng Hanuman
uNkulunkulu Kanobo Ngai Shamayim Cybele Dakini
Nataraj Pachamama Susanoo Katonda Avlukpo Eloah
Isis Temaukel Eleda Gaia Laxmi Mahmanmu-rok
Odin El-al Herukhuti Viracocha Marduk Ashira Biral
Shaddai Dzingbe Djohu-ma-di-hutu Astarte Ndengei
Koyatu Baha'u'llah Marrigan Baiame Om Pelepelewa
Durga Orisha Nyame Techaronhiawakhon Chukwu
Uvolovu Brahman Nephtys Ha-Maqom Tehuti Maat
Digambara Val Tik Chaitanya Amana Kwoth Num
Colok Nabango Fumeripitsj Shiva Varuna Lukanga
Bala Atibluku Karu Allah Sing Nainuema Artemis
Kartikeya Kuanyin Yelafaz T'ien Baal Shakti
Athena Olorun Nemesis Sheela-na-Gig Bhavartarini
Jesus Horus Izanagi Sebek Waq Ishtar Ti Seker
BegoTanutanu Sat Nam Kali Mirirul Bhavatarini
Tsui-goab Hatzur Brahman Ubusuna Tonantzin
YHVH Apollo Nana God Almighty Hu Vishnu Om

Another women's collection by Theresa King:

The Spiral Path: Explorations in Women's Spirituality
(Yes International Publishers)

THE DIVINE MOSAIC

WOMEN'S IMAGES
OF THE SACRED OTHER

Edited by
Theresa King

Yes International Publishers
Saint Paul, Minnesota

Library of Congress Cataloging in Publication Data

The Divine mosaic: women's images of the sacred other / edited by
  Theresa King
      p.   cm.
      Includes bibliographical references.
      ISBN 0-936663-10-3 : $15.95
      1. God—Comparative studies. 2. Women and religion.   I. King.
Theresa.
BL205.D58   1994
291.2'11—dc20   93-44760
                                               CIP

The editor would like to thank the following for their permission to reprint:

Excerpt from Judy Chicago, © 1979, reprinted with permission of the publishr. It is available in an illuminated poster from Through the Flower, P.O. Box 8138, Santa Fe, NM 87504.

Permission to reprint "Feminine Aspects of Divinity" is granted by Pendle Hill Publications, Wallingford, PA 19086.

"God Is a Verb" is an expansion of the chapter from *Womanpriest: A Personal Odyssey* by Alla Renée Bozarth, revised edition, Lura Media, © 1988, used with the author's permission.

"The Dark Devi" © by Kathleen Alexander. Reprinted with permission of the author.

Excerpt from the poem "The Goddess is Me" by Charlotte Kasl. Reprinted with permission of the author.

Yes International Publishers,
1317 Summit Avenue, St. Paul, MN 55105-2602.
  Phone: 612-645-6808.

Printed in the United States of America.

FIRST YES INTERNATIONAL PAPERBACK EDITION PUBLISHED IN 1994.

For my mother and father
who first showed me
the face of God.

Contents

Editor's Preface

Symbols, metaphors, and images are essential to human beings. Through them we both express and learn about reality. The more encompassing an image or symbol is, the more we can know about that reality.

If we wanted to know about a historical woman, for example, we could study a portrait of her. Through the media of paint and canvas, we could see her expression, her coloring, the shape of her eyes and lips, the style of her clothing, and from there imagine what she might have been like. If we were to examine a three-dimensional image of the same woman, we would be able to learn other things about her as well. We could tell her size and shape, her carriage, her grace, the pitch of her jaw, the strength in her arms. We could walk around the statue to experience all the angles and curves of her form, perhaps comparing her to ourselves and noting similarities and differences. We might then leave the exhibit feeling that we "know" the woman.

Of course, we would always keep in mind that the painting or statue, however well executed, is someone else's interpretation of the real woman and not the woman herself. Attempting to know any reality solely from its image yields either a limited knowledge or a confused idea of the whole.

So it is with divinity. The human mind wants to know God; the human mind knows most easily through images. Thus, over the span of human existence, people have attempted to image the Sacred One with simple drawings, primitive figures of clay, descriptions in religious scripture, stained-glass windows, inspired paintings, statues worthy of Cathedral or museum.

Religion, however, has historically claimed to present the only true image of the divine to its followers. Its sacred books have imagined God in thunderous prose and inspirational poetry. And over the centuries, thousands of religious authorities have revealed the sacred for us with certitude, if not with accuracy.

Some religious denominations claim to convey all aspects of God in a single image—rather like the distorted woman in a Picasso painting which attempts to show every side simultaneously.

Other religions claim to show all aspects of God in many images—rather like a room crammed full of statues of the same woman carved by a variety of sculptors.

But have these images yielded more than limited insight or a confused idea of the divine? Have they given us the false security of thinking we know the Unknowable? Have they inspired us to personal growth, informed our world with peace and justice, helped us relate to each other and to our creator with love and gratitude?

With the emerging spiritual power of women at the closing of this century, it has become obvious that the traditional images of God are insufficient. Women have voiced their dismay at the images of divinity used in sacred ritual and claimed by male authority to be exclusive and solely true. "If this is the image of God," they ask, "then why does it cause me such pain?"

Images of God often do not speak to the hearts of women, to the center from which and to which relationship flows like a silver thread, spiraling out to the divine and coiling back in to the self, turning inward to self and unfurling outward to the Sacred Other. Traditional God symbols do not show women that their body is sacred, that their life-giving and nurturing nature is indeed "made in the image of God." The face of God we show our children does not reflect back the faces of the children: brown and black, red and yellow, and every shade in between. It does not help us realize our connectedness to each other; it does not show us our connection to the rest of creation. Many of the images passed from teacher to student, from parent to child, from authority to subordinate no longer touch the point of instant recognition, the point where knowledge turns to love and hope and joy.

The women who form this collection have struggled with this problem. For each of them, the idea of God is not a casual question; it informs their lives in all its aspects. Some are aware of the transcendence of the divine while others search for divine immanence. Some have evolved new, compelling images that speak to their woman-ness, their values, and their place in the world; others have wrestled with a traditional image until it yielded deep meaning in their lives.

Throughout the telling, it appears that humanity's expression of God is like an intricate, yet incomplete, mosaic. Each little piece is itself an image revealing one particular characteristic of divinity manifested through one singular cultural or spiritual experience. When all the pieces are carefully placed side by side, the mosaic provides a glimpse of God as revealed in human experience and creative consciousness up to the current time.

Beautiful in its unfolding to the mind and heart, this divine mosaic is still only a limited portrait of the Sacred Other, not the Sacred Other itself. There will be more mosaic pieces as generations continue to grapple with the problem of God's image. Perhaps some central pieces will be moved to the outer edges as no longer so important as they once were. Perhaps some as yet undiscovered pieces will hold central position for a while. Perhaps humanity will long be in the position of moving and refitting the pieces into an ever-changing whole.

Yet it is by studying the mosaic, piece by piece, that we may be able to vivify with love and awareness that selfsame connecting thread that binds us to each other and to the Source of all.

Adonai Zeus Shekhinah Elim Ogun Kat Buddha
Wyame Hel Rama Mitra Odomankoma Jupiter Het
Heru Agni Cagn Thor Brahma Tangaroa Father
Lugaba Papang Diana Al-Rahman Cerridwen Ahone
Yoma' Tirawa Atius Ganesha El Mungan-ngua
Quetzalcoatl Hamakom ddai
Atibruku Moma YH Bunj aiwa
Saraswati Inanna Miriru aong
Tonantzin Yuskeha Bha Head
Olodumare Shyama Ekv Heru
Nurrundere Daramilun tzeir
Hecate Chi Musubi Hin suna
Nanderuvucu Erishkigal man
Tsui-goab Ometeotl Os chtli
Surya Elohim Nyankop Ilu
Woden Great Spirit Les goro
Poseidon Chineke Nhialic uwul

Feminine
Aspects
of
Divinity

Erminie Huntress
Lantero, Ph.D.

Makai Wakantanka Inari Ha-Qadosh barukh hu'
Tara Krishna Avaloket-iswara Rabb Goryo Qat Oke
Nurunderi Indra Shang-ti Amaterasu Ohmikami
Kannon Quan Yin Ise Lakshmi Awonawilona Bast
Omecihuatl Ruhanga Kosane Sophia Dionysus Ixchel
Mawu Ra Ardanariswara Oluwa Deng Hanuman
uNkulunkulu Kanobo Ngai Shamayim Cybele Dakini
Nataraj Pachamama Susanoo Katonda Avlukpo Eloah
Isis Temaukel Eleda Gaia Laxmi Mahmanmu-rok
Odin El-al Herukhuti Viracocha Marduk Ashira Biral
Shaddai Dzingbe Djohu-ma-di-hutu Astarte Ndengei
Koyatu Baha'u'llah Marrigan Baiame Om Pelepelewa
Durga Orisha Nyame Techaronhiawakhon Chukwu
Uvolovu Brahman Nephtys Ha-Maqom Tehuti Maat
Digambara Val Tik Chaitanya Amana Kwoth Num
Colok Nabango Fumeripitsj Shiva Varuna Lukanga
Bala Atibluku Karu Allah Sing Nainuema Artemis
Kartikeya Kuanyin Yelafaz T'ien Baal Shakti
Athena Olorun Nemesis Sheela-na-Gig Bhavartarini
Jesus Horus Izanagi Sebek Waq Ishtar Ti Seker
BegoTanutanu Sat Nam Kali Mirirul Bhavatarini
Tsui-goab Hatzur Brahman Ubusuna Tonantzin
YHVH Apollo Nana God Almighty Hu Vishnu Om

I n recent years there has been growing recognition that the religious language of the Judeo-Christian tradition is over-weighted with masculine symbolism. The transition took shape in an era of patriarchal domination, first in Hebraic and Jewish society, then in the Roman Empire. As women today become aware of their femininity as a major style of being human, they quite properly resent this. Male theologians have pointed out that masculine pronouns are used for God simply because some pronouns have to be used; the statement is annoying, if also reasonably correct. Christianity always taught that sexual distinctions are not really applicable to the transcendent mystery we call God. But the manward aspect of that mystery, the perennial experiences of divine calling, providence, shepherding, communion, made it necessary to continue to speak of God in personal terms. 'He' is at least more adequate than 'It.'

Even prior to the twentieth century, however, there were straws in the wind pointing to feminine rebellion. Mother Ann Lee, founder of the Shakers (1736-1784), claimed to be the second appearing of Christ, 'Ann the Word,' sent to complement the work of Jesus. The Lord Jesus stood before her in prison and became one with her in form and spirit, "my head and my husband, and I have no other." She had already found her earthly marriage intolerable. Mary Baker Eddy, who married three times, also claimed a direct revelation but in less personal terms. In a newspaper interview late in life (1901), she declared that "the manhood and womanhood of God have already been revealed in a degree through Christ Jesus and Christian Science, his two witnesses."[1] "In divine Science we have not as much authority for considering God masculine, as we have for considering him feminine, for love imparts the clearest idea of deity."[2] Her spiritual interpretation of the Lord's Prayer, opening with "Our Father-Mother God," is used in Christian Science services and must effectively condition any Scientist's religious consciousness.

Mary Baker Eddy went to extremes in denying the reality of evil and the material world, but if we find her balanced view of a Father-Mother God right and valuable, and if we take a close second look at our tradition, both biblical and post-biblical, we will find both. Masculine symbols are dominant and male theologians have frozen them into patterns of abstraction; but the feminine images are also there, awaiting that fuller appreciation for which we were not ready till now. What is needed is to redress the balance by restoring the feminine to its proper importance in the over-all pattern. There is such a charter available in Genesis 1:27:

> God created man in his own image, in the image of God
> created he him, male and female created he them.

While the rest of the creation chapter is written in stately prose, this verse is poetic in form, perhaps quoted from a still older tradition. Hebrew poetry follows rules of parallelism, as illustrated in the Psalms. The thought of the first line is repeated in slightly different words in the second, and the third if there is one, or if a further thought is added it is still something implicit in the first statement. "Male and female" is not a change of subject; if he created man male and female, it was because bisexuality somehow belongs to his own image.

This fact was recognized by early rabbinical commentators, one of whom concluded that God made Adam androgynous, later separating him into Adam and Eve. A parallel myth of man's original androgyncity appears in Plato's *Symposium*, where it symbolizes a lost state of wholeness. In our own time it is recognized that while individuals belong to one sex or the other, we are all androgynous in the sense of having both male and female hormones, as well as potential character traits traditionally associated with both sexes.

Some decades ago a Roman Catholic missionary, Joseph Winthuis, returned to Europe from the South Pacific and caused a stir by his diagnosis of the indifferent success of Christian missions over the years, with the social conflicts and dislocations they produced. The complementarity of the two sexes, he said, dominates the whole world view of these peoples. That a solitary male God without a consort, incomplete, should claim to be a father who begot a son, strikes the primitive as nonsense; and it seems equally bizarre to the mentality of sophisticated Far Eastern cultures. Psychotherapists find that even in the West, many suffer neurotic distortions from the lack of an adequate concept or symbol of the feminine aspect of divinity; the over-emphasis on masculine values blocks their capacity for relationship and their road to wholeness.

The Contrasexual Balance

Archeology yields abundant evidence that from Paleolithic times, from the Mediterranean lands to the Indus Valley, the ulti-

mate source of life was felt to be maternal. Religion centered in the
mysteries of birth, fecundity, and nutrition. The earliest symbols are
crude female figurines suggesting pregnancy, no doubt used as fertility charms or amulets to assist childbirth. Burial customs in some
places also indicate a belief that the dead would be reborn from the
earth. To the primitive mind, woman was the producer of life; the
role of the male partner was not immediately apparent.

In the Neolithic period the maternal principle was personified as
either a single Great Mother or several goddesses with specialized
roles. The Snake-Goddess of Minoan Crete was depicted as Earth-
Mother, Mountain-Mother, Mistress of Trees, Lady of Wild Beasts,
and Goddess of the Hunt. With the rise of agriculture and cattle-
raising in Mesopotamia and Egypt, goddesses such as Ishtar and
Isis evolved. The essential role of the male spouse was now
recognized, but in Western Asia God was usually subordinate to the
Queen of Heaven, mother of gods and men, as her servant or son.
She was the effective agent in the rebirth of vegetation and the
increase of animals or humans; she was the Cow Goddess who
nurtured kings with her milk; she was also the Goddess of the Dead,
or else her sister. Earth goddesses were usually also moon goddesses.
There were triune goddesses representing the stages of feminine life
as the maiden, the mother, and the aging hag-witch, corresponding
to the crescent, full, and waning phases of the moon. The Greek
Hecate was also defined in triune terms, as Queen of Heaven,
Earth, and Hades.

In the cosmopolitan Greco-Roman period, the goddess presided
over the issues of life and death in a new way. There was widespread
syncretism between the various local versions; a long, poetic passage
in Apuleius celebrates Isis as including them all. By this time the
communal and earthly fertility aspects had fallen into the
background. The so-called mystery religions offered symbolic roads
to an individual, spiritual type of salvation, release from the flesh
and rebirth into immortality. This transmutation took place in the
mysteries of Demeter at Eleusis and in Isiac cults throughout the
empire. The image of Isis especially was to influence the early-
medieval image of Mary; but this is getting ahead of our story.

Moses and the Hebrew prophets encountered matriarchal
religion at a time antedating these other-worldly refinements. The
indigenous mother-cult of Syria-Palestine was expressed in com-
paratively crude fertility rites, incompatible with the growing moral
sensitivity represented by the prophets. Over several centuries the
prophets carried on a heroic struggle to depose Baal and Astarte in
all forms, local or imported, to win Israel's exclusive loyalty to a

God disentangled from procreative processes. But even as they rejected divinization of the sex principle, they acknowledged a polarity of gender or 'contrasexuality' on the transcendental level in other ways.

The creation story in the first chapter of Genesis seems to be designed in deliberate contrast to the creation myths of Babylon. The battle led by the Sun-God, Marduk, against Mother Tiamat (the salt seas, the watery chaos, the primeval dragon), after which he constructs a universe out of her dead body—also the myths of Ishtar, the morally dubious goddess who produces all life from her own substance—are swept off the board. Instead, the one God serenely creates a cosmos by his word alone, unchallenged and unresisted. He makes it out of a water chaos called *tehom* (tiamat, the deep), but this is no goddess. Neither is the resultant earth. Sexuality and fertility are not his attributes but his inventions. Nature is separated off from God and made available for man's use according to divine command, even for man's 'dominion.'

Some Old Testament scholars see this story as a radical secularization of the earth; reduced to a mere creature, it is deprived of the holiness that earlier cultures revered. Critics of the Judeo-Christian tradition are right that it has been read that way, and opened a door not only to scientific investigation but to irresponsible exploitation of earth's resources. Nevertheless, the Bible still contains reverence and a sense of stewardship, and a sensitive reading of the Genesis chapter itself suggests that earth is holy, though in a way that was then entirely new.

Later the earth becomes involved in the tragedy of Adam and Eve. According to Genesis 3:17ff its original generosity is frustrated and blighted by God on their account; it did not occur to the writer that it might in the long run be done by man. Eve, the human 'mother of all living,' becomes the next feminine entity with whom God has to deal, this time not obedient but lured into estrangement. The story of our first parents' disobedience is a myth so subtle and rich in ambiguous overtones that even in these times of unbelief new literary treatments of it appear year by year. It may be, and should be, read experimentally in terms other than the traditional. Isn't a certain amount of disobedience necessary to a child's growth? Is the serpent really the devil, or something less sinister? Is God really so naive as to tell them not to put beans up to their noses and then be surprised when they do it or to feel himself threatened by their curiosity and lese-majeste? Or does he deliberately provoke the disobedience, in complicity with the serpent, because he wants to get the tortuous pilgrimage of human history under way, because whatever it costs, it will be worth it?

In any case, from the wandering sons of Eve he chooses himself a people. He devotes special attention to their deliverance from slavery; their rigorous education through Moses, the prophets, and attendant circumstances; their political development and over-throw; their spiritual refinement in the crucible of exile. The prophets speak of Israel as a son of Yahweh, but at more length as his unfaithful bride. The marital relation between Sky-God and Earth-Goddess, so basic to the fertility cult, is replaced by the mari-tal relation between an intensely ethical God and the community he loves. But the contrasexual balance gives way to precarious unbal-ance, because Israel is an adulteress. "She did not know that it was I who gave her the grain, the wine, and the oil," he mourns in Hosea 2:8, so she perennially falls back on the earlier-known, less demand-ing nature gods who care very little about personal morality or social justice. Furthermore, the two Hebrew kingdoms were so situated that they were driven to make repeated defensive alliances with one major power against another, which involved the accep-tance of their gods. This too was denounced by the prophets as adultery. Yet even as Israel suffers the whole brunt of Yahweh's wrath, and her existence as a free nation is ended, the prophets promise her survival in the Babylonian exile, reborn to a new and permanent faithfulness.

The post-exilic prophecies of the so-called Second Isaiah and his 'school' (Isa. 40-66) were written after a few Jews were back in Judah but many were widely dispersed. This man sees more clearly than any earlier prophet and lyrically proclaims not only that Israel must have no other Gods besides this one, but that only their God exists. (The Genesis creation story was written in the same century, ca. 500 B.C.) This God of incomparable power, beauty, and grace, the sole lord of a marvelous cosmos and of human history, is out to redeem not only Israel but all the world through Israel. The prophet speaks of Israel as the (masculine) servant, whose task it is to teach the world about God, but also speaks of Mother Jerusalem or Zion. Her warfare is ended and her sin pardoned (40:2); the lord has turned from his wrath and reaffirms an everlasting love for the 'wife of his youth' (54:6-8).

Chapter 62 rings the changes on the theme of triumphant marriage in several different aspects; nature, man, and God are caught up in the great reconciliation. The promised land is again fertilized and made fruitful; the returned sons of the land marry her in the spring ploughing (a widespread ancient idea) and God rejoices over his ransomed people as his bride. In 66:7ff Jerusalem becomes explicitly and rhapsodically a mother; all in a moment, before she has any time for labor pains, she brings forth a new nation which will include "all who love her."

But in the midst of her triumph, suddenly it is God who plays the mother role. Earlier (in 42:14) he had declared, "Now I will cry out like a woman in travail"—will gasp, pant, and lash about, destroying any mountains, vegetation or rivers that might hinder the delivery of his people into their own land; it is he that brings them to rebirth. Again in 49:14f he replied to Zion's complaint: "Can a woman forget her sucking child, that she should have no compassion on the son of her womb?" Even she may forget, but he won't. In 66:12ff, the mother role shifts from Jerusalem to God and back again. "For thus says the Lord, as one whom his mother comforts, so I will comfort you; you shall be comforted in Jerusalem."

Since the danger of Israel's relapse into paganism is now outgrown, it becomes possible for a prophet to find mother-love even in the austere God beside whom there is no other. But here it is not so much an experience as a hope, a hope which has to be deferred to some future consummation of history. Until then, must all the symbols of suprapersonal motherhood—discarded goddesses, a blighted earth, an unjust society, a faithless motherland, a dubious 'church'—be creaturely, imperfect, even drastically negative? Not so. In the Wisdom literature we find a different answer.

Sophia, the Friend of Man

The Old Testament wisdom literature consists primarily of the Book of Proverbs and two Apocryphal works, Sirach and The Wisdom of Solomon. Wisdom books are as a rule ascribed to Solomon, traditionally the first sage, but usually they are collections from many sources over many centuries. As we have seen, the prophetic books were forged on the anvil of historical crises. The teaching of the sages matured in less troubled times and took a more serene view of God and the world, especially of the individual's ability to live the good life and find himself suitably rewarded by his society and his God for so doing. Job and Ecclesiastes, however, are also wisdom literature, representing protests against the complacent optimism of the more orthodox teachers.

The word 'wisdom' in Proverbs is used with various shades of meaning, referring to proverbial folk wisdom, types of skill or cunning, prudent maxims, moral maxims, kingly capacity for wise rule, or the over-all quality of insight or understanding. When this last is personified, we might suppose it is done only for poetic effect. But one passage (Prov. 8:22-31) in which Wisdom speaks in the first person, carries theological implications.

> The Lord created me at the beginning of his work,
>   the first of his acts of old . . .
> Before the mountains had been shaped,
>   before the hills, I was brought forth . . .
> When he established the heavens, I was there,
>   when he drew out a circle on the face of the deep
> When he marked out the foundations of the earth,
>   then I was beside him, like a master workman;
>   and I was daily his delight,
>   playing before him always,
> rejoicing in his inhabited world
>   and delighting in the sons of men.

According to this, wisdom is a created entity, first of God's creatures, who assisted in the rest of creation. If the later verses suggest that wisdom reflects, however 'spiritually,' the earlier image of a goddess-consort, we find that some Old Testament scholars go to great lengths to explain this away. Ancient scholars as well as modern seem to have been uneasy; there are also Hebrew versions which do not have "I was daily his delight"; throughout the last four lines it is wisdom who is delighted, her delight being in the world that has been created. Still, if she was like a master workman, she supplied plans for the cosmic order as an architect would advise a king; and being an adult, her play (given the connotations of the Hebrew verb elsewhere) would be the loveplay from which the universe was born. But the word for "master workman" has the same consonants as a word for "little child," and some ancient translations take it that way. In that case she would be a daughter, God's wisdom in its exuberant beginnings, laughing and playing before him like a child.

Even if the original did carry a fleeting suggestion of marital joys, nothing more is said about it. The principal point throughout the book is Wisdom's affectionate concern for mankind. She is a teacher and counselor, the tireless instructor who teaches man how to live. "She is a tree of life to those who lay hold of her" (3:17), a tree of life and true knowledge in one. She stands in contrast to the "foolish woman," the personification of apostasy, which might involve either literal or symbolic harlotry. In contrast to the furtive revels to which Madam Folly entices the unwary, Wisdom offers a sumptuous feast and invites all passers-by. "The fear of the Lord is the beginning of wisdom" (9:10), fear, principally in the sense of reverent awe. Sober as her precepts may sound, her fruits are riches, honor, and long life; in place of false, death-dealing pleasures she offers spiritual nourishment and joy.

The book of Sirach (or Ecclesiasticus) was written in Greek around 180 B.C. It reflects a type of Judaism staunchly devoted to the Law but open to cosmopolitan influences. In Greek, Wisdom becomes Sophia. She is said to be inscrutable, known only to God, yet he has "poured her out upon all his works" and "rained down knowledge and discerning comprehension" on individuals. Again she is a tree, her branches are long life, and her fruit satisfies. To fear the lord is not only her beginning but her full measure and crown. She stands in the heavenly assembly (Sir. 24:3-9) and offers an extended self-portrait:

> I came forth from the mouth of the Most High,
>   and covered the earth like a mist . . .
> Alone I have made the circuit of the vault of heaven
>   and have walked in the depth of the abyss
> From eternity, in the beginning, he created me,
>   and for eternity I shall not cease to exist.

At first enthroned in heaven, she involved herself with man.

> In the waves of the sea, in the whole earth,
> and in every people and nation I have gotten a possession.

The evidence for this involvement with other nations is that other peoples also have wisdom literature. But the lord told her to settle in Israel, and her full expression there turned out to be the Law, the Torah given through Moses: "All this is the book of the covenant of the Most High God" (24:23). The Torah in turn was personified by later writers as God's feminine consultant at the creation.

The Wisdom of Solomon is a brief work of the first century B.C., from the cosmopolitan Jewish community in Alexandria; Greek influence pervades the book. It describes Wisdom as a spiritual entity highly exalted, yet living intimately with man. Solomon, that archetypal sage, is said to have taken her as his bride—though if he did, we can only comment that he was not particularly faithful to her. Later chapters describe how she protected Adam, Noah, and Abraham, how she led the children of Israel out of Egypt and educated them. Her universality is also emphasized in 7:25-8:1:

> For she is a breath of the power of God, and a
>   pure emanation of the glory of the Almighty . . .
> For she is a reflection of eternal light,

> a spotless mirror of the working of God,
>   and an image of his goodness.
> Though she is but one, she can do all things,
>   and while remaining in herself, she renews all things;
> In every generation she passes into holy souls
>   and makes them friends of God, and prophets
> For she is more beautiful than the sun,
>   and excels every constellation of the stars
> She reaches mightily from one end of the earth to the
>   other and she orders all things well.

Here she is seen unambiguously as more than a 'created' being. She is his wisdom, after all, as truly an attribute of God himself as the Word (Logos) or the Holy Spirit; in fact she is identified with both. Greek Logos and Hebrew Wisdom were closely parallel concepts in all but gender.

In the New Testament, wisdom is equated with the Logos, which is Christ (1 Cor. 1:24, Col. 1:5ff), and thus Wisdom loses her feminine identity. Eastern Orthodoxy however, names its mother church in Constantinople Hogia Sophia, Holy Wisdom, and a few Eastern theologians have tried to reinstate her as a principle distinct from Christ. There have also been pioneers of the inward ways who took Sophia seriously, notably Boehme and Soloviev.

Jacob Boehme (1575-1624), the shoemaker of Gorlitz, was both mystic and philosopher, as Howard Brinton showed in his comprehensive study, *The Mystic Will.* ('Philosophy' literally means "love of Sophia.") Boehme, while a devout Lutheran, had a profound sense of mysteries in the world of nature which Lutheranism did not account for, and found friends who introduced him to various underground currents of thought. In his reconstruction of the inner evolution of God-universe-man, the heavenly Virgin Sophia plays many different roles. At first an empty mirror of the formless Abyss, she becomes in turn the Mother of God, the Divine Imagination, the model of the universe (like Plato's world of forms), Eternal Nature in its actualization, man's heavenly genius, bride of the soul, and mother of the reborn. Boehme also speaks of Sophia as an aspect of the divine which he himself has experienced:

> The Virgin has given me her promise not to leave me in my need. As I lay upon the mountain at midnight and all the trees fell over me, and the storm beat upon me, and Antichrist opened wide his jaws to devour me, she came and comforted me and wedded herself to me. I am thy bride in the light [she tells him] and thy longing after my power is my drawing to myself. I sit on my throne, but thou knowest me not. I am in thee, but thy body is not in me. I am the light of the mind.

Sophia was the image of God in which Adam was created, which left him at the fall. But she knocks inwardly at the door of man's soul, or "hovers outwardly before him" in the beautiful or awe-inspiring aspects of the natural world, awaiting his acceptance of her as both bride and mother. "As God bears his son the light, as Mary bore Jesus, the virgin must bear the new man. Out of the same virginity from which Christ was born must we all be born."[3]

When American Shaker theologians worked out the implications of their experience of Ann Lee's ministry, they rejected the trinity and asserted a duality, revealed through a dual revelation in human form. "The true order and origin of our existence is from an Eternal Parentage. As Christ through Jesus manifested God as Father and Power, so Ann Lee by the second appearance of Christ through her has manifested God as the Eternal Mother and Wisdom."[4] They felt that this unlettered blacksmith's daughter's dealings with human problems were such as "only Divine Wisdom could inspire."

Vladimir Soloviev (1853-1900) was perhaps Russia's most outstanding philosopher. Long before he read Boehme he must have known about the icon of Sophia in Novgorod Cathedral, how Russians built temples to her in the Middle Ages and "worshipped this mysterious being as the Athenians once worshipped the Unknown God." His metaphysics as well as his practical religious endeavors were rooted in three visions of Sophia, his "Eternal Friend." The first occurred in Moscow on Ascension Day when he was a boy of nine. At twenty-three, as a student in London, she appeared to him in the reading room of the British Museum. He was elated, but grieved that he saw her so dimly; so she directed him to go to Egypt. "He met her this time alone in the desert at dawn, when the transfigured and reintegrated Universe appeared before him in its original splendor and glory"[5]—a vision of "all that was, and is, and ever shall be," with earth's oceans, woods, and mountains visible below him as if seen from the stratosphere, all comprised in one supernal image of feminine beauty.

Thereafter Soloviev devoted his life to the restoration of this fallen world to the transcendent state of unity that God intended. He was the first ecumenist of the nineteenth century, throwing himself into the cause of the reunion of Christendom—principally Eastern Orthodoxy and Roman Catholicism, but intending later to draw in Protestants and Jews. In his youth he envisaged an unbroken progress toward "deification of the world," but his later years were shadowed by premonitions of twentieth-century disasters. He felt, however, that both the dogma of the Immaculate Conception and Comte's 'religion of humanity' pointed to a rediscovery of Sophia.

The Holy Spirit as Feminine

In the wisdom of Solomon we read: "For wisdom is a kindly spirit" or in another translation, "a spirit that loveth man." A few lines further on, "the Spirit of the Lord has filled the world," and is "that which holds all things together" (Wis. 1:6,7). Wisdom is not only a spirit but *the* spirit, the "breath of the power of God" who "enters holy souls and makes them friends of God and prophets" (Wis.7:25ff).

The Spirit of God appears in the earlier Old Testament books in various connections—anything from the fury that empowered Samson to kill a thousand men with the jawbone of an ass (Judge. 15:14) and the frenzy that fell upon Saul as he joined a company of primitive prophets (Sam. 10:10) to the lucid inspiration that moved the great literary prophets. But it is not noticeably feminine (though grammatically it is), nor is it that which holds all things together. Till now, the feminine principle that unifies the world has been Wisdom. Only this late Apocryphal work identifies the Spirit with Sophia, though one earlier passage may have been taken as a hint.

In the Genesis creation story, in the beginning when darkness was over the deep, "the Spirit of God was moving over the face of the waters" (Gen. 1:2). This has been a subject of heated controversy among committees of translators in conclave. The primitive meaning of *ruach* is breath, and the primitive idea of the breath of God is a powerful wind. The fully developed meaning is that of the Spirit as found in late prophets and psalms, the Wisdom of Solomon, and the New Testament. The New English Bible opts for a "mighty wind" that blew across the waters, accomplishing nothing in particular but heightening the description of chaos. The Revised Standard Version and the Jerusalem Bible keep the traditional rendering, "Spirit of God." This is justifiable whatever the original writer meant, since it was understood throughout our era as meaning that Spirit which was involved in the creation and could be taken poetically as feminine.

Since the Hebrew verb is a general word for all kinds of motion, the Revised Standard Version cautiously translates it "was moving." But it is used elsewhere of birds that hover or flutter over their young; the Jerusalem Bible has "hovering." A related Syriac

verb can mean "brood." The suggestion is that of a mother bird
brooding on the mythical cosmic egg, a chaos which hatches out a
cosmos. If God as Father created by a word of command, God as
Spirit mothers the world into being. The suggestion is stronger if
the Spirit is associated with a dove, though this may not have
occurred until New Testament times.

In the New Testament the Spirit descends upon Jesus at his
baptism in the form of a dove. Centuries before, doves had been the
birds of the Mother-Goddess, expressing her gentle, pacific, loving
aspects; there is no evidence for direct derivation of the idea, but the
coincidence may be noted. The other major manifestation of the
Spirit is at Pentecost, in the sound of a mighty wind and tongues of
fire that rested on the apostles. To be "filled with the Spirit" was no
uncommon state thereafter. Speaking in tongues at Pentecost is
said to have meant utterances in languages unknown to the speaker
but known to listeners present; later in some of Paul's churches it
flourished in the form of ecstatic utterance in no known language.
Other manifestations of the Spirit were in prophecy and healing.

In all this the concept of the spirit is transmuted by the alchemy
of a unique series of historic experiences from a broad cosmic
principle to a specific dynamic associated with Christ and his
resurrection. In our own day C.G. Jung has identified the Holy
Spirit with Sophia, and we have seen that he has scriptural warrant
for doing so; but to those who have concentrated on the New
Testament it must seem a bit strange. We may regard the New
Testament phenomena as indicating a specific phase or expression
of wisdom/spirit which can and does recur (as in the Pentecostal
movement), but is not applicable to all times and places. The fruits
of the Spirit listed by Paul in Gal. 5:22, however, are consonant
with universal wisdom: "love, joy, peace, patience, kindness, goodness, faithfulness, gentleness, self-control."

According to John 14-16, Christ promised to send his disciples
another comforter, or more accurately "counselor," the Spirit of
Truth, to instruct and lead them. This Spirit is surely close to
wisdom, but is masculine. In the New Testament the Spirit is masculine where it is personal at all; in Greek it is neuter. What really
clinched it in the creeds was that *spiritus* in Latin is masculine. Only
in fringe sects whose writings are mostly lost was the Spirit still
thought of as feminine. A curious saying from a lost "Gospel
according to the Hebrews" is quoted by the Church Fathers, in
which Jesus declares that his mother, the Holy Spirit, took him by
the hair and carried him to Mount Tabor.

In any case the all-masculine Trinity became dogma. Even so, the thought of a feminine Holy Spirit recurs spontaneously in circles that probably never heard of it as an ancient minority report. Genevieve Parkhurst, a minister's wife, some years ago was healed of cancer through a vision of Christ. Later, she was led into a healing ministry. In her first book she speaks of an insight that came to her in the silence. "At last I realized that the Holy Spirit is the Mother Heart of the Holy Trinity." We all need a mother's teaching skills; and we need someone "on whose breast our tears may fall unashamed."

The Shekinah as Presence in Exile

One version of the feminine mediating principle between God and man developed in post-biblical Judaism. The abstract noun *sh'kinah*, literally "indwelling," does not appear in the Bible but the related verb does. *Mishkan* (dwelling) was one name for Moses' desert tabernacle, the tent of meeting. God's presence was manifested in quasi-physical terms in the burning bush, more spectacularly in the cloud of glory first seen on Mount Sinai, then in the tabernacle and later the temple. In the first few centuries A.D., Aramaic versions of the Old Testament introduce the word "*shekinah*" (like heaven in the Gospel of Matthew) as a reverent circumlocution for God. In Ex.25:8 the Lord's words, "I will dwell" become "I will let my Shekinah dwell among the children of Israel."

In Talmudic literature from the third century on, Shekinah is feminine in more than a grammatical sense. Theoretically she is omnipresent in the world, but more often she is physically localized. The Jerusalem temple was built to be her permanent home. When this temple was desecrated and destroyed, the Shekinah wandered to the desert or perhaps the Mount of Olives, waited vainly a few months for Israel to repent, then for awhile withdrew to heaven. After decades of exile, partial return and the building of a second temple, some say she visited it intermittently. When this too was destroyed in 70 A.D., she moved on to the principal synagogues of Babylon, where she not only appeared from time to time but made herself audible in the sound of a bell. She was believed to be a comforter of the sick, a helper of those in need, and especially tender toward repentant sinners. She would descend and rest upon any who performed good deeds, even if they were pagan idolaters, and would also "rest between" worthy husbands and wives. In this period both the Holy Spirit and the Shekinah are mentioned in the sense of a feminine entity who talks back to God, urging him to mitigate his wrath against sinners. On the other hand the Shekinah can be a disciplinarian herself, and is sent by him on punitive missions.

The full flowering of the Shekinah doctrine, or should we say the Shekinah experience, came about through the complex late-medieval phenomenon known as Kabbalism. This was partly a magical movement and partly mystical in the highest sense; it was somewhat frowned upon but never 'excommunicated' by the leaders of Jewish orthodoxy. Since the Shekinah accompanied her people through centuries of exile and mourned with them (she was seen by one mystic in widow's garb by the Wailing Wall), she came to be identified with the ideal Israel, the faithful community which awaited redemption. According to an eminent Jewish scholar, the fact that the Shekinah as a feminine element in divinity "obtained recognition in spite of the obvious difficulty of reconciling it with. . . the absolute unity of God, and that no other element of Kabbalism won such a degree of popular approval, is proof that it responded to a deep-seated religious need."[6] Among all the common folk of Eastern European Jewry, she was felt to be "a wifely and motherly, passionate and compassionate female divinity. . . no mere symbol or emanation, but a great heavenly reality whose shining countenance shoved the theoretical doctrine of the oneness of God into the background."[7]

Eastern Europe seems to have been especially fertile soil for veneration of the feminine principle; but Kabbalism started in Spain, and an especially notable group of Kabbalists settled in Safed in sixteenth-century Palestine. They used to go out in procession at dusk on Friday evenings, into the hills and fields, to greet "the Sabbath Queen." A moving hymn to the Sabbath Queen is still sung on Friday evenings in synagogues around the world.

> Come, my friends, to meet the Bride,
> Let us receive the face of Sabbath . . .
> Come, O Bride, come, O Bride!

In the principal classic of Kabbalism, the *Zohar*, not only two (or three) but ten attributes or aspects of God are distinguished, some masculine and some feminine. Among them is wisdom, now masculine, paired with feminine intelligence. The ten Sefiroth are thought of as flowing into one another in a subtle, intricate pattern of divine evolution-within-himself, reflected in turn in the physical universe and in man. The tenth and final 'face,' the most highly evolved, the most expressive, the most humanized, is the Shekinah—who is the kingdom, the mystical community, the queen, the bride. But due to a primordial fall long antedating Adam, the Shekinah is in exile while the world lasts. The banishment of the Jews from Spain in 1492 renewed their acquaintance with the horrors of exile and intensified their sense that the whole of human life is conditioned by it. "Life was conceived as Existence in Exile and in self-contradiction." Redemption and reunion with God could come about only through death, repentance, and rebirth. The individual soul goes through many stages of exile, requiring repeated reincarnations. "The exile of the Shekhinah is not a metaphor, it is a genuine symbol of the 'broken' state of things in the realm of dividing potentialities. To lead the Shekhinah back to her Master, to unite her with him, is the true purpose of the Torah." The fulfilling of every commandment, the performance of all good actions, are to be done "for the sake of uniting the Holy One, praised be he, and his Shekhinah, out of fear and love,"[8] In this type of mysticism the emphasis actually shifts to the healing of God through human action, rather than the other way round.

In the Hasidic movement in Poland in the eighteenth century from which Martin Buber derived spiritual nourishment, there was a special emphasis on discerning the Shekinah's hidden presence in morally confusing situations. Men of mystical insight were called upon to clarify them, to lift her "from the very dust of the road" and cause her "to re-approach her Source." Buber wrote a beautiful chronicle, apparently based on fairly copious records, about two gifted leaders in this movement, entitled in English translation *For the Sake of Heaven*. Leaving aside its fascinating political and historical allusions, the story brings out the relevance of the Shekinah doctrine to marital love. In Judaism, celibacy has never been encouraged; holy men especially are expected to marry. Any true marriage, according to the Kabbalah, becomes a symbolic realization of the love between the king and his Shekinah; it helps to heal the wounded heart of God.

In Buber's chronicle, the younger leader, known generally as "the Yehudi" (the Jew), is genuinely in love with Foegele, the wife of his youth, who bears him three children. But he leaves her for years on end to wander about Poland as a teacher, feeling he is called to do so; as the Shekinah wanders in exile, so must he. Returning to find Foegele on her deathbed, he promises to fulfill her request that he marry her sister, Schoendel. The second marriage results in two more children, but is full of tension and outbursts from Schoendel. She resents his treatment of her poor sister, his serene, maddening patience with herself, and his complete detachment from household problems brought on by his excessive generosity to strangers.

One night the Yehudi wakes and looks out of his window into complete darkness. This is suddenly dispersed by the blast of a heavenly shofar, and he sees "red udders exuding the milk-white light of origin." He finds himself standing by a pool full of the white radiance. A wave of it takes on the form of a woman's body swathed in a black veil, except for the bare feet, covered with dust and bleeding wounds from long wayfaring. She tells him that it is precisely the holy men, the Hasidic rabbis, who are tormenting and excluding her by their dissensions: "each of you exiles his comrades, and so together you exile me." Her word to the Yehudi himself is: "one cannot love me and abandon the created being." She raises her veil, shows the face of his beloved Foegele, and appeals to him to help her go home.[9] This vision and his repentance marked the beginning of a greatly enriched ministry of teaching and healing. We may assume his efforts toward reconciliation with the second wife. Just before his death, with his disciples and children around him, he once again asks her forgiveness, and she responds with tears.

Comfort, Life, and Fire of Love

Sophia, Spirit, and Shekinah may be seen as somewhat different but overlapping bands of the total spectrum of divinity as immanent in the universe and in man. The cosmic aspects are more prominent in Sophia. Spirit and Shekinah are more intimately concerned with experiences of inner life and human relatedness with which we are familiar, but with differences of emphasis. All three are closely related to what the Society of Friends call the Inward Light, although Friends have not clothed it in imagery nor thought of it as feminine.

Such experiences have not ceased in our own day. Those acquainted with the techniques of Jungian analytical psychology will know that "active imagination" is sometimes practiced, in the sense of opening oneself to waking dreams or fantasies. Dream symbols come to the surface to speak or act on their own; the conscious mind carries on dialogue with them and works out their meanings for situations in actual life. The fantasy figures are highly personal to start with, but as this road is followed further, universal symbols may break through with numinous effect and fantasy be intensified into genuine vision.

A friend of mine wrote me a letter years ago about a fantasy series of this kind. She had a sympathetic 'Heavenly Mother' in a gray-blue robe, who treated her as the frightened small child she inwardly was, and helped her deal with an ugly old witch who, as often in dreams, represented some unacceptable tendency in herself. Encouraged to show sympathy to the witch, she fed her with oranges; the creature turned into a cheerful old peasant woman full of folk wisdom. Later a problematic situation came up in my friend's professional life, not the sort of thing folk wisdom could cope with. In the next fantasy the peasant woman split down the back like a chrysalis, and out stepped Athena, Goddess of Wisdom. It was a powerful experience of "august, feminine authority and wisdom. Tears filled my eyes, and although she said almost nothing, her presence was calming and confidence-giving." There were later visitations, but she did not replace the tender heavenly mother. That a Mary figure and a Sophia figure were both needed has been found true also by others, perhaps because in our culture a discrepancy is felt between wisdom and compassion, between knowledge-ability and love.

A more unified dream experience is reported by a Quaker poet, Elsie Landstrom. One Halloween, she took her two small children on a trick-or-treat expedition and they met all manner of hobgoblins and ghosts. At bed-time, after singing the doxology together, the children asked, "What is a holy ghost?" On the spur of the moment she defined it as a soft breath or sigh from God toward us, conveying love and hope. Later that night she dreamed of walking down a road to a great cathedral, entering and seating herself on a bench near the altar, on which stood candles and a plain cross:

> Suddenly she was there, the Holy Ghost herself, looking less like a soft breath than anything I had ever seen: a lightning flash of living love, she leaped straight to the center where she lit and spun in flaming red. Tall, with red hair and red shoes, a red and blue gown, every slim inch of her outlined in flame, I knew she had just leapt straight from the heart of the sun, from God himself, to pirouette before me. Every move was pure ecstasy.[10]

In a later dream she asked directions from a woman in a car, to get herself out of a difficulty on a city street which probably stood for some dilemma in real life. The woman stepped out, and became the flaming Spirit, just long enough to let the dreamer know who she was. She then cooled down to a comforting human warmth, took her arm and guided her.

This story reminds me of a medieval hymn to the Holy Spirit which speaks of "comfort, life, and fire of love." The traditional term, "comforter" in the Latin is literally "strengthener"; it can suggest anything from a soft maternal bed quilt to Luther's ruggedly masculine "mighty fortress." I have heard quite a few sermons recommending that we battle against evil and forget about soft breaths and comfortable quilts; but even these can be life-savers for children and others when sorely beset. Mrs. Parkhurst's experience of the Spirit as gentle mother also carried this kind of comfort. Fire, however, is a more ancient and central symbol, and more dynamic. In this dream-vision the flames of Pentecost from above seem to blend with those of the burning bush on earth, associated in the Middle Ages with Mary as well as the Shekinah.

One last word. Nothing in this essay should be construed as recommending a relapse into polytheism. Despite the implication by one of the scholars quoted that the oneness of God is only a "theoretical doctrine," the fact that God is one in all these aspects has been and is as much a matter of vivid first-hand experience as any encounter with a specific aspect. The Inward Light's leading into unity would make no sense whatever unless God were a unity. But I believe God graciously expresses in whatever aspects are necessary to enable us to apprehend, through all our ages of cultural change. There is an element of paradox here, but no contradiction.

Erminie Huntress Lantero was born in 1907. She earned a Divinity degree from Union Theological Seminary, and a doctorate from Radcliffe in 1933. Erminie taught at Wellesley and Sweet Briar Colleges was assistant editor of the *Religion in Life,* and was administrative assistant to the president of Union Seminary in New York. In the late 60's she was research assistant to Dr. McCrea Cavert, General Secretary of the National Council of Churches, helping to compile a history of the American Church.

Erminie was married to Peter Lantero, a Roman Catholic from Genoa from 1947 until his death in 1963. One of the founders of the Friend's Annual Conference on Religion and Psychology, she also served as the editor of *Inward Light* until 1980.

During her life she explored world religions, became a Jungian astrologer, and wrote a book on the newly-discovered planet, Chiron.

Dr. Erminie Huntress Lantero died December 12, 1992 at the Fellowship Community in Spring Valley, New York.

Adonai Zeus Shekhinah Elim Ogun Kat Buddha
Wyame Hel Rama Mitra Odomankoma Jupiter Het
Heru Agni Cagn Thor Brahma Tangaroa Father
Lugaba Papang Diana Al-Rahman Cerridwen Ahone
Yoma' Tirawa Atius Ganesha El Mungan-ngua
Quetzalcoatl Hamakom *ddai*
Atibruku Moma YH Bun *aiwa*
Saraswati Inanna Miriru *aong*
Tonantzin Yuskeha Bha *Head*
Olodumare Shyama Ekv *Heru*
Nurrundere Daramilun *tzeir*
Hecate Chi Musubi Hin *suna*
Nanderuvucu Erishkigal *man*

The
Divine
Disturber

Sr. Kay O'Neil
&
Sr. Michelle Meyers

Tsui-goab Ometeotl Os *chtli*
Surya Elohim Nyankop *Ilu*
Woden Great Spirit Les *goro*
Poseidon Chineke Nhialic *uwut*
Makai Wakantanka Inari Ha-Qadosh barukh hu'
Tara Krishna Avaloket-iswara Rabb Goryo Qat Oke
Nurunderi Indra Shang-ti Amaterasu Ohmikami
Kannon Quan Yin Ise Lakshmi Awonawilona Bast
Omecihuatl Ruhanga Kosane Sophia Dionysus Ixchel
Mawu Ra Ardanariswara Oluwa Deng Hanuman
uNkulunkulu Kanobo Ngai Shamayim Cybele Dakini
Nataraj Pachamama Susanoo Katonda Avlukpo Eloah
Isis Temaukel Eleda Gaia Laxmi Mahmanmu-rok
Odin El-al Herukhuti Viracocha Marduk Ashira Biral
Shaddai Dzingbe Djohu-ma-di-hutu Astarte Ndengei
Koyatu Baha'u'llah Marrigan Baiame Om Pelepelewa
Durga Orisha Nyame Techaronhiawakhon Chukwu
Uvolovu Brahman Nephtys Ha-Maqom Tehuti Maat
Digambara Val Tik Chaitanya Amana Kwoth Num
Colok Nabango Fumeripitsj Shiva Varuna Lukanga
Bala Atibluku Karu Allah Sing Nainuema Artemis
Kartikeya Kuanyin Yelafaz T'ien Baal Shakti
Athena Olorun Nemesis Sheela-na-Gig Bhavartarini
Jesus Horus Izanagi Sebek Waq Ishtar Ti Seker
BegoTanutanu Sat Nam Kali Mirirul Bhavatarini
Tsui-goab Hatzur Brahman Ubusuna Tonantzin
YHVH Apollo Nana God Almighty Hu Vishnu Om

Women's quest for self-affirmation, survival, power, and self-determination includes the development of a positive self-esteem, as well as the development of a healthy spirituality. One's spirituality can be defined in a number of ways. It is being aware of mystery, of the Holy One in our lives. It is our relationship to God and encompasses our relationship to all of creation. It is an awesome and profound gift. In *The Color Purple* Shug says it simply: "God is in you and inside everything else. You come into the world with God. But only them that search for it inside find it."[1] Anne Carr says that "Christian spirituality includes every dimension of human life. Thus, Christian development . . . to be adequately experienced and studied, should be viewed as total human development.[2]

Spirituality is influenced by religion, but is not to be confused with religion. In our patriarchal culture, religion can be very limiting to women's spirituality and spiritual growth. To be taught that one is made in the image of the divine is limiting when all the images of the divine used in religious circles are predominantly male. For women, a first step in moving toward a healthy spirituality is to learn to image God in a way in which they are included.

Being raised female, however, has taught us well to be suspicious of our own questions if they are not validated by the religious patriarchs. Throughout the years we found differing degrees of comfort and inspiration in formal worship services, but as our feminist consciousness became brilliantly alive, our dissatisfaction and our questions concerning the fare provided for women worshippers became increasingly acute. As Mary Collins reports, "no matter how faithfully we come to this scriptural table, we are being malnourished!"[3] This was illustrated for us when a woman handed Michelle a note on passionate pink paper. It read: "Help! I'm starving. Where can I go for spiritual nourishment?"

Rosemary Radford Ruether states: ". . . religion has been not only a contributing factor, it is undoubtedly the single most important shaper and enforcer of the image and role of women in culture and society."[4] Like carbon monoxide in the air, the pollution of patriarchal religion is so subtle that it is hardly noticed until we are almost overcome. While leaving official church and synagogue practices may bring some relief, this does not guarantee clean air, since the culture is deeply tainted with the remnants of patriarchal scripture and theology. Basic to breathing and staying alive, if one chooses to espouse biblical faith as part of one's nourishment, is the belief in the *Imago Dei*. The Latin term means seeing ourselves in the image of God, and seeing that image of God as inclusive of women.

This means bidding farewell to a residue of tradition that would have us be less than God's image. Farewell to church fathers like Augustine who said women could reflect the image of God only when taken together with the male, their head; and to Thomas Aquinas, who after Aristotle's theory, viewed woman as naturally defective, a "misbegotten male." Farewell to Martin Luther who saw Eve suffering subjection to man as punishment for her sin.[5] Farewell to misogynist passages attributed to Paul such as 1 Timothy 2:12-14 wherein Eve, and consequently all women, are held more responsible for sin than men. Farewell to the patriarchal pollution of the 1990's illustrated by a male's response to the harassment of the woman sports reporter in the Boston men's locker room: "It was all her fault. Just like Eve, women are still the troublemakers!"

In the development of positive self-esteem and healthy spirituality the major concern is what we call the "God problem." Phyllis Trible said it well in her classic line: "Born and bred in the land of patriarchy, the Bible abounds in male imagery."[6] That lesson is repeatedly driven into our psyches through religious art, symbols, language, and metaphors. The next time you are at a typical religious service, count the number of references to God as male in song, prayer, scripture, and sermon while observing the art on the windows and in the sanctuary. Then check the environment and observe which sex is officiating or presiding at the altar. (Hint: the dress may be misleading!)

Several years ago we were given a tour of a Catholic cathedral by a woman sacristan who knew and treasured every inch of that church. She proudly directed our attention to all the male saints depicted on the stained glass windows. As we stood in front of the sanctuary, gazing at the gold-leaf mural above the altar, we were almost overwhelmed by the mammoth torso of an old man with a white beard who stretched above another bearded man on a throne. Between the two male figures was a small dove. At this moment, our guide pronounced with great pride: "This is God!" Not, "This is an artist's representation of the Trinity, " or "This is how we've pictured the Deity, Father, Son, and Holy Spirit in our Christian tradition." Patriarchy had taught her well: "This is God"—make no mistake. We wept for all the children and women and men who had knelt before this God for a hundred years. What effect would this God have on the self-esteem of girls and women? Scripture scholar, Sandra Schneiders, suggests that perhaps the most profoundly destructive effect of an exclusively masculine presentation of God on women is "the deep sense of exclusion from the divine that they imbibe as part of their sense of who they are."[7]

Not only picturing God as exclusively male, but using predominantly male language and titles to describe God further alienates women's spirits from an identification with the holy and reinforces male superiority and female inferiority. In the book of Isaiah alone, we find such images for God as: the Lord musters his weapons (13:4-6), Man of War (42:13), Father and Prince of Peace (9:6), Bridegroom (62:5). The litany of the manhood ascribed to God continues: Father of the Fatherless (Ps 68:5), Lord is King (Jer 10:10), Husband (Jer 31:31-32), Strong Man (Ps 78:65), Master Father (Mal 1:6). Despite all protestations to the contrary from scholars and theologians through the centuries who proclaim the God of the Jewish and Christian scriptures transcends sexuality, we continue to make God male. We have been thoroughly indoctrinated. From the person in the pew to the theologian, we hear the commonplace assertion: "God is not male, *he* is a spirit!"

As we continued to listen to our inner urgings, our questions led us to seminary. We desired to further our feminist critique while standing within mainline tradition. Often we felt totally immersed in an ocean of patriarchy. We struggled to keep afloat on little rafts of hope with several feminist classes and sisterhood experiences. One night, deep into these studies, Kay had a nightmare. She awakened with an overwhelming sense of evil in her room and looked up from her bed to see a dirty, old, bald man standing over her with an intent to rape. She screamed, and Michelle came running into her room. The old man disappeared in the light. Several years later Kay explained her interpretation of the story as her struggle to rid her psyche of patriarchy which she found almost engulfing in the seminary experience. A Methodist pastor responded: "Kay, that old man represented the rape of your psyche." Indeed he did.

That summer, while on retreat on the magnificent shores of Lake Superior in Northern Minnesota, the old man appeared again. We were feeding the gulls and listening to the gentle waves, praising God for being alive. We stumbled upon a driftwood log on which was carved the head of the old bearded man. It was a moment of great grace and growth. The old man was rotting on that log; he was disintegrating. He was no longer to be feared, because he would return to earth and new life would arise from him. He was passing on even as our psyches were being cleansed of the destruction of years of struggle against the debilitating effect of being women less valued by our patriarchal church and culture.

Schneiders names this phenomenon experienced by us with the old man on the beach.

> . . . it is the imagination which creates our God-image and our self-image. Consequently, if the demonic influence of patriarchy on the religious imagination is to be exorcised, if the neurotic repression of the feminine dimension of divinity is to be overcome, the imagination must be healed. It is absolutely imperative that language, which appeals to the imagination through metaphor, symbol, gesture, and music, be purified of patriarchal overtones, male exclusive references to God, and the presentation of male religious experiences as normative. We must learn to speak to and about God in the feminine; we must learn to image God in female metaphors; we must learn to present the religious experience of women as autonomously valid.[8]

This theme of using women's imagination is reiterated in a later work by Procter-Smith who states that we "suffer from restrictive imaginations. . . which have been "colonized" by patriarchal culture, a process Adrienne Rich calls arts of survival turned to rituals of self-hatred." In her study, the task of feminist imagination is delineated into two kinds of seeing: The first is concerned with the present and questions: Is it true for us? The second kind of seeing asks us to participate in the construction of the future, to leap past the limits of what is and what has been to what might be."[9]

From our own work with twelve step spirituality, we would add a third kind of seeing: "Let go and let God" with the seeing of the past that polluted our self-images and God-images. Refuse to dwell in the seeing of the negatives which are destructive.

Using our collective creative imagination to name our God in ways in which we can image ourselves was never more clear to us than when a dear friend shared her story of spiritual abuse. She is a gentle, spirited, beautiful woman who had been violated by her father, then married to a man who physically abused her. She recalls her son sleeping by her bedside with a gun to protect her from his father. One Sunday during a typical service where Father God imagery and male language predominated, she cried aloud from the depths of her soul: "I want my Mother!"

Women's spirits bent double by centuries of patriarchal pollution are awakening and crying with the agony of the psalmist:

"Save me, O God. . . I am weary with my crying; my throat is parched. My eyes grow dim with waiting for my God." (Ps. 69). We believe these cries have been heard in heaven and on earth, and help is on the way. The latest wave of feminist consciousness has been shaping the questions in both the theological and secular worlds and has provided the support systems of sisterhood where women's voices are being heard. Therein comes the major revisioning in our naming of God.

Once we understand the relatively simple concept that all names for God are metaphors, we can begin to speak of endless ways of relating to God. How we address our God speaks of how we propose to relate to God. Despite the multiplicity of names and language describing God in the Hebrew Bible, we in the Christian tradition have predominantly chosen Father and other male metaphors for public worship and sermons. Sallie McFague presents powerful argument for developing new models for God. "I have come to see patriarchal as well as imperialistic, triumphalist metaphors for God in an increasingly grim light: this language is not only idolatrous and irrelevant—besides being oppressive to many who do not identify with it—but it may also work against the continuation of life on our planet."[10]

When humans describe and name God, it is important to realize that women have never been metaphor makers, nor have their major social roles such as caretaker, friend, mother, wife, nurturer been objectified into primary metaphors for God. Descriptions for the Holy One in both biblical and present times reflect the positions of power held by dominant men, i.e., lord, ruler, master, king, father. As God describes God, there is neither sex nor social role given. When Moses asked God, "What is your name?" God answered, "I am who I am." (Ex. 4:13-14). Later we read a warning against idolatry: "Since you saw no form on the day God spoke to you at Horeb out of the midst of fire, beware lest you act corruptly by making a graven image for yourselves, in the form of any figure, the likeness of male or female. . ." (Deut. 4:15-16).

Not until we presume to call God Mother in a metaphor which says God is like, rather than God is, a nursing mother (Isaiah 49:15) or God is like a mother giving birth (Isaiah 42:14) does using human imagery (read female imagery) for God raise questions of idolatry. Since God transcends human sexuality and all language about God is metaphor, then why not say God/she for the next two thousand years to counterbalance all the God/he ringing in our psyche? Only then do we begin to understand the depth of patriarchal pollution when women, albeit theoretically *Imago Dei,* are not

fit images for God. Procter-Smith talks about not so much an intellectual search as a spiritual one in which women are longing to find
"God in themselves and love her fiercely."[11]

Since the publication of Carol Christ's article, "Why Women
Need the Goddess," we have made this work required reading for
our classes. The pattern is predictable. Initially many women in a
broad cross section of the population are threatened that we are
"taking their God away." After reading and discussing Christ's
thesis, the overwhelming response changes to the "yeah, yeah"
phenomenon. Christ proposes women need the Goddess to affirm
themselves and especially their bodies, to legitimate their power, to
value their own will and to celebrate women's bonds and heritage.[12]
Procter-Smith says that "the glimpse of a God whose face is like
ours opens our imaginations into another world, which is free of
'fear and woman-loathing.' Naming God as female affirms the
value and sacredness of women. If the Holy One can be named
female, then female bodies and experiences can be holy."[13] Perhaps
this is the creative imagination, the prophetic seeing that women
are en-visioning once the patriarchal blinders and restrictions have
been removed from their psyche and the urge to stand up straight
becomes irresistible. If God is not male, then why cannot the
metaphor of Goddess be enjoyed? The test is: 1) Is it true for us? 2)
Does it help us leap past the limits of what is and what has been to
what might be? 3) Can we let go and let the Holy One heal our
imagination by not dwelling in destructive God images by using this
image?

When we ask women to describe their images and names for
God, we are affirmed in our belief of the holiness of women and
their emerging from bent double to upright positions as they assert
their own experiences. God is sprite, ballet dancer, weaver, mother,
grand potter, birther, earther, mirther, mirror reflecting me back to
myself, attendant spirit, energy. Feminist theology and psychology
insist that women's experiences be their birthing ground. Nowhere
do we see this more evident than in the creative imagination
surrounding women's naming of the divine.

An empowering image is that of God as friend, a well-hidden
metaphor even though Jesus suggested it (Jn 15:12-15). Like
Schüssler Fiorenza, we might be suspicious here. Why in a
patriarchal culture has this metaphor been ignored? A quick
glimpse at male bonding both in philosophical and psychological
literature gives us a clue. As we have seen, women's identity is
defined in context of relationship; men's experience is not one of
identity through relationship. Friendship and mutuality do not serve

patriarchy. McFague defines friendship as a "free, reciprocal, trustful bonding of persons committed to a common vision."[14] She contends that having God as friend is the most adult, egalitarian and demanding of models but also a freely chosen relationship. Thus, the God in whose image we are made is a God in relationship, not a solitary abstract deity in non-relationship to the world. We recall the best of our own being lifted up in sisterhood, friendship experiences, and we reflect on an invitation from Jesus/Sophia God (Jn. 16:12-17) to be God's friend.

Schüssler Fiorenza proposes that this common vision, "not the holiness of the elect but the wholeness of all is the central vision of Jesus."[15] God's invitation that we be friends is an invitation to roll up our sleeves and go to work. We rejoice in the modeling of such women as Sojourner Truth whose name for God was Almighty Friend. Having been empowered to stand up straight and to heal and liberate the world, the admonition rings in our hearts: until all women stand straight, no woman stands straight. On the journey to positive self-esteem and healthy spirituality, how we name our God and ourselves in relationship is crucial.

An important postscript to this discussion on the naming of God is a reference to Rosemary Ruether's use of the name, God/ess, which embraces the non-patriarchal aspects of the God of biblical tradition. While some suggest the name God needs to be reclaimed by women to include an image of wholeness in which they image themselves, others, like Ruether, would propose a different naming because of the point of patriarchal history in which we find ourselves, i.e., God still carries the male image. Ruether concludes: "We have not an adequate name for the true God/ess, and 'I am who I shall become.' Intimations of her/his name will appear as we emerge from false naming of God/ess modeled on patriarchal alienation."[16]

In our own lives, one of our primary images for God is The Divine Disturber. How, you may ask, did this image of the Holy One come to permeate our spirituality?

Michelle's earliest recollection of Kay was that of "The Questioner," always asking, "Is this what I should be doing with my life?" Michelle's primary question has always been, "What is God asking of us?" As "baby nuns" nearly thirty years ago, Michelle's initial role was thinking she had some answers. The first book given to her was Frankl's *Man's Search for Meaning.* (Did that mean women had no meaning or simply that they did not need to search?) Kay was warned not to associate with Michelle because she questioned authority. A priest at Notre Dame called Kay a PIA (pain in the ass) for raising questions of inclusive language for God.

We continued to question. Together we questioned the rules and minutia of religious community which didn't make sense, the values of religious life, the authority, credit, power, and deference given to pastors while the Sisters most often did the work, and ultimately whether our actions were love and justice oriented on behalf of our students.

The formal naming of the Divine Disturber must have come in our confrontation of patriarchy and sexist practices in the early 1970's. It was our search for meaning through patriarchal pollution that knit us together in this image of God. We began to study and teach classes to answer our own questions. With the awakening of our feminist consciousness, the love and justice questions were everywhere. We welcomed neither the questions nor the distress they caused. But we had to push for answers. The Divine Disturber led us on. Believing God was in the questioning was empowering and comforting. Often we felt like the prophets of old, going forth reluctantly. We paraphrased Jeremiah 1:6, "I do not know how to speak for I am only a woman." Before going out we often pray with words of Sister Raphael Consedine: "Take down your lantern from its niche and go out! You may not rest in firelight certainties, secure from drifting fog of doubt and fear. Your pilgrim heart shall urge you still one pace beyond and love shall be your lantern flame."

Seeing God in those disturbances, in that fog of uncertainty, we begin to trust our own questions and listen to the still, small voice within ourselves and each other. We begin to hear one another into wholeness and action. It was the Divine Disturber who sent Kay searching for and reconciling with her father after eighteen years of separation and alienation. She did not want to go, but always the question arose, What does God want us to do with our lives? And always there were the disturbing answers. Somehow there was a peace in knowing who was doing the disturbing and who was making us partners in the process of global disturbance.

The peace came to an abrupt end this summer when we were involved in a tragic car accident in which a young woman was killed. What sense, what meaning can we find? The Divine Disturber sends us again on a search for personal meaning, solace, comfort. Our lives are forever in relationship with those two young people in the other car. Our souls are forever disturbed.

As we search day and night in the mist of physical, psychological, and spiritual pain for the strength to live in the present moment, we begin to claim the reality that we will live forever disturbed. And yet wanting, needing, and believing we have a birthright to inner peace, calm, love, and compassion, we are coming to accept another face of the Divine Disturber. The holy is in this disruption of life. None of us are abandoned. In the unsettling, there is a gentle settling into trusting ourselves and gathering strength in being disturbed. In our friendship with one another and the One who continues to disturb us, we will stand upright once more, praise the holy, and love those people placed in our lives.

Sisters Michelle and Kay are educators *par excellence*. They develop and teach courses and retreats in self-esteem and spirituality across the Midwest. Adjunct faculty for Mankato State University, Southwest State, St. Cloud State, St. Mary's Graduate Center, Aquinas Institute of Theology, Clarke College, Luther Northwestern, Shalom Ecumenical Center, Trinity Lutheran Seminary and many others. They are founding members of the Social Justic Committee, Presentation Sisters, and the New Ulm diocesan Task Force on Women in Ministry. They have recently received a Diocesan Distinguished Service Medal from the Diocese of New Ulm, MN, "For 21 years of service in religious education. . . for teaching rural women to have respect for who they are in society . . . and for your generous spirits of friendship and care for so many."

Adonai Zeus Shekhinah Elim Ogun Kat Buddha
Wyame Hel Rama Mitra Odomankoma Jupiter Het
Heru Agni Cagn Thor Brahma Tangaroa Father
Lugaba Papang Diana Al-Rahman Cerridwen Ahone
Yoma' Tirawa Atius Ganesha El Mungan-ngua
Quetzalcoatl Hamakom   ddai
Atibruku Moma YH Bun   aiwa
Saraswati Inanna Mirir   aong
Tonantzin Yuskeha Bha   Head
Olodumare Shyama Ekv   Heru
Nurrundere Daramilun   otzeir
Hecate Chi Musubi Him   suna
Nanderuvucu Erishkigal   man
Tsui-goab Ometeotl Os   chtli
Surya Elohim Nyankop   Ilu
Woden Great Spirit Les   goro
Poseidon Chineke Nhialic   uwut
Makai Wakantanka Ina   hu'

From Nothing to Everything Just As It Is

Nancy Ann James

Tara Krishna Avaloket-iswara Rabb Goryo Qat Oke
Nurunderi Indra Shang-ti Amaterasu Ohmikami
Kannon Quan Yin Ise Lakshmi Awonawilona Bast
Omecihuatl Ruhanga Kosane Sophia Dionysus Ixchel
Mawu Ra Ardanariswara Oluwa Deng Hanuman
uNkulunkulu Kanobo Ngai Shamayim Cybele Dakini
Nataraj Pachamama Susanoo Katonda Avlukpo Eloah
Isis Temaukel Eleda Gaia Laxmi Mahmanmu-rok
Odin El-al Herukhuti Viracocha Marduk Ashira Biral
Shaddai Dzingbe Djohu-ma-di-hutu Astarte Ndengei
Koyatu Baha'u'llah Marrigan Baiame Om Pelepelewa
Durga Orisha Nyame Techaronhiawakhon Chukwu
Uvolovu Brahman Nephtys Ha-Maqom Tehuti Maat
Digambara Val Tik Chaitanya Amana Kwoth Num
Colok Nabango Fumeripitsj Shiva Varuna Lukanga
Bala Atibluku Karu Allah Sing Nainuema Artemis
Kartikeya Kuanyin Yelafaz T'ien Baal Shakti
Athena Olorun Nemesis Sheela-na-Gig Bhavartarini
Jesus Horus Izanagi Sebek Waq Ishtar Ti Seker
BegoTanutanu Sat Nam Kali Mirirul Bhavatarini
Tsui-goab Hatzur Brahman Ubusuna Tonantzin
YHVH Apollo Nana God Almighty Hu Vishnu Om

"**G**od is great and God is good and we thank him for this food. Amen."

We are sitting around the dinner table, hands folded in our laps, eyes downcast, my sisters, 10 and 3, myself, 6, and our parents. We say "Gawd," not "Gahd," and "Ay-men." We say this verse at dinner time only.

Lest this 10-second ceremony become too solemn, daddy may be grinning. He might poke the nearest girl in the ribs while her eyes are supposed to be downcast, causing her to squeal or giggle. If you peek over at him during the verse, he might wink at you. Mother might say, "Tom!" in her chastising voice, at which he acts like he's been a bad boy and now he'll behave. But it never lasts. He lets you know this God stuff is not to be taken too seriously.

By the time we moved from Chicago to Janesville, Wisconsin, when I was 12, we were no longer saying this verse. I don't know when we stopped, but I'm surprised to remember saying it at all, given my parents' beliefs about God. We were not believers, to put it mildly. We were agnostics. We were Unitarians.

Mother and daddy had met and married in a Methodist church. They remained friends with the minister and his wife throughout our childhood. But before I had a memory, they decided they couldn't go along with traditional Christianity, and they sought a church more compatible with their beliefs and their intelligence. Someone then pointed them to the Third Unitarian Church of Chicago.

We attended every Sunday, which entailed a long half-hour drive from home. My sisters and I went to Sunday School downstairs, the adults to church in the main hall. Kids never entered the main hall, to my recollection, except once or twice a year to take part in a special program. In Sunday School, we learned about the natural world and other religions, and took field trips to visit a synagogue and different churches. We had no rituals unless potluck suppers are a ritual. We learned, above all, tolerance for different people's points of view. What we learned subtly was that other people were entitled to their beliefs even if they weren't quite as smart as we were. "Smart" meant intellectual and rational, and nothing else mattered.

During my childhood, to be a Unitarian meant:

• Always being embarrassed when asked what church I went to. No one had ever heard of Unitarianism, so they would say "What?" in a loud voice and ask what the heck *that* was. I had trouble telling them.

• Knowing there was no God, as surely as there was no Santa Claus. From earliest Christmases, when we got a present labeled "From Santa Claus," we knew it came from mother and daddy. Santa was just a little joke some people played on their younger children. God seemed to be hoodwinking a lot of adults.

• Recognizing that Jesus was a great man but not holy or supernatural. Kind of like Abraham Lincoln. He did a lot of good works, but was still just a human being. We didn't capitalize "he" when referring to Jesus.

• Enjoying certain hymns and Christmas carols that mentioned God or "our Father" while realizing that what we liked was the music, which didn't commit us to the sentiments expressed by the words. My big sister taught me that.

One summer I came into possession of a pamphlet advertising a Bible study class for children my age. I took it home and begged my mother to let me attend. She argued against it but finally gave in. I was highly excited, having heard much about the Bible and knowing virtually nothing about it. When I got to the class, the teacher asked everyone to take out their Bible and turn to Psalms such-and-such. "Does everyone have a Bible?" I raised my hand: No. Someone loaned me theirs. The teacher repeated the instructions but I was lost. Why didn't she just say what page to turn to? She had to come over and find the right section for me, embarrassing me further. It went like that all morning; every time we went to a new book, someone had to find it for me. At the end of class, the teacher asked if I had a Bible at home that I could bring next time, and I said no. When my mother heard that, she exploded. I had said what? "Of course we have a Bible, it's right here"—and she went and found it. I'd never seen it before. I never went back to Bible class.

I knew that all my friends and acquaintances believed in an all-seeing, all-knowing God who had created the universe. When they tried to pin me down on how I thought the whole thing got started, if not for God, I talked about stars and evolution and the natural order of things. Who did we pray to? We didn't pray. If further challenged, I fell back on my trusty agnostic statement: "We're not saying there is no God, just that there's no way of knowing if there is or isn't." I didn't really believe that (I knew there wasn't), but it usually got the questioner off my back.

My first year in college, I worked on the student newspaper at the university, and fell in with the wise, strident, older, left-wing journalism students. When one of them loudly castigated Unitarians as cowardly agnostics who didn't have the courage to say they were atheists, I knew I didn't want to be lumped in with that group, and immediately became an atheist. That was a relief since it meant I didn't have to look for a Unitarian church to go to. I'd hardly been to church since moving away from Chicago at age 12, since no Unitarian church existed in Janesville. Gradually I came to think that Unitarianism was, as someone put it, a fine debating society but didn't really qualify as a religion.

For many years, I was "nothing." I led a full life—married (Bob, my husband, was also "nothing"), lived in several different places, worked a year, raised two sons, went through an extremely rough period when my husband had a nervous breakdown and I had to go back to work. When our first-born was about a year old, we thought it would be nice and neighborly to attend a little nondenominational church near the town we were living in. I kept having to carry Christopher, restless and noisy, out into the vestibule. Besides, the sermon was so full of sin and salvation, we never returned.

Bob (from whom I'm now divorced) had used the G.I. Bill to live and study for a year in India, before I knew him. He had read extensively about Eastern philosophies and religions, and encouraged me to learn something about the subject. I finally read a book by Alan Watts called *The Way of Zen*. It was a huge eye-opener, filling in a lot of gaps in what I'd heard Bob talk about for years. I was especially impressed that Buddhism was the world's only great religion that didn't worship a supreme being, and that it contained no dogma, no set of fixed beliefs you had to subscribe to. Everything was open to question and to testing in one's own life. Anyone could become enlightened, not just a few people at the top of some hierarchy. Now that was my kind of philosophy!

A few years later, a small group of people convinced an authentic Japanese Zen master to move his family from San Francisco to the Twin Cities and become first abbot of the Minnesota Zen Meditation Center. By then, Bob and I had been sitting *zazen* (the Zen form of meditation) weekly with a small group in one man's suburban basement—sometimes no more than four of us. But several other small groups had also been forming around the Twin Cities, and we all came together to found the Zen Center. We formed a board of directors, raised funds to rent an apartment for the Zen master and the *zendo* (a place to practice meditation), and did all the things needed to start a formal organization and keep it running.

I'll never forget the first time I sat *zazen* in the suburban basement . . .

With about one minute of instruction in the meditation posture, and considerable qualms about being able to sit still for one 40-minute period, let alone the standard two, I find myself breathing slowly in the prescribed cross-legged position and thinking, "Now what?" I berate myself for talking to myself—but can't stop. Every time I am thinking thoughts, as if to tell someone later, I silently yell at myself "Who cares?" I know that all my life I have been carrying on a lively internal monologue that absolutely no one is interested in. And now is the time to shut up. So I tell myself, "Shut up!" along with "So what?" and "Who cares?" Over and over.

Suddenly, tears are forming and beginning to slide down my cheeks. I realize this is the first time in my whole life that I have stopped to just plain be with myself. The first time I have given myself permission to simply be. I've spent my life running and doing and trying to live up to other people's expectations, and suddenly here I am, alone with myself. Just sitting. Just being. No expectations. Listening to nothing at all.

The two 40-minute periods, separated by a 10-minute slow walk, have passed faster than I dreamed possible. Instead of experiencing agonizing impatience for the time to go by, I am startled when the bell rings announcing the end of each sitting period. I am sorry to have it end. As soon as I can get out of the room, I hurry to the bathroom, close the door, and sit sobbing for about ten minutes. I have never been so in touch with myself. I am full of pity and feeling for this poor person who has never stopped long enough to feel her body or her breath, to know her true self. I am hooked on zazen.

A year later, when the Minnesota Zen Center was formed, I got heavily involved. When it organized its first *sesshin*—three days of meditation starting at 5 a.m., with meals and work periods thrown in—I was there sitting and helping cook and having *dokusan*, a private interview with the Zen master. I didn't ask a lot of questions; I was learning too much too fast to be able to think of any. I was absorbing everything I could about Zen, about strange new ways of doing things at the zendo, and new ways of thinking about life.

Gradually, things began changing in my head. From the beginning, I had primarily thought of Zen as a meditation practice and, secondly, as a philosophy. It took several years before I began to think of it as a religion. I had started out ignoring or downplaying the Buddhism half of Zen Buddhism, but that part kept creeping in—into the Saturday lectures, the books I was reading, and finally into my consciousness. In my private definition, a religion was a world view and set of beliefs that influenced people in all their activities and thoughts and choices, in all realms of their life: it was all-pervading. Only gradually did it dawn on me: what I've got here is a religion, something I never thought I missed or wanted. And now here I was, thoroughly immersed in one.

One way in which Zen was totally different from Unitarianism, and from school, and from academia, and from my jobs, was that it dealt with the whole person: feelings, body, mind, spirit. I was not just a mind, a head! In fact, Zen stories let us know that the mind has been so overemphasized in our Western culture that we need to learn to forget about it for a while, to let other ways of knowing sink in. In *zazen,* the main thing I had to focus on was not-thinking, letting ideas and thoughts go out whenever they came into my head. All those thoughts that had so plagued me during my very first try at *zazen* were still the useless clutter of my mind years later—aptly described in Zen as "monkey mind." My focus was and still is on breathing, and on being aware of where I am and what I'm doing.

To live with awareness, with full consciousness, became a goal. Awareness of what? Of reality, of what is. Seeing; opening my eyes.

I was reminded of *Our Town,* a play I acted in as a high school junior. I was moved by the graveyard scene, but didn't really understand it at the time. That's where Emily, who has died in childbirth, is sitting with the other dead townspeople on chairs representing graves, and suddenly becomes aware that she can "go back," relive a day of her life. The other dead folk try to talk her out of it, saying it won't be what she thinks, it'll be too sad, but she won't be deterred; she'll choose a happy day, her tenth birthday. So the scene of her tenth birthday begins. But very soon, as her mother is talking to her, Emily calls out to her: "Look at me, mama— really look!" But mama doesn't, of course. And before long, Emily gives it up and goes back to her grave. Nobody was seeing what was right in front of them. They didn't know how precious everything was. They were wasting their wonderful lives in trivia and blindness, without really looking at anything.

Initially, I found my awareness would heighten whenever I was able to get quiet within. This happened most often when I sat a *sesshin,* particularly a seven-day *sesshin.* Toward the end of that time of stillness, I was super-alert to whatever came my way: the feel of water on my face, the sound of a power lawnmower next door, the taste of rice with sesame salt. What I knew was known not with my mind but with direct experience. My mind chooses a nutritious diet; my senses directly experience the food.

At the end of one *sesshin,* as participants were sitting around preparing to leave and joking about the agonizing three days we had just gone through, someone asked what each of us had learned. My mouth immediately opened and said, "I learned how to listen with my stomach." People laughed, but it felt totally true. No longer was my realm of consciousness limited to my brain, my intellect. To get to my truest feelings, I had to let them come into my awareness through my *hara,* the area of the abdomen that is one's center of gravity and equilibrium. One reason it was so important to become still and quiet was to allow myself to "hear" the messages that emanated from my *hara.*

Very gradually, I felt I was incorporating that direct experiencing into all aspects of my life; it was no longer just a temporary response to the unnatural situation of sitting *zazen.* When I ignored the *hara,* didn't slow down to get centered, my thoughts were shaky; I was nervous and unsure of myself. As time went on, I experienced the closing of a perceived gap between body and mind. I felt an equilibrium, wholeness and tranquillity never known before.

A noted Zen master is often quoted: "To study Buddhism is to study the self; to learn the self is to forget the self." Although I had always been somewhat shy and self-conscious, finally, little by little, that self-consciousness was falling away. I was finding the solid me that had been there all along, underneath the doubter and the actor, the performer—the conditioned good girl. And one day, I went beyond even the solid me.

It happens during a seven-day sesshin, on the fourth day. A lot of things have led up to it, but shortly after seating myself at 5 a.m. in the dimly lit zendo, facing the wall, it hits me that I have no problems whatsoever. "Only the small self has problems" are the words that float into my consciousness. Whereas I, or this collection of cells known as Nancy, have somehow entered the realm of the big Self.

The feeling is of complete joy and appreciation. When another sitter comes in late and sits down next to me, I gaze at his bare foot sitting on his left thigh and almost bend down to kiss it, it is so beautiful. It is a foot just being a foot. In the chanting during a service after several sittings, the words I'm chanting, and have chanted many times before, suddenly make total sense. Particularly clear is the line, accompanied by a gentle ring of the bell, "And the mind is no hindrance." My mind suddenly is no hindrance whatsoever—not getting in the way as it usually does. It is as clear as the bell. Walking outside after breakfast, I wonder how I am going to be able to explain to anyone how, walking around the block at 7:30 in the morning on a June day in southeast Minneapolis, I am the happiest I have ever been.

Seeing an old lady out sweeping her front steps, I want to go hug her, she is so completely—what? Just being herself. I restrain myself and call out to her something about the beautiful morning. Seeing lots of students and teachers walking fast and bicycling toward the university, their heads down, I want to shout something startling that will wake them up. Hearing the distant sound of a fire engine, I can only think "That poor person (with a fire) thinks they have a problem. But only the small self has problems." If only everyone could live in the big Self.

So, what was this big Self I found myself in? It was a state of being in which everything in the whole world was intimately interconnected, and everything was just fine   whatever happened. Everyone just was whatever they were, and that was perfect. It was a state in which my total being felt love, joy and compassion toward everyone I encountered. I had never expected to use the phrase 'blissed out' to describe myself, but that sounded about right. I felt truly one with the universe.

Two analogies occurred to me, as I kept struggling with how to explain what I was experiencing. In the first analogy my existence felt like that of a bean on a vine—each bean thinking itself alone and independent and isolated, whereas if it would just open its eyes and become more conscious, it would see that it was part of a vine connecting it to every other bean in the garden. Everything in the universe was subject to this vast interconnection. If people could only see it, realize it, what a difference that would make in the way they approached the world and their lives.

The second analogy was more personal. The clarity of my vision, as I meditated or ate meals or circled the blocks around the Zen Center, was as if I had spent my entire life under water and had just then surfaced, seeing sunlight in all its brilliance for the very first time. The contrast was at least that great.

Sad to say, the realizations and the direct impact of that experience didn't last long. Within a week it had all faded, although it remains strong in my memory. A major shift in my thinking, however, had occurred.

What was I—the small self, this little person who had thought herself so important, who was so self-centered, so independent? By myself, absolutely nothing at all. Nothing except in relation to other people, and animals, and things, and events. A physical form, a collection of cells, with no fixed ego or identity. A being changing thousands of times a day, responding to "my" mind or spirit and whatever situations came my way.

And how had this insight come about? Obviously, it was not something I had thought or done by myself, or controlled in any way. It had happened to me—or had been given to me. Some force I could not explain had changed my life, my understanding, my viewpoint, my world. I could no longer afford the luxury of believing I was the center of existence, and when I died that was the end of everything.

Since the great shift in my thinking, my understanding, almost two decades ago, I have felt compelled to open up to all kinds of possibilities that didn't seem sensible or rational before. Some of these are:

• We are here in this life to grow, to become more and more open, more conscious, more fully aware and awake, to strive toward becoming the most fully conscious human being we can, to really see what is all around us.

• When we're born, we don't all start out at the same place. What we do with our lives depends partly on what we did with them the last time around, and what we're here to learn this time. It may take most of our life to discover what that is, and how to go about it. We may miss it altogether.

• The energy we put into growing and learning isn't gone when we die, but changes our soul, our spirit, or life force, whatever it is that lives on after our body dies. This growth changes our next life in human form.

• Everyone in the world is making a spiritual journey whether they realize it or not; and they're doing the best they can. My job is not to compare myself with others—leading to discouragement about myself or criticism of someone else—but simply to work on me.

I have never been comfortable with the word *God* because of its simplistic image as a being, an entity, usually an old man in the sky. I do now believe in a higher power, but as a force, not an entity. It's the divine life force, beyond comprehension, that makes everything possible. That gives us free will, cause and effect, creativity, consciousness, life and death. That exists inside everyone and everything—clouds, birds, trees, people, animals, insects. When it refers to people, I also call it the big Self—the divine life force that animates me (and everyone else) and makes me what I am, who I am.

The fact that I'm on a spiritual journey doesn't mean I'm trying to act holy or something, or be serious all the time. It doesn't mean I can't do stupid things or silly ones, or laugh a lot, or get mad, or eat junk food, or lift weights, or make love. It does mean that, whatever I'm doing, I try to pay attention; to concentrate on what I'm involved in. It means I try to be as open and honest and compassionate as I can, with whoever I'm with. It means I try to tap consciously into my big Self.

It means I have a million questions, far more questions than answers—about what a truly spiritual life entails; whether animals and humans are equal or if there's a hierarchy; how to reconcile my desire to be honest with my desire not to hurt people, and on and on. It means trying to start each day from a still, centered place. I have recently begun sitting *zazen* daily again, after years of sporadic sitting. I am forever working on monkey mind, anger, hypocrisy, envy, ego.

It also means every day is a new chance to experience something miraculous and wonderful just as it is: the pounding surf, a neighbor who stops to chat, vegetables that magically turn into soup, my cherished companion, Martin (as loving after fifteen years as after six months). Everything just being itself, without any expectations or preconceptions—mine or theirs. Everything just as it is. If only I can remember to see it, to be aware. Emily from *Our Town* is right there with me: "Look at me, Mama." See how precious life is!

One unforgettable piece of advice about how to live came many years ago from Dainin Katagiri Roshi, the Zen master. In November 1979 the worst fear of any parent had just happened: my son had been killed, at the age of not quite 23. I was hit hard and unable to function well for a long, long time. But about a month after Chris's death I sat a long *sesshin* and had a private interview with Roshi. After I had poured out my sorrow, my anger, my questions, I said I couldn't find any reason for me to be alive when Chris was dead. As was so often the case, his answer was not at all what I had expected. It came out of left field, and amazed me with its simplicity and wisdom. "Don't you see?" he said. "Because Chris died, you have to live *more*."

It's hard to live fully alive and awake, spontaneous and resonating to the divine spirit inside. I know I come nowhere close to doing it. But I also know that it's possible, and I've had marvelous teachers. The attempt to realize the divine in myself and everything else, and my connectedness with the whole world, I expect to occupy the rest of my life. Every day—every moment—is an opportunity for greater aliveness.

Nancy Ann James retired in 1991 as an editor and manager and now lives in northwest Florida. She worked for eleven years at a regional government agency and a previous eleven at the University of Minnesota. She's also been a freelance writer and owner of a vegetarian restaurant.

In 1972 Ms. James was a founding member of the Minnesota Zen Meditation Center, and took part in the center's development and ongoing work until her retirement. In the 60's and 70's she was active in the civil rights movement and in furthering alternatives in education. She was part of a group that brought about a K-12 open school as part of the St. Paul public school system.

Nancy lives with her companion of 15 years, Martin Duffy. She can often be found walking on the white-sand beaches of the Gulf of Mexico near their home. She enjoys creative cooking and bakes all their own breads, including sourdough whole-wheat onion-herb bagels. She also lifts weights, does yoga, hits tennis balls, and reads as much as she wants, a lifelong dream. She also enjoys visiting her son, daughter-in-law, and grandson, aged 3, who live in Hawaii.

Adonai Zeus Shekhinah Elim Ogun Kat Buddha
Wyame Hel Rama Mitra Odomankoma Jupiter Het
Heru Agni Cagn Thor Brahma Tangaroa Father
Lugaba Papang Diana Al-Rahman Cerridwen Ahone
Yoma' Tirawa Atius Ganesha El Mungan-ngua
Quetzalcoatl Hamakom ddai
Atibruku Moma YH Bun aiwa

The Hem
of
His
Garment

**Marilyn Fullen
Collins**

Saraswati Inanna Mirir aong
Tonantzin Yuskeha Bha Head
Olodumare Shyama Ekv Heru
Nurrundere Daramilun tzeir
Hecate Chi Musubi Hin suna
Nanderuvucu Erishkigal man
Tsui-goab Ometeotl Os chtli
Surya Elohim Nyankop Ilu
Woden Great Spirit Les goro
Poseidon Chineke Nhialic uwut
Makal Wakantanka Inari Ha-Qadosh barukh hu'
Tara Krishna Avaloket-iswara Rabb Goryo Qat Oke
Nurunderi Indra Shang-ti Amaterasu Ohmikami
Kannon Quan Yin Ise Lakshmi Awonawilona Bast
Omecihuatl Ruhanga Kosane Sophia Dionysus Ixchel
Mawu Ra Ardanariswara Oluwa Deng Hanuman
uNkulunkulu Kanobo Ngai Shamayim Cybele Dakini
Nataraj Pachamama Susanoo Katonda Avlukpo Eloah
Isis Temaukel Eleda Gaia Laxmi Mahmanmu-rok
Odin El-al Herukhuti Viracocha Marduk Ashira Biral
Shaddai Dzingbe Djohu-ma-di-hutu Astarte Ndengei
Koyatu Baha'u'llah Marrigan Baiame Om Pelepelewa
Durga Orisha Nyame Techaronhiawakhon Chukwu
Uvolovu Brahman Nephtys Ha-Maqom Tehuti Maat
Digambara Val Tik Chaitanya Amana Kwoth Num
Colok Nabango Fumeripitsj Shiva Varuna Lukanga
Bala Atibluku Karu Allah Sing Nainuema Artemis
Kartikeya Kuanyin Yelafaz T'ien Baal Shakti
Athena Olorun Nemesis Sheela-na-Gig Bhavartarini
Jesus Horus Izanagi Sebek Waq Ishtar Ti Seker
BegoTanutanu Sat Nam Kali Mirirul Bhavatarini
Tsui-goab Hatzur Brahman Ubusuna Tonantzin
YHVH Apollo Nana God Almighty Hu Vishnu Om

A nd Jesus said, "She touched the hem of my garment . . ."
I heard you, as I bent to kiss it, while I was chained to
the auction block and men with greasy mustaches and
perfumed hankies forced my mouth open and counted my teeth,
saying, "Looks like a good breeder to me, $200.00."

"Touch the hem of my garment," that's what you said as I knelt
to kiss it while I picked cotton until little lakes of blood trickled from
my fingers when I pulled at its softness. Sweat rolled off my forehead like the blood at Gethsemani.

"Touch the hem of my garment," that's what you said as I
bowed to kiss it when I threw my children in the river and watched
them drown. Tiny brown hands breaking the surface, "Mama,
Mama," they screamed, but the paddyrollers were comin', faster
and faster, the pounding of their horses' hooves shook the ground. I
could see the foam dripping from the horses' mouths, they was
drivin' them so fast. Paddyrollers beatin' their horses like they would
beat my children. We run, run, run toward the river, I'm praying,
"God, don't let me and my children go back to them slavers, not
again, not no more." Paddyrollers all around us, horses kickin' up
dust and leaves by the riverbank— "No you can't have my babies—
hail Mary full of grace, the Lord is with thee—Mary, you a mother,
take care of my babies, please . . ."

"Touch the hem of my garment," that's what you said and I did
as the sheriff led me from the river—called me a murderous nigger
bitch, said, "Hell, we could have made good money off those children, but no, you decided to drown 'em, they wasn't your property
to drown. Damn niggers, just don't understand the value of a dol-
lar." I freed my children, I gave them back to you Almighty Father.
And when they whipped me, it was all right, 'cause I could see your
sweet face and I remembered, by your stripes I am healed.

My history, my Jesus. My God. My God is a strong, fierce
Mother and Father. My God and Goddess love me and all that I
am. My Africanness and my womanness. There is a saying in the
Black community, "Don't be too womanish!" That was said to me
when I was wearing crimson red lipstick (African American women
aren't allowed to do that as it makes their already full, luscious lips
look too large). Or when I allowed my hair, (note allowed) to do its

natural thing. I refused to straighten it again after Miss Willie burned me so bad, I looked like I only had one ear. She got ahold of the other one and broiled it. All the soothing words and cool witch hazel in the world could not make me go for the Barbie doll look again. You see, dear reader, it dawned on me that My God loves my juicy red lips and my undomesticated hair. He/She gave it to me as an outward sign of my spirit. I love my God and my Catholic Christianity.

My God got me through the random slaughter of the voyage through the Middle Passage. My God got me through the sweat, rape, and loss in the cane and cotton fields of Louisiana. My God got me through beholding my children being rendered from my breast leaving a trail of milk that gave nourishment to Massa's child. My God got me through paddyrollers and nightriders and trees that bore the strange fruit of the south—the fruit of lynched fathers, brothers and sons, hanging, swaying in a mystical rhythm of their own. My God brought me hope through the prophets, Garvey and DuBois, and Truth. My God gave me the gift of words during the Harlem Renaissance and Zora Neale marching through swamps of my ancestors' pasts. My God have me little brown babies with tight plaits in their hair and laughter on their lips.

My God. Where do I as an African American Catholic Christian woman fit? I am all of these things and so is my God. It took both of us a long time to get to who and what I am.

In 1958, I begged my mother to let me be on "Make Room for Daddy," starring Danny Thomas. I figured I was just as cute as Angela Cartwright and infinitely more talented. Shoot, Danny was a successful nightclub entertainer, his lovely wife Cathy was the ideal homemaker, the older brother Rusty was intelligent and irrepressible. They lived in a townhouse in New York, a real city, no Mayberry, Riverdale or Springfield for this family! Most importantly, they had a maid! A maid who cooked and cleaned so that Cathy could look beautiful; a maid, who picked up after Rusty so he could continue to be irrepressible. And she opened the door for Danny's guest stars so they could banter for our enjoyment. She was a Black woman, and I don't even remember her name. But I still wanted one of them. You see, I didn't realize my own grandmother was a maid too.

In 1958, my family and I would troop to our local parish on Sunday morning and sit in the back of the church. In the back. Because we had to. And I remember kneeling at the polished oak communion rail, stretching out my tongue to receive the heavenly

host. My eyes always fell on the crucifix at the altar. A pale, frail
Jesus with straggly blond hair and rivulets of blood dripping from
his crown of thorns eyed me so sadly, I felt sorry for him, but when
communion was over, I'd return to the back of the church and I
could feel that sickly looking Jesus stare at my bended head and
laugh. His laughter would bounce off the statues of the Blessed
Mother; St. Francis of Assisi would be in on the joke. They laughed
because here were these stupid people who had bought into the
myth of forgive and forget. People who allowed themselves to be
relegated to the back of the church. My cousins could only be baptized on Wednesday evenings, my aunts and uncles could only be
married in the rectory. I grew up knowing the only way African
Americans could come to Jesus was through the back door of the
Catholic church.

What's the connection between Mother Church and Danny
Thomas? I, Marilyn Fullen-Collins was not wanted by America
anywhere. There was no Cosby for me. I was eighteen before I saw
a Black priest. Twenty before I spied an African American nun. I
still haven't seen a Black pope. I was basically being told, "you
aren't good enough. We have no use for you, except at collection
time."

When I was at St. Mary's Academy, however, (I started the year
Martin Luther King was assassinated) my Catholicism and my
Africanness became real and viable to me. This was a turbulent
time to be a nun. They were going through changes too. Sr. Mary
Andre wore a "Free Huey Newton" button instead of a cross. She
had recently returned from the South where she had been punched,
spat upon, called a nigger-loving whore, and she kept on. She told
me she tried to find Jesus in the bigots who screamed at her, the
sharecroppers that were too afraid to register to vote, and the cor-
rupt politicians that ran the tiny towns and hamlets that made up
Alabama, Georgia, and Mississippi.

Sister Catherine Louise asked me if I'd ever read the
Autobiography of Malcolm X. It was she who told me to remember the
Mason-Dixon line began at the Canadian border, not some obscure
section of the South. Sister also reminded me that Black people
were much better off in the South because at least white people
wouldn't smile in your face and stick a razor in your back like they
do in the North. Sr. Margaret Jude reminded me to pray for Angela
Davis' safety when the FBI was looking for her.

Sisters taught me this. Sisters taught me that the University of
Ghana was the first university in the world! Sisters taught me to

think for myself, and question, question, question. The questioning included government and church authority. So, when I walked into St. Brigid's parish in South Central Los Angeles, my eyes searched the altar for another passive, pale Jesus. But to my delight, he had been replaced by a shiny, Black mahogany Jesus with a broad, flat nose, and sensual thick lips. My eyes traveled around the church and I saw icons of blessed Sojourner Truth, blessed Malcolm, blessed Harriet Tubman. And when the choir marched in on the good foot dazzling in their liberation colored robes—red from the blood my people have shed, black for the color of our skin and green for the land that will someday be ours, I wept. Wept big, copious tears, like a grateful baby. When the drummers started the procession I realized this was a piece of heaven, African American men and women walking down the main aisle of the church carrying not only the Word, but all of the dignity inherent in the kings and queens of a land that lives on in our collective memories. How did I ever worship any other way? I was home. I was free. All because I touched the hem of his garment and he/she set me free.

I believe that if we, the universal Church, could just run our fingers gently, tentatively over the hem of that garment, we could all be free. Now. Let us begin.

Marilyn Fullen Collins is a teacher and lecturer in multicultural issues, women's studies, and conflict resolution. She has facilitated workshops in numerous schools and universities in the Pacific Northwest, and has been a guest on several television talk shows giving an African American perspective to crucial national problems.

The author of many articles, she has also written *Pathblazers: Eight People Who Have Made a Difference,* published by Open Hand Press.

Marilyn lives in Seattle with her husband and children.

Adonai Zeus Shekhinah Elim Ogun Kat Buddha
Wyame Hel Rama Mitra Odomankoma Jupiter Het
Heru Agni Cagn Thor Brahma Tangaroa Father
Lugaba Papang Diana Al-Rahman Cerridwen Ahone
Yoma' Tirawa Atius Ganesha El Mungan-ngua
Quetzalcoatl Hamakom ddai
Atibruku Moma YH Bun aiwa
Saraswati Inanna Miriru aong
Tonantzin Yuskeha Bha Head
Olodumare Shyama Ekv Heru
Nurrundere Daramilun tzeir
Hecate Chi Musubi Hin suna
Nanderuvucu Erishkigal man
Tsui-goab Ometeotl Os chtli
Surya Elohim Nyankop Ilu
Woden Great Spirit Lesa goro
Poseidon Chineke Nhialic Atlek Kurt Auset Teuwut
Makai Wakantanka Inari Ha-Qadosh barukh hu'
Tara Krishna Avaloket-iswara Rabb Goryo Qat Oke
Nurunderi Indra Shang-ti Amaterasu Ohmikami
Kannon Quan Yin Ise Lakshmi Awonawilona Bast
Omecihuatl Ruhanga Kosane Sophia Dionysus Ixchel
Mawu Ra Ardanariswara Oluwa Deng Hanuman
uNkulunkulu Kanobo Ngai Shamayim Cybele Dakini
Nataraj Pachamama Susanoo Katonda Avlukpo Eloah
Isis Temaukel Eleda Gaia Laxmi Mahmanmu-rok
Odin El-al Herukhuti Viracocha Marduk Ashira Biral
Shaddai Dzingbe Djohu-ma-di-hutu Astarte Ndengei
Koyatu Baha'u'llah Marrigan Baiame Om Pelepelewa
Durga Orisha Nyame Techaronhiawakhon Chukwu
Uvolovu Brahman Nephtys Ha-Maqom Tehuti Maat
Digambara Val Tik Chaitanya Amana Kwoth Num
Colok Nabango Fumeripitsj Shiva Varuna Lukanga
Bala Atibluku Karu Allah Sing Nainuema Artemis
Kartikeya Kuanyin Yelafaz T'ien Baal Shakti
Athena Olorun Nemesis Sheela-na-Gig Bhavartarini
Jesus Horus Izanagi Sebek Waq Ishtar Ti Seker
BegoTanutanu Sat Nam Kali Mirirul Bhavatarini
Tsui-goab Hatzur Brahman Ubusuna Tonantzin
YHVH Apollo Nana God Almighty Hu Vishnu Om

God
Is a
Verb

**Rev. Alla Renée
Bozarth, Ph.D.**

God is alive and so are we. To live is to flow with feeling, to participate in the miracle of being, and to move and be moved. All life is one: experience and reflection, action and evaluation, passion and compassion. All is one. In-flow and over-flow. God and we together.

We come to birth and being from God, but mystery and meaning must unfold, and what we become depends on our response to the whole of life. We create our lives as we surrender to the larger mystery that contains us. No part of our lives can be separated from any other. The journey back to the Source never leaves the Source. All is one. All is alive. We shape our souls by the choices we make and most of all by what we love. And we never stop becoming ourselves. More and more, into eternity, we become who we are. The journey that shapes our souls is a never-ending journey. It is a journey of perpetual motion and power.

God
is
a
verb.

God is One
mighty
roaring
verb.

God is
One

God is
mighty

God is
roaring

God
Is
a verb
roaring

God-Is.

This verb named God
we now name New
Being,
solar/lunar/sidereal
MOTION
soaring
breathing burning lightning
ultrasonic
SOUND.

God is
in me
I know, being
new,
stretch strike light-
ning,
soar-sound
Godlike

sometimes I just have to
rise up and R O A R

In a dream I have just received a check in the mail for a book
that I have published. Since I have no recollection of having written
a book, let alone having published it, I decide to go out and buy a
copy to find out what I have said. I go to the grocery store and take
my cart to the book section that is between fruit and milk. I recognize my book instantly: it is a glossy black soft-covered book with
only the word SPIRIT in glossy white on the cover. I pick it up and
open it to find my name on the inside. Instead of my actual name,
the name Alice Rice is in the upper right-hand corner of the inside
leaf. I accept this pseudonym and am pleased.

When I awaken and amplify the dream with conscious associations, I realize that Alice is the name of a physician whom I greatly
admire, and Rice is the last name of a nurse I knew as a child. I

discover the etymology of the names: Alice, form Greek *alethea*, meaning "truth"; and rice, from Sanskrit *rizon*, meaning "seed." The images of the dream evoke associations—light out of darkness, the seed of truth hidden within, healing women, and nourishment—in the context of a personal spirituality that is shared with others in a public but private way through symbolic anonymity. The life of the Spirit is available in the grocery store with other food in the most natural way; there is a price on it—it is something of value which must be taken and used to be purposeful. The ecstatic and the mundane exist together unself-consciously.

Dreams have always impressed me as spontaneous works of art, produced by the unconscious parts of the psyche with breathtaking clarity. Our dreams are a valid expression of spirituality, for they tell of the life of the soul, as do our waking fantasies, images, and collective myths.

If theology is the rational attempt to describe God and our relationship with the holy, spirituality is the pararational, existential living-out of our God-experience and our relationship with the holy.

Today more than ever before in the history of spiritual consciousness, we have an opportunity to express our personal and collective spiritual life holistically. The life of the spirit is not separate from the whole of human life. The spirit is alive through the passions of the body and of the mind, and it expresses itself in living relationships with other beings, seen and unseen.

The language of the spirit is symbol, for symbolism in the psychological sense is simply the means we make for expressing the inexpressible. Symbols are charged by the aura of mystery in what they express and must leave unexpressed, but clearly felt. Mystery is the part of life that defies definition. It is not something that can be solved for, by its very nature, mystery constitutes a limitless power to exist beyond merely rational comprehension. Mystery is the part of life that cannot be captured, but which tends to capture us. As philosopher Gabriel Marcel reflected, mystery is not a problem to be solved, but a reality to be lived. Mystery is the living part of speech beyond language, of hearing beyond sound, of vision beyond sight. Mystery is where theology ends and spirituality begins. It is the threshold at which reason surrenders to the knowing capacity of the whole organism.

Theologians have always recognized the purpose of their work to be preparatory to the activity of the spirit, though occasionally the definitive language of theology has intruded upon the experience of the holy, for theology speaks and provides the context of the intellect to a process that also includes the silences of the spirit. The true theologian knows when to speak and describe experience, and when simply to experience. The challenge facing us today is to develop a valid, holistic theology—one that recognizes the female as well as the male aspects of God. Authenticating our conceptual process is the other side of re-authenticating our worship experience. Both involve expanding images and the creation of accurate language to express our present (certainly, still limited) understanding of God and our relationship to the holy.

The contribution of women and our female perceptions is absolutely essential to this process. Our approach to the task should be open, generous, honest, and creative. Above all, we should realize that the task is so great that we need to bring to it all that we have, holding back none of the materials of our dreams, myths, revelations, or longings, discriminating and choosing from among these materials those that are appropriate to our collective self-expression in faith and worship.

We need to begin by recognizing the validity and value of our own experience for the corporate good. Contrary to the distorted view of theology often communicated by our teachers in the past, our own experience is relevant to the theology of the whole community. If our theological understanding has no connection with lived experience, it has no validation of its own and becomes part of the dead weight that burdens us instead of the meaningful context that illumines our lives.

Many things in the past that have been conceptually isolated by theological language are integrated in actual experience. As modern physics now takes account of the interconnection rather than the illegitimate separation of such dynamics as space and time, matter and motion, contemporary theology begins to acknowledge that body and soul, spirit and matter, nature and grace are not rigid dichotomies that need to be reconciled but beautifully interacting forces that are experienced and perceived as one. The sensual and spiritual are the same energy playing at different speeds, like poetry and dance.

Value is determined by the way in which relationships form, not in the things themselves. The holiness of the body may be experienced as an enhancement of the holiness of the mind or spirit, and the creativity of chaos may be seen as the matrix of order.

We live in a society that values product over process, but a holistic approach views the two as one. As the medium is the message, the process is the product, a value to be loved for its own sake.

Artists and the best scientists know this functionally and theoretically.

I recall the words of my geology professor on the opening day of classes at Northwestern University: "In the beginning was the Word, and the Word was . . . hydrogen." Though some professional theologians may find the scientist's attention-grabbing statement to be offensive, those who heard him say it can testify to his reverence. As a scientist, he lives with mystery as priests and poets do, but from a different view—and the new science is eminently and wonderfully incarnational.

Creation

In the beginning was
hydrogen.
And then
the Explosion.

We, the fragments,
tumbling to Infinity,
part of the One,
expanding the Origins,
starchildren
born out of the Chaos of God.

Incarnation

In the beginning still
was the Word,
spoken into form,
being-become-motion
slow enough for us
to see and touch and hear,
bodying forth a divine love
in human glory
(God-like-Us, We-like-God),
the One, the Very,
became born
into our Chaos,
making it surely
holy for ever.

Theologian Mary Daly's fresh insight that God, like love, is a verb, gives me tremendous excitement and a sense of expansion, the temple of God at my center opening out like a morning rose. It puts me in touch with God within and God beyond; God active as fire, wind, and water inside me and beyond the universe. My own creativity becomes a sacred link with God and others, a force for healing in a broken world. The notion of a God who is motion as well as love (love-in-motion), gives me courage to face the emptiness, to meet chaos with creativity and originality, and (in a Godlike way) stretch out toward possibility. Then my own life becomes not only a work of art fashioned out of love, but a eucharistic process as well. The incarnation into a particular art form is the bodying forth of spiritual energy sacramentally into the perceptual world, and the bodying forth, the incarnation within the creative act, is always a great thanksgiving, an expression of deepest gratitude for creation itself.

My own gift to the collective theological process in the Christian community, and the gift of artists as a whole to the church, is a sacramental attitude toward life. My way of creating theology—language and concepts and metaphors which describe my experience of God—is to perceive intrinsic unities and organic wholenesses in patterns of relationship at every level of experience. These patterns of unity and wholeness take the shape of infinite diversity of expression. The dynamics of their unfolding revelation of inner relatedness through outer forms are lively and omnipresent. My mind stretches almost to breaking when I learn from modern physics that everything in the universe participates in the incomprehensible movement of God: not only do we live as organically connected with the stars—our bodies and the oldest forms in the universe, the Giant Red Stars, containing the same elements of iron, calcium and phosphorus—but at the subatomic level endless processes relate substances in a continuous pattern of interchange and creation. I consider science and scholarship at their best to be forms of art, for art itself comes from the Latin, *artus*, meaning "joint"; art is the creative joining of forms in order to create new forms. The scientists who tell me I am connected physically with the stars, and the artists who create the cosmic dance and evoke the energy of miracles with color on canvas, both open me to the sacramental dimension of life in which I perceive God moving and alive.

My very limited perception and understanding of astrophysics spills over into poetry, the area of homage to the holy:

Universal Body

Worldflesh:
my bones bones
of the Old Red Stars.

Now scientists know that while electrons fly in unimaginable
circuits around the atomic nuclei at 600 miles per second, the nuclei
themselves fly at 40,000 miles per second. Intense confinement creates intense velocity. And matter itself is nothing more than infinite
varieties and interchanges of motion, so that physicists speak of
matter's tendencies to occur rather than its absolute existence, and
they measure it by its possibilities. Everything consists of possibility
waves. This fires my intuition even when my intellect is boggled and
teaches me more about God than a hundred catechisms. It also
gets me more deeply in touch with what it means to be Godlike and
human in an intricate and expanding universe. To think of physics
as a way with a heart opens up new levels of my own reality in the
creature community:

No such thing as empty space.
No such thing as solid matter.
No such thing as one time.

    space is curved
    matter is motion
    here is possible
    now is all

The yellow canoe all by itself
without being moved is moving itself
faster than the white rapids around it.

The red velvet couch I lie on
moves a million times faster than my thoughts.

My own body and yours moving so fast
our faces cannot keep up.

Which is why they—the faces—wrinkle first,
in no-time, so the skin can get closer to itself.

These are perceptions and feelings and understandings of inexpressible realities. They are the processes which I bring to my own participation in theology-making as part of the Christian community. They are personal and experiential, intellectual and intuitive, sensual and bodily expressions of life. The unfolding discovery of these multi-level processes is what I mean by a holistic approach to theology: one which moves toward deeper wholeness through creative interplay of all available energies.

As theology is the descriptive, conceptual language of expressive, actual experience, it plays back into the experience by informing our worship. Liturgy is always created in a theological context, so that it is an accurate expression of the community's relationship to the holy. So-called 'experimental' liturgies are the creative testing field of whole-making. A philosophy of theology that defines it as a whole-making (holistic) process also assumes that the living of theology in worship will be whole-making. Spirituality manifested collectively becomes community liturgy. One of the members of our Wisdom House worshipping community recently created a Liturgy of Dreams, bringing that innermost and hidden dimension of experience openly into our corporate act of worship.

In order to be part of such collective whole-making activities in the formation of theology and liturgy, it is necessary first to have trust in one's own processes. I have to be able to trust my experience in order to share it with others. I am concerned with this more personal side of theology-making, and my concern has taken me into one more area of priestly ministry—that of therapy. Therapy—psychotherapy, in this case—is for me the process of personal whole-making. Psychotherapy is the care of the soul and aims toward the health of the soul as the person's total life center. As I bring creativity, poetry, dance, drama, and healing skills to the therapeutic encounter, my purpose is to share a relationship which tends toward the healing and growth of each person involved in it. I have experienced the priestly ministry in therapeutic encounters with my clients, but I did not know until recently of the sacred origins of the art of therapy. Before the Greeks referred to healers as therapists, the word was used in naming those who functioned as interpreters for the Oracle at Delphi. Without therapists, sacred prophecy was useless, for no one could understand it. The therapists made wholeness between prophecy and the people, working as the prophet's priests to mediate deepest healing into the community. I imagine women in ancient times filling this role.

My own personal process of whole-making has directly affected my spirituality and my contribution to my worshipping community. As I have come to own and accept and celebrate my womanhood as a gift from God, bringing my own new value for the female side of life into prayer, my experience of God has broken wide open. When I first began to use female imagery in prayer, I experienced a kind of inward leaping that was ecstatically physical as well as 'spiritual,' an inward bodily leaping that made me feel God in my nerves and blood and deep down in my bone marrow, as well as in my emotions and intellect.

As I grew in appreciation of the Hebrew and early Christian sources of reverence for the feminine in the divine, I have laid deeper claim on my own God-experience as a woman reaching back to ancient collective female roots of worship. The mystical tradition in Jewish and Christian religion has always included the feminine aspect of God's nature, and I have found validation for my own experience in Scriptures and in the saints.

The Hebrew words for spirit, wisdom, and the law are all feminine words describing the feminine energy of God. *Ruach*, the breath of the Spirit, expresses the creative energy of God. The feminine *Shekinah* is God's abiding presence, personified as the bride of Israel, as is the *Sabbath*. Israel is conversely called the bride of Yahweh, the masculine aspect of God.[1]

In the Christian tradition Julian of Norwich spoke of her relationship with Mother Jesus; Anselm described a vision in which God appeared to him as a lactating woman who fed him heavenly food from her breasts; and the Patristic description of the Persons of the Trinity as exclusively male was compensated in an underlying experience of the Holy Spirit as the feminine energy identified with *Ruach*, and the life-giving Wisdom of *Hokmah* or *Sophia*. The virtual elevation and inclusion of Mary into the Trinity by the Roman Catholic concept of her as Co-redemptrix, and by the dogmas of the Immaculate Conception and Assumption, are spontaneous corrections for the patriarchal exclusion of the feminine in the official Christian theology of the nature of God.

Describing my own theological inclusiveness and spiritual expansiveness, in keeping with those tendencies in my own religious tradition, I wrote:

Mother Christ, Sister Spirit

Christ! Thank God you
are no longer the husband/lover
icon of my inner eye
(any more than you should be
for the soul's good eros),
nor the towering Master, lowering Lord
of my early childhood sleep,
but have at last risen
within my self's reality,
One-Who-Simply-Is.

Brother Jesus, Mother Christ,
creation's climax loving me through incarnation;
you stand by without/within,
heal, nurture, strengthen,
making me possible as you are possible.

Creator, Savior, Spirit,
beyond gender yet encompassing all:
Mother Bear to this wild cub,
Brother Lion to this lamb
(or Brother Lamb to this lion);
most wonderful of all, Sister Spirit
to this wakening woman, this human star.

We recognize that worship, like theology, is a living process
subject to continuous evaluation and re-vision. It is not a fixed
object impervious to change, for liturgy and theology expand and
contract in rhythm with the rest of our lives. Currently, liturgy and
theology are expanding in some of our faith and worship communities, reflecting a life process of personal and collective self-
examination, expansion, and inclusion.

The value of inclusiveness and expansiveness in prayer—liturgical or devotional, public or private—is to help us get closer to God,
to express accurately and enhance our present relationship to the
holy. We do not presume to capture the reality of God in the language which describes our understanding of God, only to express
our limited perception of our relationship with God at this moment
in our religious lives. In the process we discover that God is truly
both immanent and transcendent, within and beyond, female and

male, light and dark, merciful and just. The only model that I know of for the paradoxical, pararational self-revelation of God, as we perceive it, is the apparently self-contradictory light theory in modern physics: light is manifested truly as waves, and truly as particles, alternately and at the same time, even though (we think) we know that waves and particles are irreconcilably different from one another in function. It is not the light which is wrong, or the theory which is lacking, but our perception which is limited, and our language which is always approximate and symbolic rather than precisely descriptive. We are faced with an even greater mystery when we approach God. This is why it is never enough to approach God with anything less than our whole selves, all our functions working together: bodily, intellectually, emotionally, with the engagement of the whole organic self, experiencing and relating to the holy in life.

I was not able to approach God with this kind of engagement until I began to open up my prayer life to the feminine aspect of God, and to celebrate my own femaleness in that aspect. And I did not suspect the wholeness that I missed until I began to experience it. Then I came alive and knew that I wanted more and more life in my relationship with God and with other persons. From increased intimacy with God, my awe of God also increased, and so did my longing for authenticity in community, the longing of depth for depth.

I do not mean to suggest that this process is possible only for women. I only know that I came to it self-consciously as a woman, open to deeper discovery of my own nature through closer contact with the nature of God and deeper contact with the nature of creation. Sexuality and spirituality interact in my own growth experience and are reunited in my religious life.

My experience of feminine imagery in prayer begins to compensate for a personal lifetime and several collective millennia of spiritual one-sidedness. Reclaiming the feminine in worship helps me reclaim my self as a person created uniquely in the image of God, female. Now I know with my whole being that I am connected with God and with all creatures, organically and naturally; the realization of this connection is the reason for which I was born.

Slowly, steadily, I am learning, through constant refinement of feeling and thought, how to worship our Creator, how to wrap the world in prayer. The way is ancient, timeless, but I have to learn it each day for the first time. It is older than the earth, newer than the first leaf of spring.

Bakerwoman God

Bakerwoman God,
I am your living bread.
Strong, brown Bakerwoman God,
I am your low, soft, and being-shaped loaf.
I am your rising
bread, well-kneaded
by some divine and knotty
pair of knuckles,
by your warm earth hands.
I am bread well-kneaded.

Put me in fire, Bakerwoman God,
put me in your own bright fire.

I am warm, warm as you from fire.
I am white, and gold, soft and hard,
brown and round.
I am so warm from fire.

Break me, Bakerwoman God!
I am broken under your caring Word.
Drop me in your special juice in pieces.
Drop me in your blood.
Drunken me in the great red flood.
Self-giving chalice, swallow me.
My skin shines in the divine wine.
My face is cup-covered and I drown.

I fall up
in a red pool
in a gold world
where your warm
sunskin hand is there
to catch and hold me.
Bakerwoman God, remake me.

As we honor the divine within the feminine, we celebrate also
that angels can take the form of other species. Non-anthropomor-
phic imagery is now for me a more immediate conduit to the
divine, as in my metaphor of the Holy Trinity:

In the Name of the Bee & the Bear & the Butterfly

In the beginning, Bee.
Bee of fertility, blessing of flowers,
high priest of pollination.
Bee of My Lady's dreaming,
dressing her eyes, ears, lips, and feet
with golden honey, feeding her
with goddess food for holy milking.

Bee, Bee, lighting on her lotus hands,
kissing her lovely toes with your silken lashes,
leaving streaks of bronze and gold,
powder from your feet on her blue mantle.
Bee, beloved pet, Angel Bee, beckoner,
messenger, bestower, wonder
of the Mother of God.

> Oh Bee, holy Bee:
> be with us and feed us
> with high-potent sweetness
> and when we grow dead
> sting us alive.

In the beginning also, the Bear.
Great Mother Bear birthing us
in your own image, you teach us
the bearness of life, unbearable
breathtaking bearness of you.
We, in your likeness, learn to survive,
learn to suckle in your furry bosom,
learn to choose within the forest
food to make us grow, growling and humming,
into the fullness of your stature:
learn to labor hard, to fight when needed,
to care for and be cared for,
to rest deep and play well
with you and one another—we your children,
we your fierce and foolish
tender cubs.

Bear, Bear, you give us teeth and claws
and make us strong with your vigor,
watch over us desiring our self-sufficiency
in healthy measure:
"Bear, I lose my way,
Bear, I fall entangled,
Bear, I feel afraid . . .
Food you give me of your self,
milk of you honey-feeding body,
berries colored of your blood.
Not only do I drink and chew—
often, with the teeth you gave me,
I bite you, God."

O Bear, Great Bear, make us your pride and joy.

And of the Butterfly.
Born of life's ending,
promised from the beginning.
All the age-old cocooning,
all the enduring of unendurable happenings,
through long beginnings and endless middle
of our worm-shaped selves:
the unborn butterfly clinging to the bark—
an ugly small worm of a thing made tight,
having no way of knowing, no way of telling
from the tree or sky hope of any change to come.

But by simply being a good and faithful worm
allowing itself to die—
surprise! breaks forth
the strangest bird
from its soft, odd-shaped egg—
from greygreen into gold,
orange, yellow, blue, vermilion,
amazing lightness and freedom
with singing wings most Christly,
slipping so lightly and so largely
into the membrane of our souls
through crevices only God can know,
filling all the soft cocoon stretching
spaces of our human hearts.

YES *International Publishers*
1317 Summit Avenue
Saint Paul, MN 55105

If you would like to receive a copy of our latest YES Books Catalog and be on our mailing list for future publications please fill in this card and return it to us.

If you would like to receive information about seminars and workshops sponsored by YES, check here. ( )

PLEASE PRINT

Name...

Address...

City, ...
State...

Zip..

Butterfly, brave Butterfly,
down the wormlike days
of all our discouragement,
give us the courage to open,
to turn into the unimaginable,
take color, unfold, make music and fly!

Blessed Sacrament

Temple-tending
sunblessed, the body
of Earth takes me
in again, cell to cell,
wind-washed cave-explorer
finding mirrored my own
dark and secret places
of deep and sacred life,
love's source in cosmos.

Here the many-wombed mother
sings ocean hymns to my worship.

I live on her breast,
drink mountain milk distilled
for children's many-eyes.

It is no secret, this ever-
present tabernacle,
star-candled by night,
a place of innocent focus,
moon-bathed votive garden
of forest—

Earth's body and each
particular mine, pure host—
the house of heaven—
my body open in adoration,
my soul a bridal bed of God.

Easter Wisdom Rite

Out of the womb of winter
she rises, welling,
the daughter reborn,
Eastre, Astarte, the Dawn.

More ancient than Night
she belongs to all Life,
dreamed before time
in the swirling Now of the sea.

Mare, Mother, holy Water,
origin of all Earthbabes living.
Here, where stillness is a song,
where waiting is every thing.

We wait now for wonder,
renewed in the dark
of our world-weary hearts.
It is she, live icon of soul,

whose name means the Source:
womb swelling full
in the spiraling
fire of a star.

Astarte, newborn, O Lover
—whom we cannot betray
or abandon in Christ—
we invoke as sleep invokes Day.

From the soulwound of our fear
From the hearthurt of endings: Begin.

Be our Golden One, our Star,
be the morning ray, the sun
of our Spring, Shekinah,
the ancient embrace

whose sabbath kiss woke the Christ,
wakes still in deep silence
the Christ within creatures,
called out of Death one by one

until, dancing your dance,
we come to, and all again
becomes
healed.

Holy Nativity

The One born to us
is a small green shoot
breaking through snow,
is a foal born to the wild mare,
is a nest of seaturtle children,
is a rubber tree in the Amazon,
a quarterton whale,
a coven of bees glistening
from the sweet Queen's body—
is a human child in the African Plain,
in a New York alley,
is you, is me, each one
not less worthy
of adoration and praise,
for God born in every living
new beginning needs the same
nurture of lovingkindness
to grow strong and happily
into its true Self.

I wish for you as I wish for myself the courage to continue to suffer your suffering and die your deaths in order to live your life more fully and enjoy your joys more completely.

The Reverend Alla Renée Bozarth was among the first eleven women ordained as Episcopal priests in 1974 in Philadelphia. She prepared for her ordination at Seabury-Western Theological Seminary in Evanston, Illinois. She also holds degrees in performing arts from Northwestern University and a certificate in Gestalt psychotherapy from the Gestalt Training Center of San Diego. She has nearly twenty years of experience as a professional counselor for individuals and groups. Her style incorporates a focus on the integration of spirituality and sexuality; dreamwork; creative inner dialogue; healing of memories and childhood wounds; recovery from addictions and abuse; women's self-empowerment;

living with loss; relationship issues; and soul-making through personal myths. Dr. Bozarth is author of numerous books, including *At the Foot of the Mountain: Discovering Images for Emotional Healing, Womanpriest: A Personal Odyssey,* and most recently, *Six Days in St. Petersburg* and *Thirty-one Commandments or Flavors of Grace.* Dr. Bozarth currently resides at Wisdom House in Sandy, Oregon, where she conducts liturgical and other special celebrations.

Adonai Zeus Shekhinah Elim Ogun Kat Buddha
Wyame Hel Rama Mitra Odomankoma Jupiter Het
Heru Agni Cagn Thor Brahma Tangaroa Father
Lugaba Papang Diana Al-Rahman Cerridwen Ahone
Yoma' Tirawa Atius *Gaoako* El Mungan ngua
Quetzalcoatl Hamakom *ddai*
Atibruku Moma YH Bun *aiwa*
Saraswati Inanna Mirir *aong*
Tonantzin Yuskeha Bha *Head*
Olodumare Shyama Ekv *Heru*
Nurrundere Daramilun *tzeir*

God
Dances

Hecate Chi Musubi Hin *suna*
Nanderuvucu Erishkigal *man*
Tsui-goab Ometeotl Os *chtli*
Surya Elohim Nyankop *Ilu*
Woden Great Spirit Lese *goro*
Poseidon Chineke Nhialic *uwut*

Akiko Kobayashi

Makai Wakantanka Inari Ha-Qadosh barukh hu'
Tara Krishna Avaloket-iswara Rabb Goryo Qat Oke
Nurunderi Indra Shang-ti Amaterasu Ohmikami
Kannon Quan Yin Ise Lakshmi Awonawilona Bast
Omecihuatl Ruhanga Kosane Sophia Dionysus Ixchel
Mawu Ra Ardanariswara Oluwa Deng Hanuman
uNkulunkulu Kanobo Ngai Shamayim Cybele Dakini
Nataraj Pachamama Susanoo Katonda Avlukpo Eloah
Isis Temaukel Eleda Gaia Laxmi Mahmanmu-rok
Odin El-al Herukhuti Viracocha Marduk Ashira Biral
Shaddai Dzingbe Djohu-ma-di-hutu Astarte Ndengei
Koyatu Baha'u'llah Marrigan Baiame Om Pelepelewa
Durga Orisha Nyame Techaronhiawakhon Chukwu
Uvolovu Brahman Nephtys Ha-Maqom Tehuti Maat
Digambara Val Tik Chaitanya Amana Kwoth Num
Colok Nabango Fumeripitsj Shiva Varuna Lukanga
Bala Atibluku Karu Allah Sing Nainuema Artemis
Kartikeya Kuanyin Yelafaz T'ien Baal Shakti
Athena Olorun Nemesis Sheela-na-Gig Bhavartarini
Jesus Horus Izanagi Sebek Waq Ishtar Ti Seker
BegoTanutanu Sat Nam Kali Mirirul Bhavatarini
Tsui-goab Hatzur Brahman Ubusuna Tonantzin
YHVH Apollo Nana God Almighty Hu Vishnu Om

K amakura is about an hour's drive from Tokyo. It is a strategic point, surrounded by hills on three sides and facing the sea on the south. The hills are low and gentle, the sea is warm and shallow for some distance. It is the ancient capital of the samurai who had formerly served nobles in Kyoto. When the government returned to Kyoto, the people in Kamakura gently resumed their agriculture and fishing, and the practice of Shinto.

Because Kamakura was regarded as an ancient capital, it was not bombed during World War II. The beautiful sea, the evergreen forests, important historic spots, the many shrines and temples remained as they were for such a long time. With the fall of imperialism, democracy came to Japan. Shinto, which had been the state religion and the unifying national symbol since the Meiji era, was disconnected from the government. It had to begin its history anew under the new freedom of religion law as one of the many religions in Japan. Shinto came to a turning point; it needed to analyze and evaluate itself as a religion and as a symbol in Japanese culture.

I was born in a small village on the shore of Kamakura, the youngest child of Guji, chief priest of the Goryo Shinto Shrine, a year after the end of World War II. I remember life then. It was somehow free and vital, even though material goods were few. I remember how the shrine looked to this little girl, the daughter of the priest who devoted himself totally to Shinto's revival.

When I was young, I ran over the hills, played in the shrine grounds, and in the summer swam in the sea every day. I had no time to feel tired. I was fascinated by the beauty of the sky and the sea at sunset, changing its color every second. I chased fish, collected seashells, and once I happened upon the spawning of a sea turtle. In the mountains, I would walk on animal's paths. I saw violets growing under the rock every spring; I found lizards, cicadas, dragonflies, and other insects. When I climbed the huge camellia tree flourishing in the shadow of the mountain at dusk and licked the nectar, I felt I was in another world. The same sensation seized me when I lay down on the shining stone among tall grass, listening to the buzz of bees. So I felt lost when I came home from school one day to find my favorite tree cut down. Memories of my childhood always include the sea, the sky, forest, grass, living creatures, and the sense of unity with all nature.

When the bright moon appeared at night, a man would sit on a stone step of my shrine and blow *shakuhachi*, the bamboo pipe. He was poorly dressed; perhaps he was a demobilized soldier. Deep, warm tones echoed over the shrine, the forest, and the mountain behind, calming even my childish spirit. Sometimes I would hear *shinobue*, the bamboo flute, played by a women behind the shrine. Even in the poverty after the war, the people couldn't help searching for beauty. In the shrine grounds they found a place where they could make their spirit calm as well as vital.

Shinto itself originated in the volcanic islands of Japan. The rich sea, the various shapes of mountains and rivers, the many kinds of trees, the temperate climate all made the Japanese people experience the mystery, spirituality, and vital power of nature. The ancient Japanese would call a divine spirit into a tree or a stone during a festival. Later, a shrine was established at that place as a dwelling for the divine existence. Even today some of the shrines regard the natural elements of mountain, forest, island, or waterfall as the real dwelling of divinity. The shrine, therefore, puts much more value on the surrounding forests, mountains, or sea rather than on the building in their midst. This makes Shinto shrines very different from churches or temples.

I believe my experience in the small world of my shrine and its circumstances made me feel the same sensitivity the ancient Japanese felt.

God's Image

For thirteen years I have served as *Kannushi*, a Shinto priest, in Goryo Shrine, my birthplace. This shrine was established 900 years ago. It is dedicated to Lord Gongoro, a samurai great both in bravery and in personality who, nonetheless, exploited the region around Kamakura. One episode from his life tells how he shot an arrow at his opponent even though he had an arrow stuck in his own eye. His highly ambitious and yet religious mind was handed down as a model of the perfect samurai in the Age of Samurai that continued for more than 700 years.

Japan has more than 82 thousand shrines, but the enshrined gods in them are all different. Some shrines are dedicated to the God of nature, climate or a particular geographical feature; others enshrine ancestors or the spirit of a human being.

The Japanese recognized the miraculous vitality of nature in the sea, mountain, river, fire, fountain, waterfall, moon, star, plant, and animal. They both feared and deified this energy as signs of God. If the ancient people found a superhuman sentiment or ability in a person, they also enshrined that person as an incarnation of God. Sometimes human beings were enshrined merely because mortification of a dead person might bring a curse on the living.

In any case, the spirits of enshrined people are purified by repeated worship; even cursing spirits are clarified into strong, divine protection in this way. The spirit of Gongoro was likewise purified by the worship of adults and children over 900 years, finally settling into our shine as a protecting and blessing God.

Recently, my daughter began to ponder the many things around her and asked the questions: "Do shrines exist for idol worship?" "Why are there so many gods?"

These are the same questions that I've been working on since I became a *Kannushi*. After innumerable worship rituals to my God, I recently realized that I prayed to one God rather than to the polytheistic gods of Shinto. When the ancient Japanese saw a sign of God in the miraculous occurrences of nature, they uttered words of praise or wonder or thanks. Those are the names of the gods. So it can actually be said that after naming the various deeds of divinity, the many names of God appeared. I myself pray not to Gongoro, but to the great life of our space—in other words, to the extreme principle of God manifest in the image of Gongoro.

The enshrined God in every shrine is actually the work of the great space, so it cannot take a particular form. When we worship, we use *gohei* (sacred matter) made of cut-paper or an evergreen tree called *sakaki* as an *iyashiro* (house of God) into which we ask God to descend. In the traditional book of myths, *Kojiki*, it is written that Amaterasu Ohmikami (the Goddess of the Sun) ordered her grandchild to "worship this mirror as my soul" when she made him descend to Japan to rule. Thus every shrine has a round mirror in its center and sometimes a sword, *magatama* (twisted jewel), or flag around it. These are the symbols or the traditional expressions of the presence of the formless God's spirit. Besides these symbols, some places enshrine *Fu*, pieces of paper with the names of God inscribed on them. These papers are also made sacred by the people's worship and became homes for the divine spirit.

In shrine festivals, bells, flutes and *koto* (the Japanese harp) have important roles. In ancient Shinto, which had many characteristics of shamanism, these instruments were used to take the shamans into ecstasy. In modern times the bells are used for the dance of the maiden, *miko,* and the other instruments accompany the *kagura* (Shinto dance). In traditional Noh drama, the tones of the flute become higher and more impressive whenever a ghost appears on the stage. It reminds me of the descent of the spirit in Shinto.

Other than the symbols such as the mirror and the twisted jewel, Shinto has no specific image of God. My private image of God in childhood, however, was that of an old man wearing scarlet *hoh* (the ancient dress of nobles and priests) carrying bells in his hands, and slowly dancing. When I was a child, I sometimes looked up at a huge tree near my house and saw, like a phantom, that image. The sound of bells echoed among the branches of the tree and faded away on the air. Even now I can remember that impressive sound.

Certainly Shinto and the image of an old man, *okina,* are closely connected. One of the most important Noh plays, also called *Okina,* is performed only on special occasions. The old man in the play dances a blessing dance; he is seen as an expression of divinity. The dancer prepares himself for the sacred dance by purifying his body for several days. The mask he wears, with the gentle smile of God carved on it, is treated like *Iyashiro,* the dwelling for the holy spirit.

Many wise, old men appear in Japanese legends and literature. In a history book from the middle ages Gongoro also was described as an *okina* with white hair who told dreams. Among the 82 thousand shrines in Japan, there are 32 thousand dedicated to the God of Rice, or the God of Food. Many of these shrines express God as an old man who carries a bunch of rice plants. The history of God's image as a elderly wise man is very old; it probably originated in the Shinsen Philosophy of China. The basic idea of the expression, however, is the worship of ancestors that Japanese people have observed from ancient times. Even I, who live in modern times, feel like worshipping an old man whenever I see one praying silently in a temple or a graveyard because it reminds me of the great spirit of the space into which he will soon dissolve.

Shinto Worship

A typical day for a Shinto priest begins with cleaning the precinct. When I wake up in the morning, I sweep my shrine and its grounds. Then I bathe in hot water and go up to the shrine for morning service. In the day time, unless a festival is held for the local community, I transmit various prayers for the people: prayers to purify the land for construction, prayers of blessing, a private rite of passage, prayers for purification of a car, prayers for safety in travel. My tasks also include preparation of shrine festivals, religious business, management of our precinct, welfare activities, training and practice of the sacred services.

Among all these tasks, the most important time for me is the cleaning at the beginning of the day. Our precinct is surrounded by forests and filled with falling leaves in autumn. Sweeping is like a battle with the leaves every day. In the summer, weeding is equally hard labor. Yet while I enthusiastically sweep and weed the land for hours, I find surprises—the buds of trees or the brightness of colored leaves. I always thank them. Looking at the soil and listening to the sound of the mountains or the sea, I exchange spirits with the wind, clouds, trees, insects, and birds. I feel myself melted into nature.

When I finish sweeping, my mind becomes empty, so my feeling is one of purity and calm. The solutions to unsolved problems from the previous day and the tasks that need doing today become apparent to me. In Zen Buddhism there is a saying that "everything starts with cleaning and ends with cleaning." This is true in Shintoism also. Every day I sweep the house and the garden of God for worshippers to face him honestly, but at the same time I clean up my inside too.

We call the cleaning of mind and body before facing God *harai*. In Shinto we say "the human being is the child of God" so he or she owns part of the divine soul. The soul of God in human beings becomes clouded and disgraced by daily life. In such situations, the human being is not allowed to contact God. Therefore recovering one's original pure soul or state of mind is the necessary preparation before facing God. In order to achieve this purity some people bathe in the sea or a river, some stand beneath waterfalls, and others retreat alone to a quiet place to calm their minds. In my case, the effective *harai* is to finish my daily cleaning and the preparations for worship one by one—politely, without earthly thought, accumulating spiritual energy. This theory of *harai* is a fundamental Japanese sentiment from ancient times.

Shinto means "the way of God." All human activities such as art, sports, work, and other aspects of daily life are expressed as *do* in Japanese (written "to"). It means the activity necessary to require full devotion. Some examples are *sado* (tea ceremony), *kado* (flower arrangement), *shodo* (calligraphy), *kendo* (Japanese fencing), *judo* (martial art), and *kyudo* (Japanese archery).

It is often said that the winning or losing of a match in *budo* (military arts) is almost decided before one actually fights. In every *do*, preparation of mind and body is the beginning. In Shinto, it is *harai*. When I was young, I learned *sado*. Whenever I went to my teacher's place for a tea lesson, she always cleaned up every room, swept and watered the garden, arranged the tea sets, and sat up straight, wearing her kimono tidily, even though she was very old. My teacher of *kado* was also old, but she waited for her pupil in the same way. The very air around my teachers seemed always to be cleared up.

In *shodo*, rubbing an ink stink can be *harai*. We rub the ink stick calmly, adding water drop by drop. Sitting ceremoniously and making our mind calm, we rub the stick on an ink slab with circular movements. When we finally write on a white paper with a brush dipped in the ink, it is not the beginning, but the end of the whole ceremony. It is the same with *sado* and *kado*.

In Shinto, there is another related concept called *makoto*. The word consists of *ma* representing beauty, greatness, and truth, and *koto* meaning "a thing or a term." Shinto is the relationship between God and human beings in which humans render *makoto* to the great service of God. If human beings face all good things created by God with *makoto*, in other words, with their entire faith, good reason, and pure mind, the whole world becomes harmonized and the ever-developing world will appear. This is the Shinto way of thinking. To render *makoto* from a pure state of mind, *harai*, is called *hataraki* (work). It is regarded as truth. In ethics it can be virtue; in arts it can be beauty.

My teacher of *shodo* often told me, "When you draw a line, there is only one way in which the angle, the thickness, and the strength are harmonized. This line is based on the whole theory of space." My old teacher of *kado* once took a branch and, looking at it closely, suddenly cut off some sprigs, straightened the branch, and put it in a vase without hesitation. She did it as if she knew the life of that branch could be expressed only in that way. She treated the flower politely, as if worshipping.

In *sado*, the host makes ceremonial tea and the guests drink it. The exchange of minds and the interchange of spirits among them is called *ichigo ichie* (the only one chance in one's life). This is also *makoto* in terms of Shinto.

Shinto is the religion that appeared with rice cultivation. The rice culture and Shinto both developed through a complicated process with the cooperation of the people in the community. A good rice crop can be realized only when human beings can achieve harmony with nature, cooperation with others, and improvement of technique. Such a view of the world established Shinto, so Shinto is the origin of all *do* in art, military art, labor, or life.

In Shinto, the human being is called *mikotomochi*, meaning "those who were sent on a special mission to realize the will of God on earth." The will of God is to establish the world of *makoto*. We worship all nature to perfect its own life. At the same time, we believe it is another form of worship to render *makoto* in order to accomplish our living.

Matsuri and Community

The Shinto shrine has always been a place of spiritual refreshment for the local people. The shrine which I serve is the same. Old people come every morning for worship and then sit on a bench and enjoy conversation.Commuters bow in front of the shrine going to and from their offices. Young mothers take their children to play in the shrine grounds, full of greenery. Because the enshrined God, Gongoro, lost sight of one eye in the battlefield, many people who suffer with eye problems come from all over the country to worship him and ask for consolation in their illness.

When a baby is about a month old in a Japanese village, it is taken to the shrine for its first worship to exchange greetings with the guardian deity. When the child is three, five, and seven years old, he or she comes again to the shrine, wearing formal kimono, to report on its growth and give thanks. At twenty years old we have the coming-of-age ceremony, and later the wedding. The shrine watches the whole lives of the people in the community, so worshippers never cease to come.

Annual shrine events include the New Year's festival, the summer festival, a memorial service for fallen soldiers, a respect-for-the-aged festival, as well as seasonal festivals of prayer and thanks for the rice crops. The most important festival is the yearly grand festival, which makes the whole community vigorous.

In our Goryo Shrine, almost all the families in the village participate in the week-long festival from preparation to clearn up. On the day of the grand festival, the ceremonial worship of thanks and hope for world peace is held in the shrine. In the middle of the precinct, sacred water is boiled in a large pot to purify the people around it through splashes. Sacred dance, *kagura*, is performed for union with God. Then a procession moves around the village with God's image on a portable shrine, *mikoshi*. It is supported by local people wearing ancient clothes, followed by children holding ornamental flags, people with unique masks to please God, players of flutes and drums. Women follow this procession dancing. Others erect booths with cotton candy, chow mein, *yakitori* (grilled meat), and games for the children.

These festivals, or *matsuri,* are actually considered to be service to the Divine Spirit. This is seen in the word itself: *tsukae matsuru* (to serve), *iwai matsuru* (to celebrate), and m*atsu* which means to receive something invisible coming to somewhere we can see. In short, *matsuri* or festival means "waiting for God." The festival welcomes the descended God as a guest, offering whatever the guest would like, and entertaining him with songs, dances, plays, and competitions. Through the festival, people try to unite with God, to exchange spirits with God.

In former times these festivals used to be rare events for ordinary people who worked hard every day. Wearing formal dress, inviting relatives, and sharing with other people in the community, people not only welcomed God in their midst, but also enjoyed themselves. In today's world the religious festival is the only occasion when people with differing occupations—farmers, teachers, artists, office workers—can work together for a common purpose. When I watch people sweeping the precinct, inflating balloons for the children, or broiling *yakitori*, I cannot but believe that the *matsuri* is the new beginning of life with the energy of origin surging down the ages.

When I was young, I was fascinated by Western culture. It was a time when Japanese people looked for a new sense of value. When Japan suddenly developed economically, I realized that we needed to know the original, spiritual culture of our country. That's why I decided to become a priest. The *matsuri*, which I used to regard as old fashioned, was actually quite radical because it retained its fundamental, original style.

The yearly village *matsuri* is similar to the act of digging a deep well. When a water vein is found, it is subterranean water, the very spirit of water, common to all the world. It makes spiritual flowers bloom in every country and in all people. This is the way to understand the unity of people all over the world on a deep spiritual level.

Women in Shinto

In the traditional Japanese myth, *Kojiki,* the divine is expressed in many ways. The Sun Goddess, *Amaterasu Omikami,* who rules the sky, has two brothers. One is the God of the Moon who rules the world of night, and the other is the Wild God called *Susanoo* who rules the world of the sea and the underground. *Amaterasu Omikami* is regarded as the supreme God, but at the same time she is the one who weaves clothes for the other gods and cultivates rice to offer to God in heaven. Her image and tasks are similar to those of a female Shinto priest.

According to the myth, *Amaterasu* became angry one day because of a wicked act done by *Susanoo*. The Sun Goddess shut herself up in a cave, closing the rock door behind her. Without the sun, the world became completely dark. The other divine beings tried to think of a way to recover light on the earth. At last, the Goddess *Ame-no-Uzume-no mikoto* began to perform a passionate, lively dance. The other gods enjoyed it and laughed loudly. Inside the cave, *Amaterasu* was curious about the strange uproar and opened the rock door to see, once more flooding the earth with light and warmth. Following upon that mythic event, female priests dance before Shinto altars to entertain the divine.

In ancient Japanese history there were often two rulers, a male and a female, who reigned over the nation cooperatively. The male ruler administered the affairs of the nation, while the female ruler (a daughter or a sister of the male ruler) took charge of divine service. The female ruler ascertained the will of God and the male ruler administered according to that will. This system was applied not only by national rulers but also by powerful regional families.

Later, the long history of exclusive male ruling was inaugurated and, except for the imperial court and special shrines, there were no female *kannushi*. Since the war, the priest's wife, his daughter or his sister is allowed to "stand in" for the dead husband, and engage in the sacred occupations. Currently the number of female *kannushi* is ten percent. There is no gender discrimination in the service itself because the duties of the *kannushi* are the same for men and women.

There is a strong ethnological rationale for women priests in Shinto. One of Shinto's basic beliefs is that the cereal spirit descends into rice plants. *Niinae matsuri*, in which people offer the first ears of the rice plants to God, is the most important event of rice cultivation. In ancient times, this ceremony was carried out by housewives. They purified their bodies and worshipped the first ear of rice all night in order to watch the birth of the new cereal spirit and ask for its growth. The people then ate the rice to ingest the divine spirit. Any woman who had borne children was recognized as a priest for this important divine service.

Another Goddess, Izanami no mikoto, is very important in the mythology of Japan. Together with the male God Izanagi, she bore the islands of Japan and formed nations. She kept on bearing children, producing the gods of mountain, river, wind, mist, field, and so forth. But when she bore the God of Fire, she burned to death. Her lamenting husband wanted to see his wife again, and followed her to the land of the dead, Yomi. There he found her dead body infested with maggots. Because he broke his promise "not to see" her dead body, Izanami became angry and chased him with the army of Yomi. Izanagi managed to escape, but at the border separating this world from the world of the dead, Izanami vowed to " kill one thousand people of your world a day." Izanagi answered, "Then I'll make 1500 a day."

Because of this myth, though Izanami was the creator of our nation, she is also called *Yomotsu Omikami*, the God of the Dead. The Sun Goddess was a gentle and forgiving virgin goddess, strong enough to hate sin, but a pacifist and negotiator. In contrast, the Goddess of Birth and Death, Izanami, toiled and became angry, covered with blood and dirt. She is special for me, probably because she is reflected in the agony and toil of everyday people who bear children, support a family, and help the sick and dying.

In *Kojiki*, there is another story of a goddess who produced food from her body, and even after she was killed, cultivated various crops from her dead body for human beings. The myth also includes many dramatic stories of childbirth. In them goddesses make spirits at the risk of their lives and then return to nature. They must be representatives of the earth itself, where all nature repeats the cycle of birth and death forever.

In the Okinawa islands on the south end of Japan, the people continue to carry out many of the original beliefs of Shinto. One of these is bone-washing. After a buried dead body becomes bones, people dig up the bones, wash them, and return them to the grave. The bone-washing is done by women. This ceremony clearly shows that women used to be priests who took charge of the life and death of their family and conducted ceremonies.

The God who ordered Izanagi and Izanami to create the nation was Musubi, which has the same meaning as *umu* (bear, create) and is a compound of *musu* meaning to create things and *hi* representing spirit, soul, day, or man. So the God who creates spirits is the God Musubi. The ancient Japanese called every awe-inspiring spirit who creates something God, or *Kami*. We still believe that every existence on the earth was created by the power of Musubi. Mountains, rivers, plants, trees, and all creatures, including human beings, represent the power of God.

Even today, many Japanese families install a family altar, called *kamidana,* in their house, and there worship the Sun Goddess, Amaterasu, or Ubusuna, the Original Creator, as well as the local protecting god. Every morning, people offer rice, salt, water, an evergreen branch, *sakaki,* and fire on the altar and pray before it. The rice is the source of energy for the Japanese, since the divine spirit descends to it. The salt is indispensable to the human body, and at the same time, it is used to purify. (Based on the ancient Japanese tradition to clean up one's body by bathing in the sea before worship, the salt is believed to have a purifying effect.) The water is regarded as the source of birth. The same is true for the fire. The evergreen branch is another recepticle for God's descending presence. In short, the altar is the symbol of the entire earth within the house.

Each day we Japanese offer elements of the earth back to God and pray: May water be clear, may trees grow thick, may the minds of human beings be innocent, may food be delivered to the whole world, and may all the people on the earth live and develop together peacefully.

Akiko Kobayashi was born in Kamakura City, near Tokyo, in 1946. Brought up in the 900-year-old Goryo Shrine with two elder brothers and elder sisters, she watched her father tend the shrine. Akiko first studied German literature at Sophia University in Tokyo, and was employed by a German firm in Japan.

In 1977 she studied Shinto for ordination at the Kokugakuin University in Tokyo and trained at the famous Meiji Shrine. Since then she has been serving as priest at the Goryo Shrine. Reverend Kobayashi is married to a publisher and has one daughter, aged 15.

Adonai Zeus Shekhinah Elim Ogun Kat Buddha
Wyame Hel Rama Mitra Odomankoma Jupiter Het
Heru Agni Cagn Thor Brahma Tangaroa Father
Lugaba Papang Diana Al-Rahman Cerridwen Ahone
Yoma' Tirawa Atius Ganesha El Mungan ngua
Quetzalcoatl Hamakom ddai
Atibruku Moma YH Bun aiwa

Porousness
in the
Web of
Indra

Judith Ragir

Saraswati Inanna Miriru aong
Tonantzin Yuskeha Bha Head
Olodumare Shyama Ekv Heru
Nurrundere Daramilun tzeir
Hecate Chi Musubi Hin una
Nanderuvucu Erishkigal man
Tsui-goab Ometeotl Os chtli
Surya Elohim Nyankop Ilu
Woden Great Spirit Les goro
Poseidon Chineke Nhialic uwut
Makai Wakantanka Inari Ha-Qadosh barukh hu'
Tara Krishna Avaloket-iswara Rabb Goryo Qat Oke
Nurunderi Indra Shang-ti Amaterasu Ohmikami
Kannon Quan Yin Ise Lakshmi Awonawilona Bast
Omecihuatl Ruhanga Kosane Sophia Dionysus Ixchel
Mawu Ra Ardanariswara Oluwa Deng Hanuman
uNkulunkulu Kanobo Ngai Shamayim Cybele Dakini
Nataraj Pachamama Susanoo Katonda Avlukpo Eloah
Isis Temaukel Eleda Gaia Laxmi Mahmanmu-rok
Odin El-al Herukhuti Viracocha Marduk Ashira Biral
Shaddai Dzingbe Djohu-ma-di-hutu Astarte Ndengei
Koyatu Baha'u'llah Marrigan Baiame Om Pelepelewa
Durga Orisha Nyame Techaronhiawakhon Chukwu
Uvolovu Brahman Nephtys Ha-Maqom Tehuti Maat
Digambara Val Tik Chaitanya Amana Kwoth Num
Colok Nabango Fumeripitsj Shiva Varuna Lukanga
Bala Atibluku Karu Allah Sing Nainuema Artemis
Kartikeya Kuanyin Yelafaz T'ien Baal Shakti
Athena Olorun Nemesis Sheela-na-Gig Bhavartarini
Jesus Horus Izanagi Sebek Waq Ishtar Ti Seker
BegoTanutanu Sat Nam Kali Mirirul Bhavatarini
Tsui-goab Hatzur Brahman Ubusuna Tonantzin
YHVH Apollo Nana God Almighty Hu Vishnu Om

A pologia:

should i write some image i conceive
and call that divine?
    the inconceivable!

the Zen ancient ones say:
should we point to the reflection of the moon in
the water
and call it the moon

can we describe

the dynamic working together of

total openness   this world of our bodies,
                        minds, trees, grasses, walls
                            and fence

without clinging
        to one or the other
as divine?

1.

the combustion of god within
the combustion of being alive

        my body blown apart
           not like a bomb,
although the movement of change can feel that
strong
but like the most exquisite psychic surgery

of softening and letting go

so that my skin is porous

the body sack
        my innards,
        empty and removed

and only spinning dynamism
    sometimes gentle, sometimes like a volcano,

running through my arms and legs and torso

and streaming
        like a fountain
           out the top of my head

spraying the whole universe with gentle life

and streaming down my skin back to my bottom

only to do it again and then again,

        pumping

2.

> cityfolk call them weeds
> but at the monastery
> we call them flowers
> and put them on the altar

on a walk in the last days of a retreat
i notice
these weeds
expressing the same movement
that i'm feeling in my body

that in spite of our differences in form,

> we flower together

3.

> i do walking meditation on the porch of the meditation hall,
>   the zendo
> 6th day of an intense meditation retreat

the wind is blowing
it does not notice my skin
my porousness allows it to blow right through me

> the Winnebago River flowing a mile away
> comes up to the zendo steps, flows onto the porch
> into my feet and up my body
> out my head and up into the sky

where is the woman
who afterwards
conceives these images?

4.

the Web of Indra
the huge systemic network of
connectedness

ah,
the glistening of the spider webs
filled with dew
in the morning sunlight
on the prairie field
like million of sails in an endless sea

can we conceive the endless sea?
can the spider see all the sails of that field?
can the spider see the beauty of his web
even with death inside, the little fly trapped and wrapped

nothing simple
yet everything simple
one sand on the bank of the Ganges.

Judith Ragir has a varied professional career. She is a writer, choreographer, an acupuncturist, and herbologist. She started studying Zen Buddhism in 1973 and is a long-standing student of the late Zen master, Katagiri Roshi. Judith is also a wife and mother. Her poetry has been published in an anthology called *The Path of Compassion: Contemporary Writings on Engaged Buddhism.*

Adonai Zeus Shekhinah Elim Ogun Kaf Buddha
Wyame Hel Rama Mitra Odomankoma Jupiter Het
Heru Agni Cagn Thor Brahma Tangaroa Father
Lugaba Papang Diana Al-Rahman Cerridwen Ahone
Yoma' Tirawa Atius Ganesha El Mungan-ngua
Quetzalcoatl Hamakom ddai
Atibruku Moma YH Bun aiwa
Saraswati Inanna Miriru uong
Tonantzin Yuskeha Bha Head
Olodumare Shyama Ekv Heru
Nurrundere Daramilun tzeir
Hecate Chi Musubi Hin una
Nanderuvucu Erishkigal man
Tsui-goab Ometeotl Os chtli
Surya Elohim Nyankop Ilu
Woden Great Spirit Leso goro
Poseidon Chineke Nhialic uwut
Makai Wakantanka Ina hu'
Tara Krishna Avaloket-iswara Rabb Goryo Qat Oke
Nurunderi Indra Shang-ti Amaterasu Ohmikami
Kannon Quan Yin Ise Lakshmi Awonawilona Bast
Omecihuatl Ruhanga Kosane Sophia Dionysus Ixchel
Mawu Ra Ardanariswara Oluwa Deng Hanuman
uNkulunkulu Kanobo Ngai Shamayim Cybele Dakini
Nataraj Pachamama Susanoo Katonda Avlukpo Eloah
Isis Temaukel Eleda Gaia Laxmi Mahmanmu-rok
Odin El-al Herukhuti Viracocha Marduk Ashira Biral
Shaddai Dzingbe Djohu-ma-di-hutu Astarte Ndengei
Koyatu Baha'u'llah Marrigan Baiame Om Pelepelewa
Durga Orisha Nyame Techaronhiawakhon Chukwu
Uvolovu Brahman Nephtys Ha-Maqom Tehuti Maat
Digambara Val Tik Chaitanya Amana Kwoth Num
Colok Nabango Fumeripitsj Shiva Varuna Lukanga
Bala Atibluku Karu Allah Sing Nainuema Artemis
Kartikeya Kuanyin Yelafaz T'ien Baal Shakti
Athena Olorun Nemesis Sheela-na-Gig Bhavartarini
Jesus Horus Izanagi Sebek Waq Ishtar Ti Seker
BegoTanutanu Sat Nam Kali Mirirul Bhavatarini
Tsui-goab Hatzur Brahman Ubusuna Tonantzin
YHVH Apollo Nana God Almighty Hu Vishnu Om

Images
of God:
Closeness
and
Power

Rabbi Sheila Weinberg

"And S/He answered, 'I will make all my goodness pass before you, and I will proclaim before you the name YHVH, and the grace that I grant and the compassion that I show.' 'But,' S/He said, 'you cannot see My face and live, for a human being may not see Me and live.' And YHVH said, 'See there is a place near Me. Station yourself on the rock and as My Presence passes by, I will put you in a cleft of the rock and shield you with My hand until I have passed by. Then I will take My hand away and you will see My back; but My face must not be seen.'" (Numbers 33:19-23)

W e long to see the face of God, to capture the presence of the divine in our finite lives.[1] As in the dialog between YHVH and Moses, we glimpse only a partial view. We pass our days in the cleft of the rock, waiting for a glance at the divine revealed in the history of our own lives. And we find many images, but they are all fleeting and partial. For a Jew, idolatry is the gravest of all sins, on a par with murder and incest. Idolatry is resting in the illusion that we have captured the divine in any image, idea, or mortal being.

The images we possess are nonetheless very precious to us. While they are human images and partial, they are subject to infinite variety, only limited by our own religious imagination. It is a joyous enterprise to talk about our understanding of the divine with one another, to spin words that may heal and inspire and connect. We partake of divinity in the motion of our images, in our willingness to entertain them, play with them and even to let them depart; to honor our own and each others'. Our various religious traditions enrich and guide our capacity to envision the divine by holding up themes and designs based on a collective experience of talking about God.

Primary Jewish events celebrate the presence of God in the life of the world and in the life of the Jewish people. Several key moments structure our view of this redemption. These are the signposts I use to relate my experience of the divine to the wisdom of my tradition. They are everywhere. Let us first look at the dance between creation and liberation.

I imagine creation as a tree, the tree in the garden, or any ordinary tree, spreading branches and leaves toward the sky and roots dug deep and far underground. Creation is the hidden potential in everything. The infant growing in the darkness of the womb, the insides of caves and oceans and human hearts. The Creator is present in the darkness as well as in the light. It is constantly moving, swirling, changing. Its variety is infinite. I am fully part of creation. I am accepted, loved, and belong in the world as long as I open to the power coursing through the earth into my own blood. I am cousins with seals and turtles, oaks and grasses. But the Creator is also the author of separation, floods, fires, and disease and calls forth my acceptance of death and loss. Creation is Spring and Autumn, Summer and Winter. Creation is joyous and painful, as distant as the stars and as near as the cells of my own body, growing and dying.

In Judaism's mystical tradition this attribute of divinity is often associated with the feminine principle. The divine indwelling presence of God, Shechinah, is identified with nature and creation. A contemporary poem by Ani Tuzman, called *Shechina*, captures this quality superbly:

Who is the dancer,
the one who moves her legs and arms
without shame, with abandon,
above all with delight.
Who is the dancer
whose secret is life, whose breath
creates, whose glance reminds the sun
to turn, the corn to form,
whose feet tell the soil to freeze.

Who is the dancer with no name
shy as the moon,
her eyes constellations,
her kneeling in the dusk;
she gathers the day and what has been
made, under her skirts,
smashing thoughts and things,
like grapes into wine.

Who is the dancer
whose body formed of silence prays,
whose laughter veils the night
with stars, the morning with dew;
whose words turn doubt into rain.
Her face, every face,

who is the one who has become
the world and each of the dancers.[2]

Moses, however, does not meet Shechinah in the burning bush. Rather, he encounters God, the liberator, who urges him to lead his people out of bondage, to become what they must become, to say no to oppression. God is YHVH—Yud Hay Vav Hay, four letters calling forth human freedom. Light, which is a metaphor for creation, flares into a flaming glow in the process of liberation. Here the human being is cousin to the angels, capable through the gifts of creation to break free of patterns, habits, denial, unconsciousness.

Liberation is less about transcending creation, in my view, than about becoming what is possible within creation. It is not antagonistic to creation, but each nourishes the other in their cosmic dance.

The divine call for freedom awakens the spirit. It is daring and filled with love of creation. As we permit ourselves to know deeply the closeness and power of creation, we open up to the sources of power within that call upon us to oppose violence, falsehood, greed, and cruelty as they manifest in our personality and in our society. We learn what it means to have a place in the world that does not encroach on the place of our neighbor. We learn how not to trespass and we learn what it means to be a friend. Knowing we belong in creation gives us the courage to let go of fear that keeps us numb, depressed, immobile. We hear the rhythm of life, our feet join the dance, we breathe fully, knowing that life is found when we can open to the beat, the pulse.

The God of my understanding, then, is both loving and limiting, a source of power and intimate tenderness. And there is more. The divine resides in the unity, the source of creation and liberation, the Ayn Sof, Without End, the ultimate mystery. We have intimations of this mystery in the unity of the dance, when we forget that there are partners, when boundaries dissolve.

In the spaces of life the sacred shines. In Hebrew, *kadosh* means holy and that root is fashioned into words that occur at the borders of life and time: the prayer that ushers in sacred time is *kidush*, the affirmation recited by loved ones in mourning and students at the completion of study is *kaddish*, and the sacred society that prepares the dead for the journey into the unknown is the *hevra kadisha*.

In the spaces and in the silence the unity resides. Jews recite at dawn and nightfall the affirmation of unity, Shma Yisrael, Listen Israel, YHVH Elohaynu, YHVH is one—the divine images of creator and liberator are unified. One experience of divine unity is known by Jews as revelation. Amidst thunder and lightening, at a mountain in the Sinai wilderness, there was a moment of encounter between finite and infinite which is remembered. It is enshrined in daily practices—reminders and signals of an ancient experience of mystery that one particular people knew.

The God of liberation is the God of redemption. The capacity to imagine unity is itself a divine gift enabling us to chart a course toward wholeness. Exile and return are united in the eternal home that we carry with us. One name for God is Makon, place. The place of unity within. The stillness always present in the dance. The balance point between inhale and exhale.

Unity, redemption, and hope are known in liberating moments of creative insight in art. Unity, redemption, and hope are known in passionate sexual union when boundaries evaporate in bliss. I also glimpse the trace of the divine shadow when I expand beyond the limits of my own imagination, in moments of empathy and compassion, when the wolf lies down with the lamb.

Judy Chicago has written a wonderful poem/prayer[3] that captures the profound hope that I identify with the divine. Images of creation and liberation fuse in a promise of oneness and peace.

> And then all that has divided us will merge
> And then compassion will be wedded to power
> And then softness will come to a world that is harsh and unkind
> And then both men and women will be gentle
> And then both men and women will be strong
> And then no person will be subject to another's will
> And then all will be rich and free and varied
> And the greed of some will give way to the needs of the many
> And then all will share equally in the Earth's abundance
> And then all will care for the sick and the weak and the old
> And then all will nourish the young
> And then all will cherish life's creatures
> And then all will live in harmony with each other and the Earth
> And then everywhere will be called Eden once again.

As I look back upon my life from the momentary calm of the rock's shelter, what do I see? I see signs of a presence, footprints in the sand, glimpses of a back, a face, a hand, a moment of risking liberation, a moment of embracing creation. There were times in my life when I was ready to say yes or no in a strong enough voice to make a new boundary. This is how I understand the God of liberation. There were other moments when the truth of my own belonging burst through into the light of awareness. This is how I understand the God of creation.

These accumulated moments pass through times of change, fear, loss, uncertainty, and pain. They teach me that I am worthy and responsible. My actions matter. I am a part of something much greater than myself. I am not alone and I am not lost. It occurs to me that I could speak from one of at least four different, but interrelated, identity perspectives as I share some stories that illustrate the recurring presence of the divine in my life. They are: as a woman, as a Jewish leader and rabbi, as a recovering addict, as a parent.

As a woman, the divine has manifest for me in the ongoing struggle to value myself independently, not primarily in relationship to men and male approval. I learned as a young girl that the most important thing in life was to be married. All the stories ended with the princess being rescued by the prince and then living happily ever after. Power, prestige, indeed legitimacy for a female were derived from their masculine source. My job was to secure access to this masculine source through the manipulation of my feminine sexuality and whatever other methods I could improvise.

This way of looking at the world was enforced by culture, society and religion. Almost all sources of leadership and authority on earth and above were male, from president to pope to principal. If women used power it was behind the scenes or behind the backs of their men.

I rushed into marriage, still shy of twenty years old, feeling I was home safe. Eleven years later I left the marriage and began a journey toward and with the divine liberator and creator calling me to envision the world and myself anew. The liberator was present when I became willing to say no: no to the idea that any relationship with a man was better than being a woman alone; no to the fears that assailed me; no to the absence of alternatives; no to my own suffering. The liberator was present when I was able to say yes: yes to facing the unknown; yes to driving my own car on the super highway; yes to forfeiting the world's approval.

The creator was present in this act as well because only through a sense of inner connectedness, call it faith in creation, could I take the leap that I did, out, not only of a marriage, but ultimately, out of an entire mindset. This affirmation of my independent value as a woman has been repeated many times since the day I left my marriage. A tiny spark has grown to a flickering flame through numerous acts of saying no and saying yes, especially in relations with men, where the temptation has been great to sell my soul and my body for approval, security, and reflected power.

The implications are potentially earth- and heaven-shattering when multiplied by all women's lives. For me the slow, often painful and glorious spiritual process has been supported by other women telling their stories and reimagining God. I remember the first time I saw Rabbi Lynn Gottlieb tell the story of Lilith, created together with Adam and endowed with equal power. Lilith, who in later Judaism is demonized for her independent strength and called the murderer of infants, has been returned to Jewish consciousness by women reclaiming their own power to say no and yes. I also remember signing up for a course in 1980 entitled "Feminist Jewish Theology" taught by Judith Plaskow. I was incredulous that those words could be used together. What was so amazing? I think what struck me so deeply was the willingness of women to say we are worthy enough to share our images of God in our lives in full voice. We also are created in God's image.

The class became a Jewish feminist spiritual community where a group of women have committed to meeting regularly to support each other and create a language to share our images of the divine and how they are moving us in our lives. I have been challenged, prodded and nurtured by this group and others along the way to relinquish my own unworthiness and my own passivity. I continue to experience my emergence as a woman into self confidence, partaking of the divine, feeling at home in my own skin as I am at home in creation.

As a rabbi, my professional and spiritual journeys intersect at many points. First, I came to know myself to be fundamentally a teacher of Torah and then I became willing to name this publicly and assert that it represents continuity, as well as a radical break with tradition. As a woman rabbi, I immediately challenge my own and other people's images of God. I believe, however, that the expansion of Judaism to embrace women as teachers and leaders is a manifestation of the divine liberator active in our time, in our lives. For me, the choice to become a rabbi is an ongoing affirmation of all women whose insights and understandings of the divine now rest on an equal plane with the wisdom of our male ancestors.

Serving a congregation is an ongoing challenge to my spiritual life. It becomes very easy to pretend to piety and to hoard authority. It is easy to forget one's humanity when one is sought after as an intimate and looked at with awe. It is alluring to attempt to take responsibility for everyone's relationship with the divine, their Jewish tradition, and their Jewish identity. It is tempting to incorporate people's confusion about being a Jew in the modern world into my own soul, to become overwhelmed by the isolation, fear, anger, embarrassment, guilt, grief, and longing that I touch. It is seductive to get angry at the absence of commitment, the lack of knowledge, the impotence of spiritual leadership.

The most enticing pitfall for a rabbi is confusion between self and role and between role and God. How does the rabbi celebrate Shabbat? This is an issue, I think, of boundaries. Saying no and saying yes. The latter has no meaning without the former. I am not solely responsible for the survival and creative renewal of the Jewish people. Everything that happens or does not happen in the synagogue is not about me. The enthusiasm, the criticism, the praise and the complaints all need to be worn as a loose fitting robe.

The divine speaks to me as the voice of a friend telling me to take the day off, to risk freedom from escalating self-imposed expectations. The voice contradicts an inner voice that is using the role of rabbi, using any external achievement as a means of feeling more worthy. The inability to stop, to feed my own spirit, to respect the boundaries between personal and professional, is a denial of the divine creator, the flowing spring that grows stronger and stronger as I become more willing to drink of its cool waters.

One of the core experiences of the divine in my life has been the struggle with my addictions. To be addicted means to be enslaved to a substance, a person, or an activity despite the awareness that the addiction is causing considerable misery. One is unable to change one's behavior. Cigarette smoking is an example. Each time I took a cigarette, I knew that I was hurting myself. Yet, I experienced such pleasure in feeling the smoke fill my lungs that I simply could not imagine relinquishing it.

Compulsive use of cigarettes, drugs, alcohol, gambling, sex, are ways of grabbing for momentary pleasures. They are ways of filling an inner emptiness, a yearning for approval, worthiness, and belonging.

I know what it feels like to be in a primary relationship with an addictive substance. I know how it works well for a while, how I am lulled into believing that I have found my best friend, my way to make it through the world, my secret for feeling okay, full. I know what it feels like to keep a secret from myself and from the world, how to hide the addiction in clever ways, how to explain it away. I know how it feels when it turns on you. How I try to stop and can't. How I begin to feel more and more like a failure, a fraud, a fool, less worthy, more alone.

There is little room in addiction for the divine as creator or as liberator. The addiction is the *yetzer hara*, the evil inclination, telling us we don't need help, we can handle it by ourselves. The *yetzer hara*, crowding out faith with fear, tells us that we can't live without it as it plans our slow death.

The divine is found in recovery. I know that when I took the leap across the abyss of my addictions, I was not alone. Somehow I allowed a door to open to the divine liberator. Somehow, the divine creator carried me across the chasm of despair with the message of renewed life. The messengers of hope and freedom are often those who have suffered and have known the miracle of liberation. Who else could I trust with the dreadful secret? Who else could understand me so well?

Most of us in one way or another struggle with thought patterns or behaviors that hurt us and keep us afraid and separate. I believe that the process of becoming free from those binds is a spiritual process. As we become free we can turn our energy outward toward the world. We can assume more responsibility for our part in creation. As we emerge from behind our private walls, we learn to feel more deeply and become more willing to use our knowledge, energy and talents for the betterment of life on earth, for the pursuit of peace, justice and healing.

The fourth identity to explore is the fact of my having been blessed in life to be a parent of two children. For most of their lives I was a single parent and therefore did not have the opportunity to divide parenting functions in the classic mode of mother as nurturer and father as source of authority. I think this was a great teaching for me in guiding me to overcome this dichotomy in my own life and to embrace the richness of worshipping the divine liberator and the divine creator.

One of the classic images of God is as father. Jewish liturgy often casts father in the intimate divine role in contradistinction to king, source of limits. Yet, father for many of us is the distant parent and hence echoes a distant God. As a single parent I needed to learn how to embrace and adore my children while at the same time set clear limits and structures for them. I had a chance to envision and emulate an integrated God, father/mother/God. I learned that there is as much love in the no saying as in the yes saying; as much care in defining boundaries as in grounding the children in unconditional love.

While parents are co-creators of our children, parents are not

God. The divine may be an eternal flowing fountain of both love and discipline, but no parent is everflowing or eternal. Parenting is a wonderful opportunity to cope with my own humanity. I am always being reminded of it by my children.

Between the enormous power that parents wield in the early years and the ongoing process of separation and letting go dwell life's lessons. My children's life passages were profound challenges to my faith. Bar and bat mitzvah, leaving home, driving a car, and their entrance into intimate relationships were moments in my children's lives when I experienced fear, joy, loneliness, and sadness. Their growing up allowed me to face the mystery of life and to choose to flee into panic or to turn my face toward the mystery, to remember that i am a part of creation as are they, to renew my own lifeline of spirit, and to trust the divine liberator, the divine creator, to manifest in the lives of my children in their own way.

Looking back we can name the divine image. But how do we continue to choose a life that will put us in presence of the divine? Must we all be like Jacob, when he awakes from his dream of the ladder of holy messengers ascending and descending and says: "God was in this place and I, I did not know?"[4] How can we prevent ourselves from falling asleep again and forgetting? This is one of the ultimate questions of religion and philosophy. Perhaps, it is the ultimate human question.

What follows is a list of actions, tools, approaches to remembering the divine presence in the present. These are methods that I try to use and that I know work, when I use them, to keep me from hiding, from running, from forgetting.

1. The company we keep is of utmost importance. We live amidst airwaves crowded with messages promising escape and illusion. Cynicism, selfishness, and materialism abound. We must actively choose to reach out to people who are seeking something beyond themselves, people who are trying to become honest, who are willing to stand up for values rather than profit. Seeking the company of common spirits is the origin of church, synagogue, and ashram. But no institutions are filled with people fostering their relationship with the divine. Those people are found here and there. They become our teachers and our guides. We model our lives on theirs. We seek their counsel. We listen to their advice.

We also can forge relationships with the God seekers of the ages through study of sacred texts, poetry, and song. We can open our hearts to these soulmates of eternity. This approach also asks us to distance ourselves from harmful influences. A recovering alcoholic is wise not to hang out in bars. A person who chooses to prepare to live in the presence of the divine would do well to avoid all forms of deceit, exploitation, ridicule, and arrogance.

2. For me God is found in the relationship between God and Israel. While in the earlier discussion I emphasized God's presence in my life in very personal terms, I also claim to be part of a collective relationship with the divine. I crossed the Red Sea, I stood at Sinai, and wandered through the wilderness with my people. This in no way negates the fact that many other peoples and cultures claim a relationship with the divine. To live a life filled with the holy daily and seasonal practices of my people affords me the opportunity to be present to the divine in my life. Identifying with the triumphs, sacrifices, visions, and losses of a people marching through time enormously enriches my life and ties me to a dimension that far transcends my limited span here on earth.

In our day Jewish people must grapple with the inevitable question: How can you believe in God after Auschwitz? I have no adequate response except to say that the Holocaust itself was an absolute desecration of the divine image; to surrender to meaninglessness, chaos, and despair is to fail to challenge that desecration. To defy the forces in the world that seek to blot out the unique magnificence of any group or individual is the only adequate response I can make to the gas chambers.

3. Through prayer and meditation we place ourselves in the presence of the divine. I utilize the ancient words encoded in the Jewish prayerbook, words from other new and old sources, my words and no words. What is essential is regularity. I need to devote some moments of prayer at least upon rising and before going to sleep.

Prayer's main content is asking for help and saying thank you. My major goal is to admit that I am not fully in control of what goes on in my day, but I can allow myself to be open to the power of the creator/liberator to lead me forward. It doesn't really matter to whom or what I think I am praying as long as it is beyond me. Prayer can help me uncover dishonesty within myself, or detach from some of life's seriousness. Prayer is about lightness, although it is seen as something somber. It is about loosening the bonds that chain us to our own self importance, whether that be expressed in self-congratulations or self-deprecation. Prayer is an extraordinary gift for living a happy life as long as I pray for what can be granted by prayer—things like honesty, courage, willingness, and patience. Prayer is free. Perhaps that is why it is so devalued in our culture.

4. Human creativity partakes of the soul of the creator. We are used to thinking of creativity as the gift of geniuses, Beethoven and Picasso. But we all can create. We simply need permission to find our mode. It may be inventing a new recipe or writing a poem, designing a dress, a garage, or a garden, solving a dilemma or settling an argument. It may come as we teach in the classroom or in a therapy session, or in a court room. It comes when something new breaks through. This is the spark of divine light. Let it be! Let us appreciate our participation in creation as an opportunity to catch a glimpse of the divine countenance.

5. I asked a class of third grade Sunday school children to fill in this sentence: "I feel God is with me when_____." About half the children wrote, "when I am asleep." I think we vastly undervalue sleep, rest, and solitude as forms of being in the divine presence. Jews have Sabbath, an entire day in the week to rest, to allow ourselves to empty, to allow room to return to the over-full vessel of the self. I find that I need time without doing anything, afternoon naps in the sunshine, time snatched from the jaws of expectation. Most of us have to get sick to find this time in our lives. Even the Sabbath gets overcrowded with communal activities, eating, visiting, learning.

What a joy to allow myself to fade into the twilight of awareness, into a dream world, into another dimension, spending time alone and getting enough rest replenishes the soul. It is a form of being in contact with pure being. If we never rest enough, our waking time is absorbed in longing for sleep, edged in anxiety. If we allow ourselves true rest, we can be present and awake to the rest of our lives.

6. I feel the divine presence when I receive and return loving attention with another human being. In those moments I know I belong and partake in the goodness of creation. Times of closeness are often filled with laughter or with tears, as the body cleanses itself of the holding patterns we develop to keep us safe, or so we think. The frustrations and disappointments of growing up are melted away, time and again, in the warm smile of a beloved friend.

It is not surprising that the sensuous, passionate language of lovers is often used to describe the divine-human encounter. The classic text is "The Song of Songs." Each relationship is transparent to the other. I see God in my beloved and my beloved in God.

7. I believe that God is found in the world when we say no to injustice and cruelty. Here we encounter the God that liberated the Israelites from Egyptian slavery. This is the God of Rosa Parks who said no to sitting in the back of the bus and the God of Anita Hill who said no to keeping silence about sexual harassment. Every time a veil of denial is removed, the divine image is revealed. When we say no to racism, sexism, homophobia, antisemitism, militarism, pollution, we are raising the image of the divine and the value of a human life increases.

When a battered wife reports the batterer, I see the image of the divine in the world, although many others are happy to see this activity as a simple triumph for human dignity without the transcendent presence. Whatever we call the action need not be a source of controversy. I chose to relate it to God's image but do not demand that of anyone else.

8. The image of the divine may be found when we face someone very different from ourselves and agree to share our wounds and our hopes. This can happen between genders, races, religions, people of different classes or sexual orientations, people of different political stands. When we open up to the experience of another, we have left our self. If we don't pounce in with defenses, explanations, and solutions, if we learn to listen, our humanity expands, we are changed. As our perspective now includes another's from a distant point on the circle, we are closer to the perspective of the divine who sees the circle complete, as we never do.

9. I left for last our capacity to partake of the natural world as a window to the divine. Our world is full of colors. Who can count the kinds of birds, or fish, or flowers, or rocks? Would that we could cherish the variety flowing out of divine unity.

Every day the quality of light undergoes a symphony of change. Every year the earth dies and is reborn in startling patterns, textures, fragrances, and hues. The earth is resonant with sounds that mute orchestras, monumental movements of air and water, and microscopic universes. Whether we can care for and enjoy this wonder is one of the most profound questions of our moment in history. I see the earth itself as an image of the divine and our present task is to connect to her life, her wisdom, and her wholeness.

The infinite God appears to us in infinite disguises. Or perhaps we are the ones hidden behind dark glasses, blind to that which is close as the next breath. The divine is both power and closeness, creation and liberation and reconciliation. Each time we speak of the One, we find the sound fractured into many. But we can peer beyond the many and catch the glow of the One.

Rabbi Sheila Peltz Weinberg is the rabbi of the Jewish Community of Amherst, Massachusetts. A graduate of the Reconstructionist Rabbinical College, she served previously as rabbi of Congregation Beth Am Israel in Narberth, Pennsylvania. She has worked in the field of Jewish community relations and was Hillel director on campuses in the Philadelphia area for seven years.

Rabbi Weinberg has published poetry and a variety of articles on subjects including feminism and Judaism, spirituality, single parenting, and the pursuit of peace. She served as commentaries editor of *Kol NaNeshama,* the New Reconstructionist prayerbook and as a founding member of B'not Esh, a Jewish feminist-spiritual collective.

She has been associated with Equity Institute, a non-profit organization devoted to the em-powerment of all people through teaching an appreciation for diversity.

Rabbi Weinberg is the mother of Abigail and Ezra.

Adonai Zeus Shekhinah Elim Ogun Kat Buddha
Wyame Hel Rama Mitra Odomankoma Jupiter Het
Heru Agni Cagn Thor Brahma Tangaroa Father
Lugaba Papang Diana Al-Rahman Cerridwen Ahone
Yoma' Tirawa Atius Ganesha El Mungan ngua
Quetzalcoatl Hamakom ddai
Atibruku Moma YH Bun aiwa
Saraswati Inanna Mirir uong
Tonantzin Yuskeha Bha Head
Olodumare Shyama Ekv Heru
Nurrundere Daramilun tzeir
Hecate Chi Musubi Hin suna
Nanderuvucu Erishkigal man
Tsui-goab Ometeotl Os chtli
Surya Elohim Nyankop Ilu
Woden Great Spirit Lesa Boyjerh El Dan Gongoro
Poseidon Chineke Nhialic Aciek Kąri Auset Tcuwut
Makai Wakantanka Inari Ha-Qadosh barukh hu'
Tara Krishna Avaloket-iswara Rabb Goryo Qat Oke
Nurunderi Indra Shang-ti Amaterasu Ohmikami
Kannon Quan Yin Ise Lakshmi Awonawilona Bast
Omecihuatl Ruhanga Kosane Sophia Dionysus Ixchel
Mawu Ra Ardanariswara Oluwa Deng Hanuman
uNkulunkulu Kanobo Ngai Shamayim Cybele Dakini
Nataraj Pachamama Susanoo Katonda Avlukpo Eloah
Isis Temaukel Eleda Gaia Laxmi Mahmanmu-rok
Odin El-al Herukhuti Viracocha Marduk Ashira Biral
Shaddai Dzingbe Djohu-ma-di-hutu Astarte Ndengei
Koyatu Baha'u'llah Marrigan Baiame Om Pelepelewa
Durga Orisha Nyame Techaronhiawakhon Chukwu
Uvolovu Brahman Nephtys Ha-Maqom Tehuti Maat
Digambara Val Tik Chaitanya Amana Kwoth Num
Colok Nabango Fumeripitsj Shiva Varuna Lukanga
Bala Atibluku Karu Allah Sing Nainuema Artemis
Kartikeya Kuanyin Yelafaz T'ien Baal Shakti
Athena Olorun Nemesis Sheela-na-Gig Bhavartarini
Jesus Horus Izanagi Sebek Waq Ishtar Ti Seker
BegoTanutanu Sat Nam Kali Mirirul Bhavatarini
Tsui-goab Hatzur Brahman Ubusuna Tonantzin
YHVH Apollo Nana God Almighty Hu Vishnu Om

This
God
Is

Wabun Wind

I conceive of God as being the great and eternal spirit that is within all things and around all things, that has no beginning and no ending but always is, is manifesting, shifting, changing, illuminating, expanding, contracting, creating and evolving. This God is neither male nor female, human nor animal, element nor plant. This God is made in no image but its own. That image is as illusive as the firefly in daylight, the mist after the sun rises, the smoke from a fire long in embers. This God is as vast as the universe, and as small as an atom. This God judges no one, but encourages all life to become as shining as the smile on a newborn's face. This God is a God of life, not death. This God is all things and no things. This God is.

I have not always had this view. Like most people growing up in the thrall of the worldwide patriarchal culture, I was taught to believe in a God made in the image of man, and man at his worst. The God of my childhood was a malicious, vengeful deity who seemed to derive the purest pleasure from torturing his worshippers. This God seemed to be jealous of all other Gods, and of man. This God had a lengthy history of inspiring hatred, not love, although I was taught he was the God of love. This God seemed to enjoy war, even though I was taught he was the prince of peace. This God espoused compassion but sentenced women to having pain in childbirth. This God who was reputed to care about the condition of the sparrows in the fields encouraged parents to use the rod so as not to "spoil the child." What a confusing God of hypocrisy!

Yet I bought the idea that this God of dominance and fear was worthy of my worship. What alternative did I have? I read the "inspirational" work of this religion, the Bible, three full times while I was still in high school, even though I normally avoided violent books. I dutifully went to Sunday school and church believing that the alternative was to burn in hell for all eternity. I learned the commandments and attempted to obey them, even when they conflicted with each other. Thou shall have no other Gods—unless the church sanctions them. Honor your parents—unless they don't worship properly. There were many such inconsistencies in the religion of my youth. Still, it seemed the only option I had.

My great grandparents had come to this country from Wales

carrying with them belief in a Protestant denomination (the particular one is lost to my knowledge) that allowed them to justify working themselves to death in the coal mines of Pennsylvania. All of the grandparent generation I encountered were religious to a fault. Several of the women seemed to love their church more than their family. There were rumors of family fortunes being given to the church in some mysterious circumstances.

Both my parents became lapsed church people as soon as they moved away from their families. The lapse lasted until I became Sunday school age. Then I was dutifully taken to a local traditional Lutheran church. That was okay until I reached confirmation age.

The following story of how I became a lapsed Lutheran at eleven is so foolish it will sound as though I am taking literary license, but I am not. This is one of the few childhood incidents of which I have a perfectly clear memory. I was a bright child, and a writer since I was six. Both these facts made me an easy target for children who had already learned that the God of their fathers favored brawn over brain.

Around Christmastime of my eleventh year I wrote a story about a young girl making a gingerbread house with her mother. Another young woman in the confirmation class began to ridicule me and my story. I did not take the bait so she began physically pushing me. I looked at her, and told her she was an ignoramus. My statement stopped her in her tracks, and she ran to tell the minister what I had said. Hearing the circumstances of the disagreement, the old, stern-lipped minister pronounced that he was going to come to my home and tell my parents I was engaging in the sin of cursing. He did so. My mother, however, knew my vocabulary and believed my side of the story. She informed him that ignoramus was not a curse word. I refused to go back to the confirmation class or the church, contending I could not learn much from a man with such a limited vocabulary and intelligence. My parents agreed.

For a while after my lapse from traditionally organized Protestantism, my father and I would occasionally go to revival meetings with a friend inclined to that old-time, holy-roller religion. I loved them. There was so much emotion present it was palpable. I enjoyed giving my life to Jesus each time. But he didn't seem to want it. Being in the midst of an emotional adolescence in a society that bars most rational outlets for that fervor, I tried to become a religious fanatic for a time. But the promised rapture always eluded me. So did the sense of fulfillment, unity, and purpose that I sought.

We moved from the city to the suburbs and I began to attend a

Presbyterian church. Because I was too old for the normal confirmation proceedings and because the boy down the street who was then the object of my fervor was also doing so, I joined the church by admitting my faith in front of the congregation along with said boy. I loved the emotion of again giving my life to Jesus, and the romance of doing so with my current fantasy prince. Being confirmed was also the normal thing to do in my neighborhood and, like most teens, I wanted to appear to be normal. I dutifully attended the church and went to the expected teen activities.

Then a new minister came to that church, one I fondly remember even now. He was one of the few adults who really was willing to listen to what I felt about life. Consequently, he was such a big influence that I ended up attending a midwestern Presbyterian college for my freshman year. It was a mistake, and one I corrected as soon as possible. The homogeneity and saccharine 'niceness' I perceived in my fellow students made me feel fenced in by the neat corn rows growing around the perimeters of the college. I didn't know what I wanted at age 18, but I knew I wouldn't find it at that school.

Yet religion and belief still mattered a great deal to me. If women had not been ignored as potential carriers of the word of God at that school, I probably would have stayed there and attempted to become the type of caring minister I saw in my home reverend (who became an early part of the charismatic movement and carried my parents along with his enthusiasm). But women were considered fit minister's wives, not fit ministers in the mid 1960s.

I transferred to a large university in Washington, D.C. and much of my fervor went into politics, increasingly of the left variety, and into the men I met through politics. I still faithfully attended church (better an hour on Sunday than eternity in hell I reasoned), usually high Episcopal because I liked their sense of ceremony.

That continued for a few years until my own hypocrisy became unbearable. I realized I was not going to church because I wanted to. I was only going because I was afraid of losing my "eternal soul" if I did not. By this time in my life I had had plenty of firsthand experience of the lies society told me about sex, relationships, education, finances, the American dream, politics, childhood, and most other areas of life. I figured if I had been deceived in all of these, it was very possible I had also been lied to about the state of my soul. Besides, social injustice was all around me and the war in Vietnam was heating up. Why should I take time to go to church when I could use that time for more meaningful pursuits. Politics became my religion.

I debated. I lobbied. I wrote. I demonstrated. I got tear gassed. I picketed. I boycotted. I got clean for Gene in the 1968 election. I leafleted. I got cited for littering. I took it to court. I wrote more. I spent a year working on my first book—one about lawyers of the left.

At the same time this political revolution was brewing, so was a social one, and I wanted to be on the front lines of both. I went to encounter groups and encounter theater. I threw away my heels and bought earth shoes. I studied yoga. I dabbled in the psychedelic world. I searched for the hidden meanings in music and poetry. I purchased diaphanous white Indian shirts and wore them braless on the subways. I found a variety of other ways to help my guardian angels collect overtime.

At one point I realized my efforts were going to help men become equal—and I wasn't a man. I joined forces with the burgeoning feminist movement. I sponsored consciousness-raising groups. I wrote more about the inequalities between the sexes.

I did everything I could think of in the political arena, and I saw little change in my own world, or in the world-at-large. I became a lapsed radical, and turned my energy back to religion. But this time I would not explore the God of my fathers. This time I would explore the new religious ideas pouring into this country from all parts of the globe. I went to lectures about Sufism, Buddhism, Tibetan Buddhism, Yoga, Tantra, Arica, Gurdjieff, other fourth-way schools, interesting combinations thereof, and stuff so strange my guardian angels threatened to boycott me. At that point I decided to pick A WAY, one that seemed relatively safe and straight. I got involved with a Gurdjieffian school.

My mind was enthralled. I used to tell people Gurdjieff had answered all the questions I had and some I had not thought of. I looked forward to learning the movements and bringing my body more into the equation. Life seemed settled. I felt safe and as though I was progressing on my path.

Then I started to get odd experiences of earthquakes happening that no one else felt, or of tidal waves coming that no one else could see. I feared for my safety and sanity. After trying to get the opinion of others about what was happening and meeting only with scorn, I kept my mouth shut about these experiences and learned to get through them.

That summer Sun Bear came to New York City and totally

shattered my illusions of life being settled. I had first heard about Sun Bear and his Bear Tribe when I was in California researching my book about lawyers. From what I heard, I thought Sun Bear was an eighty-year-old Hopi who believed he was bringing together a tribe of reincarnated Indians who would help and teach people during the time of earth changes. I wasn't sure how I felt about reincarnation; I knew nothing about the Hopis or other Indians; I had no idea what the earth changes were. Months later I got a letter saying Sun Bear was touring the country to talk about his beliefs. Not only could I interview him during his New York visit, but also he would take me up on the offer I barely remembered making saying he could stay at my place if he came to New York.

When a handsome, virile 40-year-old man came to my door instead of an 80-year-old supported by an assistant, my life tilted. When he explained the meaning of my strange earthquake and other experiences (before I told him about them), my life shifted. From the moment I laid eyes on Sun Bear I loved him. I believed this was what I had been taught was love at first sight, the romantic event of a lifetime. I knew very little about other kinds of love at that time.

In his own way Sun Bear loved me too. And he saw much more clearly than I how our destinies were entwined. He knew that I was supposed to be with him. He knew how I would help the vision that was the driving force of his life. There was no way I could have understood his need to serve his vision. I had little idea of what vision was.

The force of the feelings I had for Sun Bear was stronger than my resistance to deep change. I left the life I had built for myself as a writer in New York City and went West to explore what was a new world to me.

I went from an urban, technological existence in which mankind was the only important part of the universe to something very different. Sun Bear rarely sat down to give lectures about opposing worldviews, but he showed me the world through his eyes, which is the greatest gift any teacher can give.

I began to notice that his world was much larger than mine. He did not limit his interest to humans and what they were doing. He found the progress of an ant or the flight of an eagle just as fascinating. His interest was neither pedantic nor condescending. He simply enjoyed watching what his relations did. Sun Bear's world contained more happiness than the one I had come from. And more laughter. There was little guilt nor desire to impress. He believed that every part of the creation had a right to exist and enjoy.

I began to understand the circular view of life, the idea that everything is interconnected. Even more, I began to feel the connections between me and the rest of the earth. I could hug a tree and feel its energy. I could touch my hands to the earth and feel the pulsing there. I could open my eyes and see the energy that dances in the sky. I began to hear the subtle yet distinct songs of nature.

No longer did I perceive humans to be the jewel in the crown of creation. In fact, it seemed more often that we were the thorn in the crown.

As I opened my mind and heart to the earth I began to truly learn about the creator, about the God who eluded me when I only searched in mankind's thoughts and works. There was a very familiar feeling inside me when I felt this earth connection. I could not understand why at first. Then I remembered. It was the same feeling I had had as a child when I rolled in the grass, watched honeybees on hollyhocks, walked by a gentle stream, jumped from rock to rock, watched a bird build a nest, coaxed an earthworm out of its hole, saw the shapes in the clouds, gazed in wonder at the stars in the sky.

Being with Sun Bear certainly speeded my learning about the creator. He and his native friends were vast repositories of the wisdom of the earth. The energy of the earth seemed to course through them so that they exuded an aura of naturalness and simplicity. This was so different from the energy of people I had known in the cities. There is a story I heard may times through the years about a white man who encountered an Indian wandering through the forest. The Indian was an elderly man and the white man was concerned that he might be lost. When he asked the elder whether he was lost the old man looked at him and replied, "I'm not lost. My teepee is lost."

Many of the native people I have met over the years do seem very at home on the earth wherever they are. They have a confidence in the earth and a sense of place lacking in most folks from the dominant culture. This earth wisdom always seems to guide them to the creator.

When the first European immigrants came to this land they would see a native person praying to a tree or a stone and they would think that the Indian felt that the tree or stone was a God. With the arrogance that marks so much of the patriarchal culture they made an assumption and never asked the native people whether the assumption was true. If they had, they would have learned that the native person only believed in one great spirit or great mystery. However, natives knew that the energy of that mystery was present in all beings in all of the kingdoms upon the earth. They knew that you never assumed that you could just take from one of these kingdoms. Rather, you asked the tree or the stone whether they wanted to give. If they did, then you took the gift you were so generously offered whether it was a healing stone or a branch for the fire.

Native peoples here and all around the earth knew that life was a circle, that everything was interconnected. They knew that if you affected one part of the circle, you affected the whole circle. This knowledge permeated all parts of their lives. They built their homes in a circle, they made their music upon the circle of the drum, they danced and chanted in a circle, they used the circle in their art. They knew about the different kingdoms upon the earth and also celebrated this in their life and art.

This is part of the reason that the number four was so sacred to many native people. They knew that there were four sacred directions, four elements, and four kingdoms of life upon earth. The first kingdom is that of the elemental people: the earth, the water, the fire and the air. This kingdom provides the building block for all the rest of life. The elements are the first beings, and the most independent beings. They can exist alone, without the help of the other kingdoms. The second kingdom is that of the plant peoples: the grasses, the trees, the land plants, and the sea plants. The plant beings are more dependent than the elementals. They cannot exist without the earth, water, fire from the sun, and air. The third earthly kingdom is that of the animals: the crawlers, the swimmers, the winged ones, and the four-leggeds. These beings are even more dependent. They need the help of both the elements and the plants for their lives to continue.

We humans are the fourth kingdom upon the earth, and the most dependent. Like the others we can be divided into four: the four races. We need the help of all the other kingdoms for our lives to continue. Without the elements we would have no life: without the plants we would have no food or medicine, without the animals we would lose our closest allies in the circle of life. We would lose the companionship, the teachings, the songs, the food, shelter and clothing which our animal relations give to us so generously.

I learned from native teaching that we humans are the most dependent beings upon the earth, not the independent creators of manifest destiny society teaches us we are.

When I began to realize just how dependent I was myself, I learned one of the most important lessons there is in life. I learned how to give sincere thanks. Through this lesson I learned a great deal about the creator.

I've heard a number of people say that native people made a prayer of thanks with every step they took. Over the years I have come to understand what that simple sentence means. When you realize your own dependence, you come to appreciate the wonderful gifts the creation is constantly giving to you. The earth allows you to have something solid upon which to stand. The water satisfies your thirst and allows you body to function. The fire warms you. The air allows you to breathe. The plants give a feast to your senses. The animals teach you, guide you, protect you, give you energy. Together these beings give you life and allow you to sustain this life. When you learn to respect the life, you begin to give your appreciation to those who bestow this gift upon you.

At first giving thanks was a rather clumsy effort on my part. When I needed to make my offerings and thanks to another of earth's children I would try to do so with the pomp and circumstance I associated with the prayers of churchmen. Eventually one of my teachers suggested that I pray in the way I remembered doing when I was a child. That seemed much more comfortable. Still I had a rather ritualized idea of how prayers of thanks should be made.

I remember being shocked at the way one elderly Indian herbalist would go along and pick plants without taking the time to make the elaborate offerings I thought were necessary. I felt she was being disrespectful to the plants because she wasn't doing things in the way I expected. One day I asked her about her way. She told me that the longer you worked with the plants, the shorter time it took you to thank each one. The communication and respect was already there. When every step you take is a prayer, each prayer can be simple.

How did we get from there to here? From a place of natural thanksgiving to one of contrived religiosity? From a God of life to a God of death? I pondered this question as my understanding of ancient ways grew. I opened myself to hearing the answer in whatever way it would come to me. Like most contemporary visions, it came in small pieces. Some pieces came while I prayed or meditated. Others came while I listened with or spoke with my heart's wisdom. Some came through words I would read; others, through myths or stories I would hear. Still more come in a way I don't have words to explain—what is best described as the whispering of my muse.

When I had accepted enough pieces I realized I had a vision of how human beings have developed and changed over the past 20,000 years. My vision gave me a view of history much broader than that of this society's historians: a view that took me back to our earliest evolution as humans. I came to value history and to believe if we don't understand the mistakes we've made in the past, we become prisoners of those mistakes. Only through understanding do we have a chance to evolve both in our understanding of the creator and in our ability to relate in a better way to one another and to the earth mother.

It's difficult to learn about the history of our far past as human beings because most of the records of those times have been destroyed. It is the victor who gets to write the history books, and one of the ways of assuring continued victory is to be certain people believe the way life now is being lived is the only way life can be lived. To keep a system in power—particularly an authoritarian one—it is very helpful to keep people in ignorance.

The more I studied, both with other people and by going within myself, the more I became convinced that at least 20,000 years ago we all lived together in harmony, spending much of our time having visions. The dividing line between the visionary state and what we now call waking reality was not nearly as defined as it is in today's world. We had visions, we fulfilled them. Life was simple. One of the things I believe contributed to the simplicity was that in those early times we did not have the ability to speak, or to differentiate. I don't think our brains were formed then in such a way that differentiation or speech were important to us. We communicated, but we communicated in a way we have no good words for in the English language today.

"Telepathy" begins to describe this method of communication, except telepathy implies we thought the same thoughts. I believe in this earliest stage of our history we didn't think as we do today. Rather, we felt and we sensed, and from our feelings and sensations we were able to know what was needed by any of our other selves, our brothers and sisters. To the best of our ability, we would strive to fulfill whatever that need was.

Time passed and change occurred. We learned how to differentiate. We learned how to speak. We learned the difference between "me" and "you." As time went on, that difference became more important than "us."

In this early period of our social history, I believe all humans lived in what we would now call matriarchal systems. Because women had the ability to give birth, to bring forth new life, women were considered to be very magical creatures. I've heard it said by native people that women have the first medicine, and that medicine is the ability to bring forth life. Everything having to do with this ability was considered to be sacred. The time of menstruation was considered to be particularly powerful. After all, in those days most people who bled as much as a woman bleeds during her menstruation would die. But a woman had the ability to bleed, to heal herself, to go on, to bleed, and to heal herself again. Some anthropologists believe many of the later rituals of bloodletting and the patriarchal practices of making blood sacrifices were men's attempts to emulate the power of menstruating women.

In our early times in the matriarchy, I believe we all lived together in harmony and peace. Everything was considered to be a gift of the great mother. People shared what they had, and everyone had what they needed. Children were welcomed into the world with great joy, and childhoods were wonderful times, very different from what they later became. In matriarchal times, it's likely we lived a very agrarian existence, close to the land. People respected the earth mother, who was so much like the human female; both could bring forth life.

I believe at this point of human history men did not know they had anything to do with the conception of children. Consequently, they felt they were second-rate humans, unable to participate in life's most sacred mystery. At one point in the history of the matriarchy, it is almost certain the priestesses found out the truth about conception, and thus knew of the part men did play. However, those who learned this decided to hide their knowledge. That kept culture developing in the way it was, and kept men in their place. It also set the stage for the later downfall of matriarchal cultures.

In order for the priestesses to keep their secret, they had to create a religion based upon lies. In order to keep the power they had begun to savor, they had to keep men from knowing the truth they had learned. And they did so successfully for many years.

Now, please understand I am not speaking in a historical sense here. I am speaking in a mythological sense that relates to our collective unconscious. I don't believe there was one woman or one group of women who made this decision; I believe it is just the way the consciousness of the world streamed right then.

At some point of the stream of consciousness, a man or group of men probably watched the animals and observed that in a period of time after they mated, the females would give birth. This observant mythological man eventually became obsessed with the idea of knowing which child he helped to father. So he plotted to be sure the woman with whom he mated would mate with no one else. In this way he could ascertain which child was his. This mythological man was able to fulfill his scheme, and by doing so he established his own paternity and became the first father. He also introduced the concept of ownership, which became the underlying concept of the patriarchy.

In humanity's egalitarian times, and then in its matriarchal times, no one owned anything. The land, the earth was there to be taken care of by the family, by the clan, by the tribe. The plants were there to be shared by those who needed them. Animals were their own beings. Children were not considered to be the property of the mother but the gift of life renewing itself.

All that changed when this mythological man plotted to assert his paternity. By doing so he made a radical statement. He purported to own the womb of the woman. And the Goddess or her priestesses did not strike him dead. When man saw he could own a woman's womb, he began a frenzy of ownership. The land was divided up. The plants, the animals, and the children became property. When man created so many possessions, so many borders, so many boundaries, he had something to fight about. The concept of war came into the world, and violent behavior burgeoned.

When patriarchy gained a toehold, it soon got a foothold and then overcame the matriarchal religion. Likewise, people living in matriarchy did not believe in war, so they had few weapons effective against the followers of the new and violent patriarchal religions. And the patriarchy was born of a rage that was murderous.

When men, who had been denied the knowledge they had anything to do with creating life, were told they did, they became very enraged at women for withholding this fact from them. That rage, mixed with the concept of possession, of ownership, became the basis of the religions they introduced in the world. I am again speaking mythologically.

I don't believe the matriarchal times were perfect. If they had been, they would have had built into their philosophy the ability to embrace whatever changes occurred. But in many ways, they were superior to the patriarchal periods that followed. Matriarchy was a lot gentler and kinder to the earth, and to all the children of the earth.

The creator, the great mother of the matriarchy, began as an all-loving, all-forgiving compassionate being. Later, when her priestesses practiced falsehood, the great mother was depicted as having the power of destruction as well as creation. But she was beneficent when compared to the Gods that came with the patriarchy.

If you study the mythologies and oral histories of people around the world, it appears the patriarchal religions began in what is now called the Orient, and spread in a westward direction around the earth. This means the last places the patriarchy reached were Europe and the Americas. That gave the native peoples of these areas the opportunity to live with the matriarchal philosophy and consciousness a lot longer than people in other parts of the world.

I found that by studying the philosophy, the religion, of the Native American people, I learned a lot about what earth-centered, women-loving cultures were like. Many of the Native American cultures have remnants left of their matriarchal times. Even today, there are tribes where property is held by the women, where the name passes through the woman's line, where clan membership is determined by the clan of the mother. What a joy it was to learn about these ways that promised some relief from the patriarchal God of my youth: a God of vengeance, a God of rage, a God who values possessions above people and who hates women as much as did the men who created him. What freedom came with identifying the underlying lie of the patriarchy: the lie that contends that you can possess anything. Just as the lie that men did not help to bring forth new life became both a foundation for the matriarchy and a major thrust in its downfall, so the concept of ownership is the foundation of patriarchy, and its greatest flaw.

The truth is we can't possess anything of substance. We come into the world with our unique energy, our unique vision. We leave the world with the visions we have loved. Aside from that, we bring or take nothing. Everything else is a gift: a gift of the creator, a gift of the Goddess, a gift of God, a gift of the earth mother, a gift of life.

Life seems to have a way of continuing itself, of intertwining, of weaving humans, animals, plants, elementals together in ever-changing, ever-beautiful patterns. When I learned to appreciate the beauty of each moment of patterning to which I could open my eyes, I began to really understand God, the creator, who is always changing, growing, expanding, contracting, just like we are.

I love the God I have found. My God is a God of love, not of fear; a God of compassion, not of vengeance; a God of gentleness, not violence; a God of acceptance, not jealousy. My God is not a prejudiced God, but a discriminating one. My God doesn't believe you turn your eyes the other way when you see something hurtful happening that you might have the power to change. My God looks to alleviate human suffering, not to cause it. My God is not found enclosed in any church or temple; my God is everywhere, in everything—me, you, and all of creation. My God does not require any prescribed ritual from followers. Rather, the creator recognizes there are many tools to help people come to understand the creation, and all of these tools are fine for the people who use them.

I don't need to set apart particular times for worshipping. When I notice a tiny flower coming through the cracks of the sidewalk, I know it's sign from my God. When I see a wisp of clean white cloud in the sky, or watch the dance of the lightning bugs as they rise to the tops of the pine trees, when I hear the laughter of children or see them with their clear, vivid eyes, when I open myself to the song of the birds, to the smell of the roses, in all these ways I worship the creator. Sometimes I sing beautiful songs for the creator; other times I might drum or rattle, or smudge, or use my pipe, or go into the sweat lodge to intensify my ability to envision the creator. Other times, standing under the shower, tasting a delicious fruit, embracing my loved ones, enjoying a piece of candy, I know the creator is there too.

The more I've come to know the creator, the more I realize that there is no one right way to worship, and there are few wrong ways to worship. Like breathing, worship is now part of my life whenever I can bring my consciousness away from all the bustle of the busy world around me and remember the wonderful place where the creator always is inside me.

Wabun Wind is the Director and Keeper of the Vision for the Bear Tribe, the organization founded by native American shaman and teacher, Sun Bear. She is also a writer, teacher, ceremonial designer, counsellor, wife, mother, student of earth cultures, and wise woman.

Wabun has authored or co-authored nine books, including *The Medicine Wheel: Earth Astrology* and *Black Dawn/Bright Day*. Her spiritual autobiography, *Woman of the Dawn,* has inspired countless people to find and follow their own dawning visions. Wabun believes that through personal understanding and responsibility we can heal ourselves and help heal the earth. Wabun is one of the most powerful contemporary teachers about the feminine, earth cultures, and ceremonies.

Adonai Zeus Shekhinah Elim Ogun Kat Buddha
Wyame Hel Rama Mitra Odomankoma Jupiter Het
Heru Agni Cagn Thor Brahma Tangaroa Father
Lugaba Papang Diana Al-Rahman Cerridwen Ahone
Yoma' Tirawa Atius Cagoaba El Mungan-ngua
Quetzalcoatl Hamakom ddai
Atibruku Moma YH Bunj aiwa
Saraswati Inanna Miriru aong

God is Always Pregnant

Jeanette Rodriguez, Ph.D.

Tonantzin Yuskeha Bha Head
Olodumare Shyama Ekv Heru
Nurrundere Daramilun tzeir
Hecate Chi Musubi Hin suna
Nanderuvucu Erishkigal man
Tsui-goab Ometeotl Os chtli
Surya Elohim Nyankop Ilu
Woden Great Spirit Lese goro
Poseidon Chineke Nhialic Aciek Kari Ausel Tcuwut
Makai Wakantanka Inari Ha-Qadosh barukh hu'
Tara Krishna Avaloket-iswara Rabb Goryo Qat Oke
Nurunderi Indra Shang-ti Amaterasu Ohmikami
Kannon Quan Yin Ise Lakshmi Awonawilona Bast
Omecihuatl Ruhanga Kosane Sophia Dionysus Ixchel
Mawu Ra Ardanariswara Oluwa Deng Hanuman
uNkulunkulu Kanobo Ngai Shamayim Cybele Dakini
Nataraj Pachamama Susanoo Katonda Avlukpo Eloah
Isis Temaukel Eleda Gaia Laxmi Mahmanmu-rok
Odin El-al Herukhuti Viracocha Marduk Ashira Biral
Shaddai Dzingbe Djohu-ma-di-hutu Astarte Ndengei
Koyatu Baha'u'llah Marrigan Baiame Om Pelepelewa
Durga Orisha Nyame Techaronhiawakhon Chukwu
Uvolovu Brahman Nephtys Ha-Maqom Tehuti Maat
Digambara Val Tik Chaitanya Amana Kwoth Num
Colok Nabango Fumeripitsj Shiva Varuna Lukanga
Bala Atibluku Karu Allah Sing Nainuema Artemis
Kartikeya Kuanyin Yelafaz T'ien Baal Shakti
Athena Olorun Nemesis Sheela-na-Gig Bhavartarini
Jesus Horus Izanagi Sebek Waq Ishtar Ti Seker
BegoTanutanu Sat Nam Kali Mirirul Bhavatarini
Tsui-goab Hatzur Brahman Ubusuna Tonantzin
YHVH Apollo Nana God Almighty Hu Vishnu Om

I walk into a cave, not sure why I am there. Deep inside, I notice movement to my left. Turning, I see monks, maybe twelve or fifteen, dressed in full, coarse robes of brown and white, their faces hidden in the shadow of their hoods. They move together pushing a large mural across the floor of the cave. Wanting to see what it is, I come from behind and see an image of Our Lady of Guadalupe.

"What are you doing? Where are you going with this image?" I ask them.

But they don't answer, only keep pushing it forward. I see that the monks are heading toward a large vault. They push the image in and slam the door shut. Then they turn the lock and build a wall, a brick one, sealing off the vault.

"No, no! You can't do this," I scream. "Why are you doing this? Please answer me."

No one answers. They continue their sad task, now sealing the bricks with plaster, covering all trace of the vault and the image. I continue my wailing, "No, please stop! This is the life of the people. They need this image; it is their truth, their wisdom, their hope, their power."

The monks move away from the plastered wall, continuing on their way deep into the tunnel. I run after them, screaming and crying, "Please show me that you have hearts. Respond to me."

They continue on, but one monk, still walking in unison with his brothers, turns around. I see a huge tear rolling down his cheek. And for one moment I feel relief, perhaps even hope: "Ah, he understands." But he is incapable of answering or acting on his own outside the system. I know he knows, and if he knows, others *must* know also.

§

At that point I woke up to find that I had been crying. The pillow on my bed is soaking wet, the echoes of the dream's last words are strong in my mind: "I know he knows and others must also know."

What I know is the result of six years of research, interviews, and shared daily life with the Mexican and Mexican-American populations of California and Mexico. What I know, I know from contemplation as well as from study of the image of Our Lady of Guadalupe. Now I wish to share with you the fruit of my years of journeying to her.

Let's go back in time—more than ten years. In 1981 I arrived in Berkeley to pursue doctoral studies after serving, for three and a half years, in the missions of Guam, Micronesia, Japan, Taiwan, and the Philippines. Wishing to continue my ministry when I returned to the States, I accepted a leadership position as consultant for Hispanic catechesis and Hispanic development for the diocese of Oakland. Up to that time I had been exposed to Hispanics of many different backgrounds, but this was the first time that I had been exposed to Hispanics of Mexican and Mexican-American descent. Within the six years that I had the privilege of working and growing with them, I have come to learn and be devoted to the vision of Guadalupe.

Among the 12.1 million people of Mexican descent in the United States, she is everywhere—the brown-skinned woman surrounded by the sun, cloaked in a blue mantle covered with stars, standing on a crescent moon held by an angel. Our Lady of Guadalupe. She gazes downwards, and her face expresses compassion and strength. Her image pervades all Mexican-American neighborhoods—as a statue in a sacred corner of the home, as a medallion worn around the necks of young and old, as an image on T-shirts, on the sides of buildings, and even on business logos. Parents bestow her name, Guadalupe, on both girls and boys, and the name adorns not only parishes and churches but also streets, towns, cities, rivers, and mountains.

Almost all persons of Mexican descent, whether in Mexico or in the Mexican diaspora, recognize the name and image of Our Lady of Guadalupe. In the United States, Guadalupe has found a prominent niche in the barrios, homes, and businesses of Mexican-Americans. She has found a place within the technological, fast-paced, elitist, and secular milieu shared by so many who also share her dark skin and her language. She is everywhere, and it is obvious that she has a profound impact on the people. You can see it on their faces, hear it in the way they speak about her; you can feel it in their ritualistic, endearing, and reverential behavior towards her image. But who is she? And what is this power that she holds over them?

Of Ecuadorian descent, I grew up with the image of Mary as La Madre Dolorosa, the Sorrowful Mother. I have grown to understand that image and see it lived out, incarnated in the women I grew up with. But I knew nothing about Our Lady of Guadalupe, who she was, nor what her story meant. I did know, or at least felt in my bones, that if somehow I could tap this power, this influence

she had, then I could use it to help motivate the people to participate in their own liberation. I admit there was an egocentric moti-
vaton in my quest for understanding the impact of the image. What
I did not know was that I would come back from the investigation a
devotee.

When I first heard the story of Guadalupe, I was not convinced
that it was enough to warrant the kind of devotion and affective
response that I witnessed in the people to whom I ministered, so I
decided to conduct my own investigation. I began by reading, asking questions, attending fiestas. In the process, I became so seduced
by the impact, influence, and power of the image that I decided to
make it the focus of my doctoral dissertation.

The following pages record what I found. I want to make quite
clear that it was the faithfulness of the people and the obvious
response that they have to this image that motivated me. The
scholarly investigation is fascinating and may even make the hair on
your head stand up as mine did, but that is not what initially moved
me. There is something about this image that touches deeply, not
so much while praying to the image, but in contemplating it. She
speaks, she expresses herself. I'm not sure I can access and articulate
the depth of the feelings that I now have when I look upon the
image; I am even nervous about the consequences of a fuller understanding of the story and image, but I offer you a glimpse of my
musing.

Background

Our Lady of Guadalupe appeared in 1531. Her appearance
dates from before the age of newspapers and mass-media, but the
story is recorded in a text titled, The Nican Mopohua. In order to
appreciate the significance of the Guadalupe event, it is important
to understand the context in which it occurred. History records that
Hernando Cortez began the Spanish conquest of the Aztec empire
in 1519.[1] The encounter between the 16th century Spaniards and
the 16th century Aztecs is an example of an extreme clash of
cultures. This clash, coupled with the Spaniards' military superiority
and disdain for the indigenous people, led to the devastation of the
Aztec Nahuatl[2] and their culture. Physical violence and massacre at
the hands of the Spaniards were common experiences as attested by
Aztec paintings of that era showing Spaniards in the act of dis-
membering Aztec and Nahuatl alike. Intense suffering in the form
of hunger and lack of fresh water was caused by Spanish blockades;

abuse of indigenous women was widespread.³

The indigenous people were forced into a state of hopelessness, powerlessness, anger, fear, and eventually self-hatred.

> Their gods had been defeated, their temples had been destroyed, their women had been violated. They, who considered themselves the chosen people of the gods, had been defeated. Their honor and glory, their power and government had disappeared. This traumatic experience of a total conquest would be deeply imprinted in the very soul of the new Mexican people.⁴

One need only review the poetry that came out of post-conquest Aztec literature to find similiar cries of an oppressed and pain-filled people: broken spears lying in the roads, roofless houses covered with blood, the sound of pounding despair, cries of grief rising up, cities in darkness and destruction, and the calls to God, the Giver of Life. "Nothing but flowers and songs of sorrow are left in Mexico," wrote the Aztec poets.⁵

The most profound aspect of the conquest, however, was the spiritual dimension: the spiritual devastation of an entire people. With the destruction of their temples, and thus their pride, and with the murder of their people, the Aztecs felt that the gods were angry with them and had deserted them. The people had nothing to live for. "If, as you say, our gods are dead, it is better that you allow us to die too."⁶

How do we even begin to get in touch with this kind of devastation? Reflect on a time in your life when for even a moment you felt like you wanted to die, when you felt you had nothing to live for because of some tragedy in your life. If you then take that feeling and multiply it to a whole people, to a whole nation, to a whole civilization, then you will begin to understand what the indigenous people felt as a consequence of the Spanish conquest. Perhaps the strongest proof of the conquest's destruction was the chief theological question occupying the Spanish minds of the time: Are the Indians human? Do they have a soul? ⁷

The Spaniards wanted not only to impose their political power on the Indians, but their religious belief system as well. In doing so, they obliterated a most essential element of the native culture, namely, its spirituality. It was in the midst of this terible clash of cultures and religion that Our Lady of Guadalupe made her appearance.

The Story

Early on a Sunday morning in northern Mexico City, ten years after the Spanish conquest of the new world, Juan Diego was on his way to church. Suddenly, he heard music in the air, and a bit startled, he looked to the East, the home of the Sun God, and the source of the music. There he saw a "Lady," as he said later, clothed with the radiance of the sun.

The Lady spoke to Juan Diego, "Know and be assured, the smallest of my children, that I am the ever Virgin Mary, Mother of the true God, for whom one lives." She further identified herself as the Mother of God, who is the God of Truth; the Mother of the Giver of Life; the Mother of the Creator; the Mother of the One who makes the sun and the earth; and the Mother of the One who is near.

She told Juan Diego that she wanted a temple to be built for her where she could bestow her love, compassion, strength, and defense to all those who came to her. She wished her house to be at Tepeyac, a site of great significance, for the spot previously housed the shrine of Tonantzin, one of the major Earth Mother divinities of the Aztec people.

At her mandate, Juan Diego went to the bishop only to be told to return at a more convenient time. Disappointed, Juan went back to the Lady, telling her to send someone "who is of great importance, who is known, who is respected, and who is esteemed." He also asked forgiveness from her for any pain he may have caused her by failing to convince the bishop of her message. He thought it was his fault that he was not accepted. Juan Diego's self-depreciation and lack of self-worth exhibited in this passage is a tragic result of the conquest.

But the Lady absolutely refused to choose another messenger. She reaffirmed her desire that Juan be the one, even though she had "many servants and messengers." She did not negate or deny the oppression that Juan Diego was experiencing, nonetheless she both insisted upon and begged for his involvement. Juan Diego re-embraced the mission and returned to the bishop's home in Mexico City. Once again, he experienced difficulties, but he subjected himself to the distrust, humiliation, and disbelief for the sake of the mission. When the bishop finally interrogated Juan Diego, he said that the could not build the temple on the Indian's word alone, and sent Juan back to the Lady for a sign.

After agreeing to elicit a sign from the Lady so that the bishop might believe him, Juan Diego returned home. When he arrived there, however, he found that his uncle, Juan Bernardino, was very sick, pleading with his nephew to bring a priest from Mexico City to administer the last rites.

Juan Diego was caught in a dilemma: should he fulfill his uncle's request or meet the Lady to receive the sign? He decided to get help for his uncle, while taking an alternate route so as not to meet and have to "disappoint the Lady." As he walked along, he once again heard the Lady calling to him. Juan told the Lady about his concern for his uncle and she said, "No temas esa enfermedad, ni otra algune enfermedad y angusita." That is, "Do not fear this sickness, or any other sickness or anguish. Am I not here, your Mother? Are you not under my shadow and protection? Am I not your fountain of life? Are you not in the folds of my mantle, in the crossing of my arms? Is there anything else that you need?" Her words expanded the uncle's illness to include all sickness and anguish, to embrace all the needs of her children.

Once Juan Diego surrendered to the Lady's authority, Juan Bernardino was cured. This was Guadalupe's first miracle. It brought healing not only for Juan Bernardino, but also for Juan Diego, and ultimately the whole Nahuatl people. The healing and the miracle of the uncle extended itself to the nephew who "felt much consoled and was left feeling contented."

At peace with the assurance that his uncle was healed, Juan Diego asked the Lady to send him back to the bishop with a sign. Guadalupe ordered him to go to the top of Tepeyac and look for roses. He should cut, gather, and bring them to her. When the roses were brought, she arranged them in Juan Diego's tilma (cloak) and sent him back to the bishop.

Filled with faith and new commitment, Juan Diego returned to the bishop's palace. The servants made him wait for a long time, but finally informed the bishop of his presence and allowed him to enter. Once again, Juan told his story to the bishop. He implied that by doubting him and asking for a sign, the bishop had, in fact, questioned and made demands of the Lady. Juan Diego said that the Lady, "sent me up to this hill to get flowers, but I know it was not the season, yet I did not doubt." After stating this, Juan handed over the proof, the roses, and asked the bishop to receive them.

As the flowers fell from Juan's tilma, the image of Our Lady of Guadalupe appeared imprinted on it. When the bishop and those around him in the room saw this, they fell to their knees admiring the image and repenting for not believing earlier.

The bishop immediately took the tilma into his private chapel. He then offered hospitality to Juan Diego, ordering his assistants to follow Juan to determine the place where the temple was to be built. They also went to the uncle's house where they heard testimony about his healing.

Significance of the Apparition

Our Lady of Guadalupe responds to the deepest instincts of the Mexican psyche. The symbols used are theirs; the words belong to their gods; the woman who speaks touches the deepest beliefs of their culture.

The Nican Mopohua text records Saturday, December 9, 1531, early in the morning *(muy de madrugada)* as the time of the apparition. In the Nahuatl culture, the words referred not only to daybreak, but also to the beginning of time. Thus, the image represents the beginning of something new. To the native people, therefore, the Guadalupe event has the significance of a foundational experience equal in importance to the origin of the world and the cosmos.

The titles the Lady uses to introduce herself—Mother of the God of Truth, the Mother of the Giver of Life, the Mother of the Creator, the Mother of the One who makes the sun and the earth, the Mother of the One who is near—coincide precisely with the names given the ancient Mexican gods. The five names of the gods were well known to the Nahuatl. Guadalupe stated who she was and where she came from using Nahuatl duality and phrases, thus utilizing what the Nahuatls understood to be the operative essence as well as the cosmological and historical dimension of their gods.[8]

Guadalupe thus represents compassion, relief, and a means of reconciliation between different groups of people. She is also much more. By identifying herself as "Mother of the true God through whom one lives," Guadalupe identified herself with the supreme creative power, that is, the creative and creating presence. She is a symbol of a new creation, a new people. "Only in an event that clearly originated in heaven could the conquest and rape of the people of Mexico be reversed and a people become truly proud of their new existence." [9]

The drama of Our Lady of Guadalupe addresses a deep need for dignity and restoration of self, that self being the image and likeness of the creator. It speaks of unconditional love and a place in salvific history. Perhaps most significantly, it affirms a need to experience the maternal face of God.

This maternal face of God is made visible by the key words used by Guadalupe: she is here to demonstrate all of her love, compassion, help, and defense; she hears and heals all of our laments, miseries, pains, and sufferings. She does not bring her presence or message initially to the center of power and domination, but to where the poor and abandoned are found. She made herself present in the roses Juan Diego gathered from the mountains, and thus remained within the logical symbolic culture of the Indian: flowers, truth and divinity. For the Nahuatl, flower and song together manifested the presence of the divine. From the midst of the poor (personified in Juan Diego) comes our call to conversion and faith. To believe in Guadalupe is to believe in the poor and the God who stands among them.

The preferential love of the God of life, the God of salvation, is beautifully expressed in Mary's song, the Magnificat (Luke 1:46-55) and in the words and deeds of Jesus. God, as both Father and Mother, the Lord and Lady of Near at our Side (the Nahuatl Ometcotl), comes as the new Tonantzin (our Mother). In Guadalupe, God appears before our eyes as woman and mother, as the sacramental presence of the maternal features of God."[10]

The Image

The image of Our Lady of Guadalupe hangs today in the cathedral in Mexico City. Millions of people come each year to stand before the old tilma of Juan Diego, hanging high above the altar, and look at the beauty of the young woman depicted there. The image is extraordinary in many ways; it is unusual among the many images of Our Lady in Catholic churches around the world. It is obviously an image for the people of Mexico. As a way of exploring this image I would like to share a sample of the artistic, scientific, and symbolic elements that compose it. For those who believe, the explanation is simple: the image of Guadalupe was made supernaturally. No artist painted it, and it was not made with human hands.

The Face: A person's face held great importance for the indigenous people of Mexico because they felt it was through the face that one could come to understand the inner person. A child was considered to be born faceless and with a nameless heart. It was through education that the child was introduced into the tradition of the group and thus his face was gradually formed. It received individuality through the unique way in which the child assimilated unto itself the tradition of the group. Thus the face could be defined as the embodiment of the self as it had been assumed and developed through education. Face and heart *(rostro y corazón)* for the Nahuatl, could then be approximated by our contemporary notion of personality. The face reflected the internal physiognomy.

By looking upon the face of the Lady of Guadalupe and seeing compassion, the Nahuatl saw her person as being compassionate. She was young in face "with mature eyes and a smile of compassion." Her face also told the indigenous people that she was not a Spaniard; she was one of their own. Artistically, the face is one of the most intriguing aspects of the image of Our Lady of Guadalupe. Researcher Philip Callahan says,

The expression suddenly appears reverent yet joyous, Indian yet European, olive-skinned yet white of hue. The feeling is that of a face as rugged as the deserts of Mexico yet gentle as a maiden on her wedding night. It is a face that intermingles the Christianity of Byzantine Europe with the overpowering naturalism of new world Indian; a fitting symbol for all the people of the great continent.[11]
His scientific analysis of the face reaches the following conclusions:

1. The entire face is of unknown pigments that are blended in such a manner as to take advantage of the light refraction qualities of the unsized fabric and impart the olive-skinned hue to the skin.

2. This technique utilizes the rough imperfections of the tilma weave to impart great depth to the painting.

3. The face is of such beauty and unique execution as to render it inexplicable in terms of present-day science.

The Eyes: As with most human images, the eyes of Our Lady of Guadalupe are both intriguing and revealing. The eyes of the image are looking down, indicating that she was not a proud creature. Neither did she show the impersonalism of the Mayan gods nor the masked presence of the Aztec gods. She had her eyes cast down looking upon the people and even allowing them to be reflected there.

Between 1950 and 1980 several ophthalmologists analyzed the eyes of the image. They used infrared photography and a computer to photograph the eyes and amplify them. In this way, they discovered a human figure in the eyes of the Lady, positioned at precisely the locations that they would have to be if she were looking at the figure.

All of the figures found in the eyes of the Lady could conceivably be attributable to "ink blot" speculations were it not for the fact that the same figures appear in both eyes at precisely the positions demanded by the law of optics and two-eyed physiology.[12]

To investigate this phenomenon, Doctor Jose Aste Tonsmann, a computer engineer, used a process called "digitalization." This type of photo enhancing involves the assignment of numerical equivalents to originally qualitative values, and the resulting printout allows evaluation of images too small to be interpreted visually.[13] The enhancement has revealed images of people in both eyes. The shapes are genuine images although difficult to explain. It is almost as if when the Lady appeared she took a picture of the people who were before her.

The most startling discovery in this analysis is the hypothesis about the identity of the images. It was previously thought that there was only the image of Juan Diego in the eyes. Doctor Aste, however, uncovered several more images. There is an image of a cross-legged, bare-chested Indian holding his hands in prayer. The muscles of the legs, abdomen, and arms can be seen clearly. The unusually high forehead of the profiled face is typical of the Aztec "Cuacuacultin" priests, who shaved their foreheads as a badge of rank.

Another image identified was the face of Spanish Bishop Juan de Zumarraga. His face was characterized by a white beard, high cheek bones, and an aquiline nose. The features of the face have been identified as Basque by anthropologists; Bishop Zumarraga was a Basque.

One of the most fascinating images discovered by Doctor Aste is the indistinct form of a black woman. This raised questions, given that the presence of a black woman in 1531 in Mexico was most unusual. Father Maurillo Montemayor, of the Center of Guadalupan Studies, however, confirms the presence of two black female slaves among the household of the bishop.

The Hands: Another aspect of the image of Our Lady of Guadalupe that draws attention is her hands, which are not poised in the traditional Western manner of praying, but rather in an Indian offering. The Nahuatl would have known that something was being offered, that something would come to them from her. A further anatomical study concluded that Guadalupe's arms were not only offering, but were resting on her stomach, much in the way a pregnant woman would hold them.

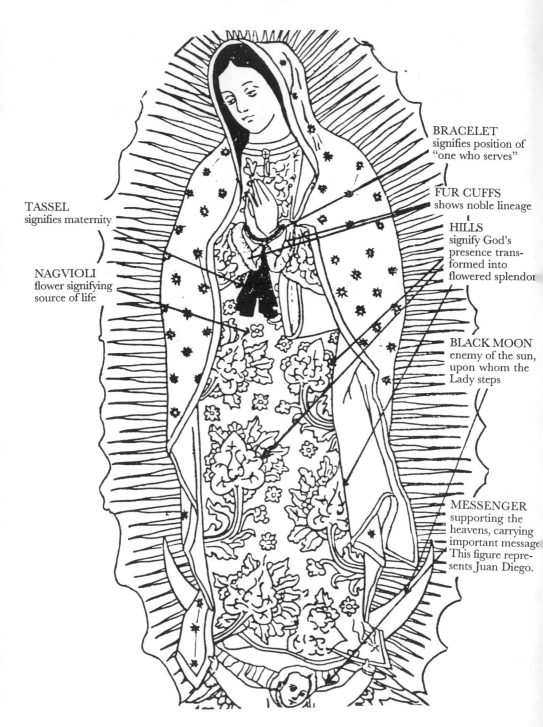

BRACELET
signifies position of
"one who serves"

FUR CUFFS
shows noble lineage

HILLS
signify God's
presence trans-
formed into
flowered splendor

BLACK MOON
enemy of the sun,
upon whom the
Lady steps

MESSENGER
supporting the
heavens, carrying
important message.
This figure repre-
sents Juan Diego.

TASSEL
signifies maternity

NAGVIOLI
flower signifying
source of life

The Pregnancy: The element that sets the image of Our Lady of Guadalupe apart from other apparitions of God's Mother is the fact that she is pregnant. Her pregnancy is indicated by an important element of the image: the tassel, or maternity band *(cinta)* that she wears around her waist. The current Mexican saying, Estoy en cinta, "I am pregnant," attests to the use of this band. Some disagreement exists as to whether or not the waist tassel was added to the painting some time after the original image was formed. This presents a dilemma for us: Was the original image of Our Lady of Guadalupe one of a pregnant woman or not?[14] Further investigation of the symbolism of the image gives us a clue. Below the tassel there is a small flower which is called nagvioli; and signifies the birth of the Sun God. To the Nahuatl, this flower was the Sun God's symbol. They recognized it as having been on the Aztec calendar. The flower's position above Our Lady of Guadalupe's womb verified for the Nahuatl that she was pregnant. Perhaps the cinta was added to make the Nahuatl symbol of the flower clear to Spanish missionaries who already understood the symbol of the maternity band.

Other Aspects: Other significant parts of the image are the stars, the gold sun rays, the moon, and the angel. Each of them relate directly to some aspect of Aztec divinity.

The stars refer to the skirt wrapped about the feminine aspect of the God Ometeotl. The rays of the sun expressed the presence of the Sun God, Quetzalcoatl. The fact that Guadalupe is standing on the moon reminded the Nahuatl of the God of Night, the Moon God. Finally, the fact that Guadalupe is held aloft by an angel relates her to Aztec divinity because royalty and representatives of the deities were always carried by others. The fact that she was carried by heavenly creatures also meant that she came on her own and not with the Spaniards.

The color of Guadalupe's mantle is another aspect of the image that clearly connects her with Aztec divinity. It is turquoise, which was reserved for the great God, Omecihuatl. Current scientific analysis reveals that the blue mantle appears to be original and of semi-transparent pigment while the gold and blue edges of the mantle were added in the sixteenth or early seventeenth century.

A notable aspect of the image is the red robe. Elizondo contends that the color of the robe was the color "of spilled blood of sacrifices . . . the color of Huitzilopochtli, the Sun God, who gives and preserves life and was himself nourished with the precious liquid of life blood."[15]

From an artistic viewpoint, the robe of Our Lady of Guadalupe is especially notable because of its unusual luminosity. "It is highly reflective of visible radiation, yet transparent to the infrared rays. . . . as in the case of the blue mantle the shadowing of the pink robe is blended into the paint layer and no drawing or sketch is evident under the pink pigment."[16]

These artistic and scientific explanations are a testimony to the extraordinary nature of the image. The description makes clear that the image is not simply a picture, but is a story made up of a number of symbols, symbols which spoke to the Nahuatl people in the sixteenth century, and still speak to us in the twentieth.

The Meaning of Guadalupe

Our Lady of Guadalupe is a prism capable of being approached from many perspectives. From one perspective she is an historical event. Sociologically and anthropologically, she forms and supports both cultural and religious identity; theologically, she is the mother of God and the great evangelizer. From another perspective, what one will see depends on the person who is looking at her—within a particular political, cultural, and historical context.

My experience of her is that Our Lady of Guadalupe manifests God as Mother. She identifies herself as our loving mother, a maternal presence, consoling, nurturing, strengthening, and offering unconditional love. She has access to my heart in the way that other things simply do not.

She shares intimacy in pain and joy. Guadalupe captures both the pain and joy of the people. She holds it and transforms it. In my experience, this holding of one's pain and presence is deeply intimate. With the acknowledgment and recognition of that pain, that joy, one is no longer alone in it. When I look at her she reminds me of all the pain our people are in, yet in the midst of that pain there is great joy because she is like us. She is woman; she is mestiza, that is, she hold together different, if not conflicting, worlds. She wants to love and be compassionate and defend and help. She is like me. In a world that negates me, I am imaged in the divine.

All that is creative and generative of life nurtures and is nourishing. Kolhenschlag makes this point in her book, *Lost in the Land of Oz*[17] She identifies orphanhood metaphorically as the deepest, most fundamental reality. If this is the case, then Guadalupe offers something towards the spirituality of the twentieth century because she offers one a *lugar* (place or home). One moves from isolation to belonging. In our alienated society, she offers a place where all can come and feel loved and empowered, a place where they belong, where they can grow and be transformed. Guadalupe offers what Vatican II documents call for: a reason to live, and a reason to hope.

The point of import of Our Lady of Guadalupe is that she not only tells us something about who we are, but says something of what God is. If one looks at her as a Marian image rather than as the maternal face of God, the fact that she is pregnant is significant. She is the only pregnant image of Mary that exists in the Catholic tradition. This image is mother; this image is pregnant divinity.

Meinrad Craighead says, "A mother has but one law: to create . . . transform one substance into another . . . transmute blood into child, fiber into cloth, stone into crystal, memory into image, body into worship."[18] In our world, to long for mother is an embarrassment. It might mean one is not grown up or independent. And yet the archetype of mother is associated with everything that gives life, sustenance, security, stability. Mother accepts us as we are: our warrior side as well as our surrendering side, our strength and our weakness.

For me, being pregnant means to love another so much that it is scary. It is a form of dying. Dying to self. Yet in the very act of such loving one becomes more than one is. If the child hurts, the mother hurts; if the child laughs, the mother laughs. When you have children, you begin to worry about everyone's children. Guadalupe shows us that.

God is always pregnant. What does this mean? This metaphor reveals a God always there to transform, to transmute an experience of pain into an abundance of life. When people discover Guadalupe, they turn to her for that nourishment, that acceptance, that "being fed" that they do not receive in the world. And as she carries their pain, they are transformed. Empowered with their own dignity and humanity, they can then move to transform the world by offering whatever is life-sustaining, i.e., birth, teaching, organizing, uniting for justice, etc.

Understanding the maternal face of God and the call to be pregnant as God is, we have the opportunity to answer Guadalupe's question to us: "Is there anything else that you need?"

My hope is that after you answer this question, you will join me in releasing the original meaning of Guadalupe out of the vault.

Dr. Jeanette Rodriguez is a faculty member at the Institute for Theological Studies, Seattle University. She is a member of ACHTUS, the Academy of Catholic Hispanic Theologians in the U.S. and dedicates her professional life to the articulation of U.S. Hispanic theology with an emphasis on women's experience and spirituality as well as theologies of liberation.

Her doctorate is from the Graduate Theological Union in Berkeley; she earned M.A. degrees in counseling education and religion from the University of Guam and Fordham, respectively, and a B. A degree from Queens College.

In addition to her interest in religion and culture, Dr. Rodriguez is a licensed marriage, family and child therapist. Since 1986 she has worked primarily with Latina women on issues of family, identiy, and acculturation issues.

She is married to Tomas Halguin and has two children, Gabriella, six, and Joshua, three.

Adonai Zeus Shekhinah Elim Ogun Kat Buddha
Wyame Hel Rama Mitra Odomankoma Jupiter Het
Heru Agni Cagn Thor Brahma Tangaroa Father
Lugaba Papang Diana Al-Rahman Cerridwen Ahone
Yoma' Tirawa Atius ~~Gunaoba Ela Musogonguа~~
Quetzalcoatl Hamakom ~~_ddai_~~
Atibruku Moma YH Bun ~~iwa~~

The
Dark Devi

An Interview with
Shuma
Chakravarty

Kathleen Alexander

Saraswati Inanna Mirir ~~uong~~
Tonantzin Yuskeha Bha ~~Head~~
Olodumare Shyama Ekv ~~Ieru~~
Nurrundere Daramilun ~~tzeir~~
Hecate Chi Musubi Him ~~una~~
Nanderuvucu Erishkigal ~~man~~
Tsui-goab Ometeotl Os ~~chtli~~
Surya Elohim Nyankop ~~Ilu~~
Woden Great Spirit Lese ~~goro~~
Poseidon Chineke Nhialic ~~uwut~~
Makai Wakantanka Inari Ha-Qaaosh barakh hu'
Tara Krishna Avaloket-iswara Rabb Goryo Qat Oke
Nurunderi Indra Shang-ti Amaterasu Ohmikami
Kannon Quan Yin Ise Lakshmi Awonawilona Bast
Omecihuatl Ruhanga Kosane Sophia Dionysus Ixchel
Mawu Ra Ardanariswara Oluwa Deng Hanuman
uNkulunkulu Kanobo Ngai Shamayim Cybele Dakini
Nataraj Pachamama Susanoo Katonda Avlukpo Eloah
Isis Temaukel Eleda Gaia Laxmi Mahmanmu-rok
Odin El-al Herukhuti Viracocha Marduk Ashira Biral
Shaddai Dzingbe Djohu-ma-di-hutu Astarte Ndengei
Koyatu Baha'u'llah Marrigan Baiame Om Pelepelewa
Durga Orisha Nyame Techaronhiawakhon Chukwu
Uvolovu Brahman Nephtys Ha-Maqom Tehuti Maat
Digambara Val Tik Chaitanya Amana Kwoth Num
Colok Nabango Fumeripitsj Shiva Varuna Lukanga
Bala Atibluku Karu Allah Sing Nainuema Artemis
Kartikeya Kuanyin Yelafaz T'ien Baal Shakti
Athena Olorun Nemesis Sheela-na-Gig Bhavartarini
Jesus Horus Izanagi Sebek Waq Ishtar Ti Seker
BegoTanutanu Sat Nam Kali Mirirul Bhavatarini
Tsui-goab Hatzur Brahman Ubusuna Tonantzin
YHVH Apollo Nana God Almighty Hu Vishnu Om

K ali, the Dark Devi, is as black as the void of space or the
fathomless depths of a black hole. She is the divine matrix
out of which life emerges and the dark vortex into which all
created things return in death. She is described by the mystical
poets of India as a beautiful woman, nude, voluptuous, with flowing
black hair. Her "dark body boils up and out like a storm cloud"[1] as
she dances with ecstatic abandon, laughing wildly, intoxicated with
bliss. Her epithets include Digambara, "clad in space," and
Shyama, "The Dark One." Her ineffable beauty is evoked through
lyrical images of the dark, which suggest the infinity, the mystery,
the transcendence of the Dark Devi.

> [Her] Body is imagined to be blue of color
> Because like the blue sky she pervades the world
> [She] is imagined to be black
> Because she is colorless . . .[2]

The Dark Mother is self-luminous, lit by an inner radiance: "The
hue of her skin is a dark that lights the world"[3]

Historically, Kali's dark color suggests her ancient origins as a
tribal Goddess worshipped by the dark-skinned indigenous peoples
of India, who inhabited the subcontinent before the Aryan inva-
sions.[4] Her black color also indicates her chthonic connection to the
earth and its fertility.[5] Yet Kali eludes any attempt to place her in
any historical, ethnic, or cultural perspective. As a numen of the
untamed feminine, the Dark Devi is the embodiment of the powers
of women which have been so long suppressed, denigrated, or
denied by patriarchy—our spirituality, our sexuality, our fertility,
our anger, and our inherent freedom. She gives expression to the
primordial depths of the unconscious and the non-rational, sources
of feminine wisdom which have been devalued by patriarchy. Kali
presents us with an alternative to the "purified feminine"[6] held up to
us as an ideal model by patriarchy. She offers us an opportunity to
reclaim and celebrate the power, the beauty, and mystery of the
dark as an inseparable part of our own being. The Dark Mother
teaches us to honor our feminine nature, in all of its aspects, as
sacred.

In India, the worship of Kali is a living tradition, an integral part of the lives of Indian women. Kali's presence is especially pervasive in the state of Bengal. A great Bengali devotee of Kali once said, "All women are the embodiment of Shakti. It is the Primal Power that has become women and appears to us in the form of women."[7] In this cultural context, it is not surprising to find that Bengal has a particularly rich tradition of women saints and spiritual teachers, some of whom are regarded by their devotees as the very embodiment of Kali. Sri Anandamayi Ma (1896-1982), a Bengali woman and one of India's most beloved spiritual figures of this century, was revered by many as an incarnation of Kali in human form. Contemporary Bengali guru, Shobha Ma, is similarly looked upon by her disciples as a personal manifestation of Kali.[8]

What is your concept of the dark, both personally and within your own spiritual tradition?

In the context of my own spiritual heritage as a woman of India, the dark is synonymous with the Goddess Kali. The word Kali means "The Black One" in Bengali. To me personally, the dark symbolizes the unknown, evoking the fears, ambiguities, uncertainties, and vulnerabilities which the unknown implies to most people. The initial confrontation with the dark in the form of Kali, the Dark Mother, arouses fear in the superficial or casual beholder. Our fear of the dark Goddess is a projection of that fear.

In her terrifying aspect, Kali invites us to confront our deepest fears, embrace them, and go beyond them. To acknowledge and accept our fears is the first step to freeing ourselves from them, I think. As a symbol of our worst fears, Kali teaches us to face the inevitability of death, the inescapable extinction of our own personal identity.

Yes. Kali is frightening only when we deny the totality of life in all its aspects. When one accepts, not with grim resignation but with clarity, the coexistence of life and death, joy and sorrow, one truly becomes free and thereby fearless.

What powers are associated with the dark, in the form of Kali?

Above all, fearlessness. The Dark Mother reminds us that it is only by accepting death, change, and our fears of the unknown, the dark, that we can experience the empowerment that comes with fearlessness. I think that it is only then that we can truly celebrate the beauty, bounty, and creative opportunities that life offers us.

Would you share something about Kali's presence in the city of Calcutta where you grew up?

The very word Calcutta is an English adaptation of the name Kalighat, a famous place of Kali worship in the city of my birth. The Dark Mother's presence permeates Calcutta, a city in which the horrific and the beautiful are inextricably intermingled. Of the many temples dedicated to Kali, perhaps the most wonderful is found at Dakshineswar, on the banks of the Ganges, a short distance from the city. Here, Kali is worshipped as Bhavatarini, the Savior of the Universe. Many pilgrims travel great distances to come to the Kali temple at Dakshineswar. Devotees wait patiently in line for a brief glimpse of the exquisitely beautiful image of the Dark Mother in the inner shrine of the temple. She is of black basalt, dressed in gold brocade, and adorned with ornaments of gold and precious jewels. The majesty and numinosity of this image, regarded as the living presence of the Mother herself by her devotees, makes an indelible impression on the beholder.

What is the inner meaning of the symbolism associated with the Dark Devi?

In one upraised hand, Kali brandishes a naked sword. It is the sword of wisdom, with which she cuts the fetters of personal and societal deceit which bind us, if we dare come close to her. She holds a severed head dripping with blood in another hand, to show us in graphic terms that true wisdom and intellectual cleverness are poles apart. It is only when a person is willing to recognize the limits of finite, rational thinking that the deeper process of developing our inherent wisdom can begin. For that, we must be willing to listen, to open our hearts to the wellspring of wisdom within.

Within one of her right hands, Kali says, "Fear not." With the other she beckons, "Come unto me." These gestures symbolize the benign bounty that life also holds out to us, in addition to the chisel of pain. Her garland of skulls conveys the same message to the beholder as the severed head—the surrender of the intellect and the annihilation of the ego, allowing her devotees to merge into the universal consciousness of the Divine Mother.

Kali's waistband of human arms symbolizes the necessity to perform action without harboring any attachment for harvesting the fruits of one's deeds. If one is attached to one's actions, one cannot be free, or fearless. Determination to possess the rewards of one's actions chains one to an ever-changing cycle of elation and disappointment. In order to be efficient, caring, but non-clinging and unpossessive, one must be prepared to surrender the fruits of action to the Goddess, that invincible spark of integrity within oneself.

What is the spiritual and philosophical significance of Kali as the embodiment of the dark?

Kali is conceived of as black because she represents the state where time, space, and causation have disappeared without a trace, rather like the phenomenon of a "black hole" as described by modern physicists. Kali is represented as black because she is the primordial energy responsible for the dissolution of the created universe. Kali ultimately withdraws her entire creation back into herself, just as black absorbs, resolves all colors and forms.

A metaphorical explanation of Kali's dark hue is given by certain mystical poets and philosophers of India. According to them, the ocean, when viewed from afar, looks very dark indeed. Similarly, when we distance ourselves from divinity—that invincible core of truth which dwells within us, in nature, and in all that lives reality then appears as a dark haze to our myopic sight. However, when one wades into the ocean and scoops up some water in her hand, that water is seen to be colorless. In the same way, the sky appears blue in the distance, but look at the atmosphere around you and you will see that it has no color. Kali, too, appears dark when she is viewed from a distance, but when she is intimately known, she is no longer so. In essence, Kali is *Sat Chit Ananda*: pure existence, knowledge, and bliss. She is unqualified and absolute reality, transcending all names, forms, colors and attributes which the human mind imposes on her infinitude. The Dark Mother cannot be understood, only experienced.

How does Kali relate to cycles of transformation, death, and rebirth?

Profoundly. A great Bengali devotee of Kali once had a vision which vividly illustrates the Dark Mother's role in the endless cycle of creation, transformation, and death, so intrinsic to the process of life. In this vision, a beautiful pregnant woman, the Goddess herself, emerges from the waters of the Ganges River, and upon the river bank gives birth to a lovely baby. Mother Kali lovingly embraces her child and nurses it at her breast. Then, without warning, the Mother suddenly changes form, assuming a terrifying, horrific appearance. She then devours the baby and reenters the river. Although one may at first find this vision of the Goddess frightening and repellent, it nevertheless contains a profound philosophical truth about the nature of existence. It symbolizes the inexorable cycles of creation, preservation, and destruction: birth, growth, decay, and death; and the never-ending transmutation and transformation of the one divine energy, the ground of being, out of which everything comes into manifestation, by which everything is sustained, and to which everything returns in death before beginning the next cycle. Kali reminds us that death, although an inescapable fact of life, is also ultimately an illusion. In Ma Kali's universe, nothing is ever really lost or destroyed, but only "renewed, transfigured in another pattern." We are all her children. She gives birth to us, nurtures us, and ultimately reabsorbs us into herself. Light and darkness, joy and sorrow, procreation and destruction, life and death are but different aspects of Kali's all pervading energy.

As Sarojini Naidu, one of the great Indian women of this century wrote, "Life is a prism of My light/And Death the shadow of My face." In India, Kali is worshipped as the blissful Mother of the Universe, the refuge and comforter of her devotees. How do Indian women achieve their intimate rapport with this awesome Goddess and how does she empower them?

One might well ask, "Why should anyone, female or male, adult or child, wish to approach so formidable a form as Kali?" An Indian woman would answer, "Why not?" Kali is life, nature, and fearless femininity. She is unafraid of her body, and uninhibited by the narrow rules and parameters so often imposed on the feminine. Her nudity is far from being a sexual provocation. It is a challenge to us to confront ourselves without mask, cloak, deceit, or mannerism.

At a time when many Western women are also seeking empowerment, what better symbol of female empowerment can be found than Mother Kali? She obviously debunks any attempt at artifice or concealment. Kali reminds us that any attempt to hide from nature by denying, masking, trivializing, or deodorizing our female identity is clearly debilitating and ineffectual. Kali is nature in all of its

multiplicity, and seemingly contradictory, but ultimately paradoxical, reality.

* What role does Kali play in the individual spiritual practice of Bengali
women and the religious life of their community?*

Many Bengali women choose Kali as their *ishta*,[9] the aspect of
the divine which they worship as their chosen ideal. For these
women, the form and attributes of Kali become the focus of their
spiritual practice. Any external worship of Kali, through the contemplation of her image on the altar and the loving offering of fruit,
flowers, water, and other articles of worship to the Goddess, is
intended to remind the devotee that the Divine Mother resides in
her own heart, as the very essence of her own being. Through devotion to the Dark Mother, women may realize their own
identification with the Goddess within. The profound spiritual
practices of chanting, singing, and *japa* (the repetition of the name
or *mantra* of the Goddess) also encourage remembrance of the
Divine Mother as an intimate, loving presence, both within and
without.

Kali, the dispeller of fear and the dispenser of boons, is
worshipped as the presiding deity in the *thakur ghar*, or household
shrine, of many Bengali homes. The daily worship of the Dark
Mother as a tangible, personal reality in these shrines is usually
carried out by the older women and young girls of the family.

In addition to this daily domestic worship, and the widespread
temple worship of the Dark Mother, there is the annual Kali Puja,
one of the most important religious festivals in Bengal. Over and
above the many, many permanent Kali images in temples and
household shrines, thousands of temporary images of the Dark Devi
are set up in *pandals*, or open pavilions, all over Bengal for this great
occasion. These evanescent images are immersed in the water of a
nearby river or pond at the conclusion of the *puja*,[10] as the Goddess
returns to her formless state after having blessed her devotees with
her *darshan*.[11] Kali Puja is celebrated on the darkest night of the
year. Throngs of devotees gather as the Dark Devi is worshipped
throughout the night. She is joyfully welcomed as the divine guest,
with offerings of food, flowers, and *kirtan*, or devotional singing. The
beauty of her image on the altar, set perhaps against the backdrop
of a richly brocaded silk sari, surrounded by red flowers, and the
light of flickering oil lamps or candles, is dazzling.

In this charged atmosphere, the poetic imagery of the

devotional songs extolling the beauty of the Dark Mother become especially vivid. "The black bee of my mind is drawn to the blue lotus flower of Ma Kali's feet/See how black is made one with Black." This traditional Bengali song expresses the irresistible attraction which draws the devotee, like a bee seeking nectar, ever closer to the beautiful Dark Devi, until complete identity, or union with the Beloved, is achieved. Those who have reached this state tell us that to realize our oneness with Mother Kali is the supreme bliss, the goal of all spiritual practice.

What is Kali's special significance for Indian women?

Kali is more than a symbol to millions of Indian women—she is life itself, in all its paradoxical, challenging, seemingly terrifying nudity. The Dark Mother teaches us to be courageous, enduring and creative. Perhaps her message can have similar significance for Western women who are seriously seeking the actualization of their own inner potential.

Yet in spite of various problems in Western society, Western women, by and large, do not have to experience the grinding poverty which is a daily reality in the lives of millions of Indian women. For many Indian women, faced with a leaky roof, one threadbare sari, and one meager meal a day, daily survival is a victory of life over death.

As sister Nivedita wrote in her beautiful book, *Kali the Mother,* "Our daily life creates our symbol of God." The religious model of Kali is especially empowering for women dealing viscerally with life and death issues of survival on a daily basis. Such stark living conditions compel many Indian women to live without the clutter of personal and social pretensions. Having experienced and endured yesterday, they face today with the strength that comes from close companionship with Kali, the Dark Mother, the undisguised power of the feminine.[12]

Jai Ma. ["Victory to the Mother"].

Poems to the Dark Devi
by
Shuma Chakravarty

I

Often the epiphany
of pain announces
the advent of your presence—
slicing my heart
with its tumultuous surge.
Yet my mourning
turns into
morning
when the sea-swell subsides—
leaving only the
opalescence
of dawn.

II

I asked for death
so I could have peace
at last.
You gave me a
quizzical glance and
your opal chalice to quaff;
a goldfish draught
of incandescent joy
and vivid pain.

III

Petalled with joy,
I lie laughing
In your mantling love.

IV

Lashed and leashed
by poverty and pain,
gashed by grief
I stand alone
on the heaving floor of life,
wondering when this rain will end,
wondering why?
Do you thrash me
only to thresh me?
To separate grain from chaff?

V

Mother of the universe,
Fools pity me,
Worldlings mock me.
Devi, they don't know
that I am healed and held,
held and healed
only by You.

Shuma Chakravarty was born in Calcutta, India in a family distinguished for its contributions in social reform literature, business, the arts, and education. Shuma earned her B.A. from Calcutta University and an M.A. in English Literature from Boston's Simmons College. She also holds two graduate degrees in theology from Boston University and Harvard University.

Shuma was teaching assistant to Nobel Laureate, Elie Wiesel from 1981-86. She is an ordained Unitarian Universalist minister and serves as such as First Parish Church in Bridgewater, Massachusetts. She is also assistant minister at the Vedanta Center in Cohasset.

Shuma describes herself as "a poet, pilgrim and pastor; a bridge between different cultures and world views."

Kathleen Alexander is a freelance writer and tutor to students with learning disabilities. She holds an M.A. degree in Art History from Northwestern University. From her home in Framingham, Massachusetts, Kathleen writes articles on the archetypal feminine in art and mythology. Her special interest lies in the imagery of the feminine as expressed in the visual arts, mythology, and religion. Her articles have been published in *Lady-Unique-Inclination-of-the-Night*, *Woman of Power*, and *SageWoman*.

Adonai Zeus Shekhinah Elim Ogun Kat Buddha
Wyame Hel Rama Mitra Odomankoma Jupiter Het
Heru Agni Cagn Thor Brahma Tangaroa Father
Lugaba Papang Diana Al-Rahman Cerridwen Ahone
Yoma' Tirawa Atius Ganesha El Mungan ngua
Quetzalcoatl Hamakom ddai
Atibruku Moma YH Bun aiwa
Saraswati Inanna Miriru uong
Tonantzin Yuskeha Bha Head
Olodumare Shyama Ekv Heru
Nurrundere Daramilun tzeir

Where Is God
for the Lutheran Girl Who Turned to Zen?

Karen Sunna

Hecate Chi Musubi Hin una
Nanderuvucu Erishkigal man
Tsui-goab Ometeotl Os chtli
Surya Elohim Nyankop Ilu
Woden Great Spirit Lesa goro
Poseidon Chineke Nhialic uwut
Makai Wakantanka Inari hu'
Tara Krishna Avaloket-iswara Rabb Goryo Qat Oke
Nurunderi Indra Shang-ti Amaterasu Ohmikami
Kannon Quan Yin Ise Lakshmi Awonawilona Bast
Omecihuatl Ruhanga Kosane Sophia Dionysus Ixchel
Mawu Ra Ardanariswara Oluwa Deng Hanuman
uNkulunkulu Kanobo Ngai Shamayim Cybele Dakini
Nataraj Pachamama Susanoo Katonda Avlukpo Eloah
Isis Temaukel Eleda Gaia Laxmi Mahmanmu-rok
Odin El-al Herukhuti Viracocha Marduk Ashira Biral
Shaddai Dzingbe Djohu-ma-di-hutu Astarte Ndengei
Koyatu Baha'u'llah Marrigan Baiame Om Pelepelewa
Durga Orisha Nyame Techaronhiawakhon Chukwu
Uvolovu Brahman Nephtys Ha-Maqom Tehuti Maat
Digambara Val Tik Chaitanya Amana Kwoth Num
Colok Nabango Fumeripitsj Shiva Varuna Lukanga
Bala Atibluku Karu Allah Sing Nainuema Artemis
Kartikeya Kuanyin Yelafaz T'ien Baal Shakti
Athena Olorun Nemesis Sheela-na-Gig Bhavartarini
Jesus Horus Izanagi Sebek Waq Ishtar Ti Seker
BegoTanutanu Sat Nam Kali Mirirul Bhavatarini
Tsui-goab Hatzur Brahman Ubusuna Tonantzin
YHVH Apollo Nana God Almighty Hu Vishnu Om

As a young girl I always wondered where God was. Once I went and sat in the Lutheran church to see if he was there, but all that happened was that the pastor came and invited me to his office to ask why my father never came to church—sort of like church social work. I never could find God in the hymns or the prayers or anything. Finally I gave up and stopped going to church. Later, when I was in graduate school I found out that there is a way to sit down on the ground and fold my legs and arms together in a way that my parents never taught me, and then if I sat long enough with no thought, God might come to me. I sat that way for a long time. At last I came to realize that no matter where I was sitting I was always in the palm of the hand that we call God or Buddha or Allah or whatever. That was a big discovery.

To experience really being right here it has become important to have no agenda. Ordinarily, I have a big head jumping full of beta waves. Worry is my best friend and worst enemy. Over time, I went to see a number of psychotherapists, even became one myself and did that as my work for years. It was reassuring, but it didn't touch Deep Worry. My teacher, Katagiri Roshi, talked about freedom, but it took a long time to get a taste of it. Early on, I began to realize that freedom meant letting go, putting down my burden, but I never could do it. My burden is my familiar, a secure presence that I can curl up with. I can turn on the TV of my worry and concern and keep things normal for another day. Using the remote, I don't even have to move. Freedom means being able to move, turn, spin, in every direction. It is scary at first to be weightless in space and to have no agenda. Having a burden could seem something like being grounded, having some baggage, not being without a toothbrush, sleeping bag and pajamas. Sleeping under the stars could be dangerous or uncomfortable. Letting go may seem simple, but it always seems that I want to know what the menu is, to keep some control over what is about to strike the palate.

I learned by doing psychotherapy that the best way to get over neurotic patterns is to get good and tired of them. Letting go of my burden is like that. When I get really tired of my small-self concerns, such as how well am I doing, what will people think, what if I don't get this or that done in time, where is my money going to come from, etc. sometimes the burden drops and a moment of space

appears. Sometimes there are stretches of time when everything is
fresh at every moment, everything encountered is new bright and
shiny. When I am doing the same dishes in the same kitchen as
yesterday, it is all new and all fully alive. This is the way I want to
live. This is living in the palm of the Buddhas, walking with Jesus,
dancing with Shiva.

For this bright and shiny life to live, my teachers all recommend
constant *zazen*. Sitting *zazen* is to sit down with legs and arms and
body in order, and to have no agenda—just be present. Standing
zazen is to just be present in standing position. For walking *zazen*,
just walk. For lying *zazen*, just lie down. And so forth, for all the
activities of daily life. In my tradition, I have learned always to do
the sitting *zazen* in a formal way every day, because it is an ancient
reminder not to get off track.

As a priest, there are a certain number of ceremonies that
become part of life's ordinary activities. Like the hymns and prayers
of my childhood, they are ways that kind teachers once gave for
being intimate with All while standing right here in this particular
spot. Now such intimacy is present for me whether I am shoveling
the walk or singing hymns at a church, or doing chants in the *zendo*.
Bowing is important. In Zen the formal bow is a way of laying
down the burden. Every day I can remind myself to put down the
burden of my ego through the bow.

For my future spiritual life, I expect to continue in this way,
walking, sitting and lying on the ground, getting wet in the fog and
warm in the sunlight.

Karen Sunna was born a
Lutheran girl in a Midwest city.
After attending a liberal arts college
and graduating, she began to do
her adult life without any particular
sense of direction. One Ph.D. and
a baby later, she was doing Zen
meditation and feeling much more
grounded. She helped to bring
Dainin Katagiri Roshi to Minneapolis and participated in founding
the Minnesota Zen Meditation
Center. In 1980 she was ordained
a Zen monk and in 1989 received
Dharma transmission from Katagiri
Roshi. She practices at the Minnesota Zen Meditation Center.

PHOTO BY VIRGINIA HANS

Adonai Zeus Shekhinah Elim Ogun Kat Buddha
Wyame Hel Rama Mitra Odomankoma Jupiter Het
Heru Agni Cagn Thor Brahma Tangaroa Father
Lugaba Papang Diana Al-Rahman Cerridwen Ahone
Yoma' Tirawa Atius G̲a̲n̲e̲s̲h̲a̲ E̲l̲ M̲u̲n̲g̲a̲n̲ ngua
Quetzalcoatl Hamakom ddai
Atibruku Moma YH Bunj aiwa
Saraswati Inanna Miriru aong

The Voice of God, The Mother of Life

Dr. Lily Siou
(Zhang I Hsien)

Tonantzin Yuskeha Bha Head
Olodumare Shyama Ekv Heru
Nurrundere Daramilun otzeir
Hecate Chi Musubi Hin una
Nanderuvucu Erishkigal man
Tsui-goab Ometeotl Os chtli
Surya Elohim Nyankop Ilu
Woden Great Spirit Lesa goro
Poseidon Chineke Nhialic uwut
Makai Wakantanka Inari Ha-Qadosh barukh hu'
Tara Krishna Avaloket-iswara Rabb Goryo Qat Oke
Nurunderi Indra Shang-ti Amaterasu Ohmikami
Kannon Quan Yin Ise Lakshmi Awonawilona Bast
Omecihuatl Ruhanga Kosane Sophia Dionysus Ixchel
Mawu Ra Ardanariswara Oluwa Deng Hanuman
uNkulunkulu Kanobo Ngai Shamayim Cybele Dakini
Nataraj Pachamama Susanoo Katonda Avlukpo Eloah
Isis Temaukel Eleda Gaiu Laxmi Mahmanmu-rok
Odin El-al Herukhuti Viracocha Marduk Ashira Biral
Shaddai Dzingbe Djohu-ma-di-hutu Astarte Ndengei
Koyatu Baha'u'llah Marrigan Baiame Om Pelepelewa
Durga Orisha Nyame Techaronhiawakhon Chukwu
Uvolovu Brahman Nephtys Ha-Maqom Tehuti Maat
Digambara Val Tik Chaitanya Amana Kwoth Num
Colok Nabango Fumeripitsj Shiva Varuna Lukanga
Bala Atibluku Karu Allah Sing Nainuema Artemis
Kartikeya Kuanyin Yelafaz T'ien Baal Shakti
Athena Olorun Nemesis Sheela-na-Gig Bhavartarini
Jesus Horus Izanagi Sebek Waq Ishtar Ti Seker
BegoTanutanu Sat Nam Kali Mirirul Bhavatarini
Tsui-goab Hatzur Brahman Ubusuna Tonantzin
YHVH Apollo Nana God Almighty Hu Vishnu Om

To know all women takes a wise man,
To know all men takes an enlightened woman.
Mastering all women requires intelligence,
Mastering all men requires discipline.
Overcoming others requires solidity,
Overcoming the self requires fearlessness.
The contented woman or man is rich.
When everyone stays where they belong,
All men and women last.
Do not forget, life has no end;
Do not forget, death is a part of longevity.
When the wheel of the chariot spins around,
The wheel of life keeps turning around and around.
It is the Tao that gives birth to immortality,
Therefore, Lao Tzu, the sage, speaks what Tao is.

Tao. The path of harmony. The Way. The source of life. Some say Tao is nature. Others say Tao is the voice of God. Tao is the ancient Chinese philosophy of creating excellence in life and eventually attaining immortality.

Since the Chou Dynasty, some 2500 years ago, scholars who want to know the Tao have consulted the *Tao of I Ching*. In the first chapter of this book, Lao Tzu, the father of Taoism, says: "The Tao that can be described is not the eternal Tao." What is so mysterious and difficult to understand about Tao?

For me, Tao is the mother of life. She nourishes the ten-thousand beings and makes no claim on them; she wakes up her children early in the morning by lifting her silken curtain to suggest the beginning of a new day. With a gentle kiss, she wakes up the trees, leaves and branches, streams, rivers and seas and orchestrates the symphony of nature.

As the first wind stirs, she calls it the power of the tiger, which manifests in the ever-changing shape silken clouds suspended between heaven and earth. We call her clouds the dragon. The mother provides life-giving sunlight and healing energy, she provides flowing water. Water, constantly searching the lowest level, nourishes the ten-thousand things.

Water is the most adaptable of all elements and most symbolic of the mother. She calls it her middle son because she likes the gentle, caring aspect of the male nature. Flowing water always tries to balance its level, filling in holes, forming a lake. She calls the lake her youngest daughter. The little girl can help to balance things, to fill all depressions with life-giving water energy.

At other times the mother makes loud noises. She has a large family and to get their attention, she makes announcements with a thunderous voice. She calls thunder her eldest son.

The mother of life has to let some people ebb away because others are ready to be born. This metamorphosis manifests in fire, the beautiful middle daughter who makes more life possible.

The mother now transforms the power of the tiger into the wind, calling it eldest daughter. It moves over the seas to the mountains and valleys, carrying pollen on its wings and blowing a cool, fresh breeze to delight all living beings.

Now comes the mother's last job. She wants us to be still, to be rooted in life. So she gives birth to her youngest son, mountain, whose qualities are strength and silence.

Above the silken cloud is heaven. We called him father, symbolized by three solid lines, long before there was a written language. Below is earth, the mother, symbolized by three soft lines. From this union springs the family of Tao:

1.	Earth	Mother	K'un	N
2.	Heaven	Father	Chien	S
3.	Lake	Youngest Daughter	Tui	SE
4.	Fire	Middle Daughter	Li	E
5.	Thunder	Eldest Son	Chen	NE
6.	Wind	Eldest Daughter	Sun	SW
7.	Water	Middle Son	K'an	W
8.	Mountain	Youngest Son	Ken	NW

The birth order was determined by the oracle bones in the *Liang Shan I Ching, The Book of Changes,* when the ancient Chinese were living in the hills. Other symbols are taken from the *Kwei Ch'ang I Ching,* when the ancients were living in caves. The family relationships were established in the *Chou I Ching,* after the Chinese had attained a higher degree of civilization and sophistication.

Later on, when Confucius was in charge of the eternal teachings, he wrote six classic Chinese doctoral dissertations on the six arts. Confucius was born from a romantic union, out of wedlock. His mother and father were actually quite modern; they met in a wild field, not too different from what's going on in today's world. But Confucius was not happy with his home life. He observed how his mother worked hard as the bread-winner, while his father lounged around drinking tea with his friends, chatting and reciting poetry, passing time with calligraphy and catching butterflies. His father's long silk robes were too impractical to allow any physical work.

Thus, twenty five hundred years ago, Confucius revolutionized the structure of society by prioritizing family relationships: The father must go out to work to support the family, the mother stays home because she is the more capable homemaker, the younger generations show respect and give financial support to the elderly, including paying for funeral expenses.

Out of this philosophy developed our modern-day ideas that men make all the decisions, are the leaders of society, and receive the best education. Women, on the other hand, must no longer leave the home but are to be revered for their ornamental value in the inner chambers. Songs were written extolling the beauty of small feet, and the custom of foot binding was initiated, rendering women totally useless. A foot size of less than three inches was the beauty ideal of the time.

Confucius' revolutionary, original ideas of creating a balanced, equal relationship between men and women was taken to the extreme and blown out of proportion, creating a male-dominated society. Lao Tzu, the father of Taoism, totally disagreed with this idea of gender roles. He espoused the idea that each person should find what is natural for her or him to do, regardless of gender. It holds that as much as men are capable of doing women's work, women are capable of doing men's work. Needless to say, women have always gravitated more towards this philosophy. Women have an important contribution to make to society and should not be hindered in their execution of this role. They must realize that it is high time they wore shoes their own size again in order to fulfill their natural destinies. The law of Tao is the law of nature.

Tao is everywhere and in everything one feels, sees, touches, hears and smells; it is invisible. Good and evil, day and night, light and dark, soft and hard, women and men—all are part of Tao.

The Tao fits all circumstances and has never failed to perform its duty. It reaches out and touches everything, day in and day out, breathing life into all things in the universe. Tao calls everything her children. All things under the heaven benefit from the Tao, yet the Tao makes no claims on them. It provides all basic needs through water, air, and sunshine and forms a strong family bond, yet expects no rewards. It is the Tao, the mother, who gives life to all beings. All are treated equally by their divine mother.

A Life in Harmony

When I was a child of six, I left home and did not see my family again for 27 years. For ten years, until the age of sixteen, I lived with Taoist Master E.F. Chang and attended "Chen I" Taoist School, located in Lung Fu Shan in the southwest province of Chiangse, 200 miles from the nearest community. Then I received training in medical school for another five years. When I left mainland China, I continued to search for the meaning of Tao in the department of Chinese philosophy at the Chinese University of Hong Kong.

I had no desire to become a doctor; I wanted to deal with nature, flowers, rocks, and trees. In fact I wanted to study law—the law of the universe, the interconnection of everything. In this present incarnation I was destined to be of service to humanity. I hate disease, and my own personal mythology holds that in a world where there are no patients, there are also no doctors and there is no disease. However, in researching my previous lifetimes I discovered that this time around I did not have much choice other than to become a doctor of Oriental medicine. I was told I must give service for at least twenty five years. This obligation is almost fulfilled.

During my ten years of childhood education at the monastery I was taught the skill of how to negotiate—negotiating the best possible contract for others for their life on earth now. You might say I was appointed a Heavenly Senator by the Heavenly Master, Master Chang Tao Ling of the Han Dynasty, 2000 years ago. It so happens that I have the same celestial birth year, month, day and hour as he. As Headmaster of a Tai Hsuan Taoist Monastery, I am the 64th generation holder of that title.

Over the last 2000 years I have had many lifetimes in many different countries, including a number of lifetimes in Hawaii. What is important to remember is that we all have been around many, many times, in many different forms. Although in this life I was born in China and look Chinese, all my experiences contribute to who I am today—Hawaiian, Thai, European.

If, as a society, we placed a high value on family history and would trace our ancestors, know our ancestors dating back beyond great-grandparents, we would be surprised at what we find. According to a recent wire story, newly discovered scientific proof exists to show that our last communal mother—the woman from whom descended everyone born over the past 200,000 years—was a native of Africa.

How can we wage war on one another or feel superior to another race when, in fact, we're all related and share the same ancestor? I feel fortunate to have been raised with such a sweeping world view.

My monastic curriculum included the study of galactic communication—penetrating through 36 layers of heavens, moons, and stars to help find solutions for the transformation of the planet. In this practice we were trained to look beyond the obvious, beyond the visible, beyond our own universe, in order to connect with powers that can offer solutions to better our planet. Part of this process was learning to negotiate for allowances of resources, including air, water, sunlight, food, healing energy, and commitment to the search for excellence on the planet. This includes negotiating for life extensions for some people who have not yet completed their work. According to Taoist philosophy, all resources are finite. In order to keep the balance, if one person lives beyond her or his originally negotiated time, another person will have fewer years.

Negotiating for better world leadership is part of this process as well, and it involves identifying leaders in each country who should be empowered to help make a better life for their own people.

In my training, heavy emphasis was put on the development of psychic powers, which I have since applied successfully in my profession for diagnosis and prescription. Taoist telepathic communication was another part of the monastic curriculum. The Taoist title Chien Li Yuan means "eyesight of one thousand miles." After five years of study, one becomes Wan Li Yuan meaning, "eyesight of ten thousand miles." Having completed ten years of studies, one becomes Chien Wan Li Yuan, which means "eyesight of tens of thousands of miles." Over the years we developed the ability to see not only across the miles but also into the future. Each year, for example, I compile an astrology book for the members of Tai Hsuan Monastery. As early as September of 1989, I predicted the Middle East war. My 1990 astrology book contains information regarding the extraordinary developments in the Soviet Union.

In Taoist philosophy, death is very much part of the natural cycle of life, and assisting in a person's transition is considered a privilege. In the monastery we were trained both to educate people about death of the body as a natural aspect of life, as well as to assist the deceased in returning to their spiritual home.

Taoism for Today

For twenty-one years, I have traveled around the world, through Asia, the Middle East, Europe, and the United States, always searching for knowledge of Tao. I have taken two to six trips each year, or three, four, or even ten thousand miles each. Sometimes I have felt that I live more in heaven than on earth because I fly so much! I have visited philosophers in many universities. I have never found a complete description of Tao, but I have never felt frustrated, or that I was wasting my time, because I have always enjoyed what I am doing. I am always learning. But no matter how many more years I go to school, no matter how many more libraries I visit, no matter how many more minds I meet, I still find that Tao is a difficult subject.

On each of my visits to China, I ask who is master of the local district. Who is familiar with Tao? On a recent visit I had a chance to talk with Master Huang, a Taoist monk in Hsuen Yang Taoist Monastery. He has been practicing for seventy-two years. He told me that my heavenly master, Chang En Fu, 63rd generation lineage-holder of the Tai Hsuan Taoist tradition, had visited him at this monastery for about a month almost forty years before. I was very excited to find someone who was not only friendly, but who was respected by my teacher. We began to discuss Tao.

"Why is Taoism not as popular as some other practices, like Buddhism, for example," I asked him.

He answered that Tao does not try to attract anyone. Yet, Tao will never die, he said, because there is always at least one master who will pass on the teachings to one student. That Tao will never die has been proven by 5000 years of Chinese culture; this is the key to China's longevity.

Tao does not try to attract anyone, yet Tao is attractive. For me the feeling of Tao is joyful contentment, combined with an ever-challenging, always new experience of life. I look at the beautiful green mountains of Hawaii. Even after they have been destroyed by fire, once the rain comes, they turn green again.

The forms are dancing and the wind manifests in the spirit, which has its own agenda. Free as the wind, beautiful as fire, powerful as thunder, still as the mountain, adjustable as water, creative as heaven and receptive as earth. What more does one need to know of Tao?

We can experience Tao in many simple ways—the rushing of a river, wind blowing through the trees, the heady fragrance of flowers, birds singing, fish jumping in the lake, turtles carrying their babies—the endless beauty of nature. When I walk through the mountains and my bare feet touch the soft earth, I feel rooted and enjoy the moment. Looking up, I see blue sky and white cloud. Seconds, minutes, and hours of continuous change pass by while I admire this beautiful scenery; it is as though millions of pictures were rotating in the gigantic museum of nature.

At such a moment, the greatness of nature makes me feel like the most important person in the world. I feel rich and I enjoy myself more than most rich people. I feel beautiful because I help to decorate this wild naturalness of scenery. I flow so naturally with the wind and the clouds, not only with my mind and spirit, but also with my physical body.

While dancing with Tao, my breath, my arms and legs are moving and meditating with the superior spirit—I am part of the universal movement and I feel so alive! While doing Chi Kung moving meditation, my breath, my arms and legs are moving and dancing—I am a part of the universal movement and I feel alive! It is such a beautiful feeling when your mind, body, emotions, compassion, actions and creations all come together and are one with nature.

Female and male, called yin and yang in Tao, give joy to each other. They support each other and give life to the next generations. They also share the darkness of night so their mother can provide light for the other side of the earth. During her absence they experience not only dark, cold, sickness, disappointment, depression, loss and frustration, but they also discover there are no ladders that connect to heaven, no tunnel that connects to the depths of the earth. Sometimes we go against the will of Tao and then complain that life is not treating us fairly. Some of us do not receive good treatment from our siblings, our loved ones, our best friends or neighbors, our colleagues, doctors or teachers, our government agencies, or society. Some of us commit crimes, take drugs or alcohol. Some of us lie, steal, or abuse others. Without realizing it, many people misuse the Tao.

Perhaps some people have never appreciated these simple things. Perhaps some people, seeking happiness or wealth, do not realize that they are just one heartbeat away. Perhaps happiness, contentment, wealth, abundance and satisfaction are right in front of you or perhaps just behind you or to the right or left of you and all you need to do is look in a different direction.

I have observed that in the West, people tend to look more at external manifestations. For instance, in martial arts in the West, often times all effort is concentrated on achieving perfect form. I call these "big action people" because they pay very little attention to the internal or unseen manifestations. They have lost the most important part of art, and the most valuable aspect of martial arts is the gentle action because it contains more strength.

Non-action contains even more power and strength then inner action. Non-action is the real action, and the big action is no action at all, it has neither power nor strength.

It seems that with just a little effort or with no effort at all, you can attain Tao and feel free. You can feel free as God and share a part of God's intelligence. You will become a wise person if you apply this intelligence. For instance, as a doctor, sometimes all that is necessary is to touch a patient and the patient gets well. Sometimes you can shake hands with a patient and the patient gets well. And sometimes, you have no results. This is something Tao may perform every day. It all depends on the limitlessness of your thinking.

You may think a patient will get well through exercise, through herbal prescriptions, acupuncture or traditional Western medicine. Maybe you don't have an acupuncture needle or a scalpel or you are feeling too exhausted to treat anyone. Now suppose you are this patient's last resort. The patient may just sit next to you and get well. It is possible for you to sit by me and experience this. In fact, you may only be thinking of me and get well. Because all I have to do is think of Tao and you get well.

Tao is inexhaustible and it always helps you. The tremendous life-energy that exists in the universe is ever-changing and yet it always exists. Within the Tao are the yin and yang. A universal law of Tao is that when the yin is complete, it gives birth to the yang. When yang is complete, it reaches satisfaction and gives energy to the yin; yin is the mother of yang. Both reach the fullness of their own potential and give birth to the opposite. This is the law of nature. Although there is no perfect and complete explanation of Tao, this is a very important concept and partial definition. All things in the universe, when reaching their potential, give birth.

When a doctor reaches fullness of potential, the doctor gives birth to the wellness of her or his patients. When patients get very sick and need help, they give birth and become a doctor and are healed. That is why you may pass by my door and get well, because what you need is to get well. I am part of Tao. I have been among the wind, the trees, fish, flowers, rivers and clouds. I was part of that, and that can give birth to all changes. You were sick and you needed to change. And so you get well and you give birth to your own wellness.

Of course, wellness does not give birth to sickness. Lao Tzu says: "The nameless is the beginning of heaven and earth. The named is the mother of the ten-thousand things." What does this mean? When you get well you give birth to a new phase, birth to other kinds of challenges and you have other types of satisfaction. Perhaps you come across me and it's just like the rain and the sun forming the rainbow. I am rain and you are sun and when we meet, we form light—you get enlightenment, just like the rainbow. Physical and spiritual wellness grow from the same root. To some people, the body is most important, and there is spirit and maybe not. To others, the body is not important and the spirit is the main focus. They think of the body as a house and the spirit as the master living inside the house. Even so, the house is not just a shell, it is very important. The house must be clean and there must be circulation through the doors and windows; it must be livable, so one can enjoy, feel safe, feel satisfied, feel fulfilled. The house must have good foundations and be solidly built to withstand heavy rains and typhoons. The body has to be able to tolerate all kinds of external conditions, viruses, and bacteria.

The spirit is equally important. It wants to be creative and receptive; it wants to be with lots of people, yet private at the same time. The spirit must be able to communicate freely with the universe. That is, it can send a fax out to anywhere in the world and also be open to receive all the various communications from the corners of the universe.

Taoist practices are grounded in this philosophy. Let me give an example of this ancient practice as it was successfully applied to current conditions:

As part of my service at the Tai Hsuan College of Acupuncture and Herbal Medicine, where I teach, I offer consultations to students when problems arise. One of my students had financial difficulties. He asked for help in selling his house in Yugoslavia so he would be able to pay tuition.

I knew the student was sincere and wanted to complete his training, so I offered to make a Taoist charm to help him sell the house which had been on the market for the past eight years. Tu Ti Kung, the "God of Land" charm, is made by a Taoist priest and is burned at a "God of Land" temple. Since there is no such temple in Yugoslavia, the student's relatives in that country would take the charm and burn it outside the land office.

The student felt very pressured to begin, and even though I did not have calligraphy brush and ink with me, he insisted I prepare the charm right away. Taoists usually like to use implements fashioned by their own hands from materials found in nature. Due to the urgency, however, I simply used what was at hand, a modern-day highlighter. I took the charm to the altar in our clinic and explained that the student needed money for his training and that the charm would be burned in Yugoslavia outside the land office. Then I asked the student to copy the charm in his own hand. He protested that this would be too difficult to do. Could he use a copying machine instead? I laughed out loud. A Chinese student would never think of this! But because this student was not lazy, and sincerely wanted the message to be very accurate, I agreed. He made a color copy of the charm and sent it off by overnight mail.

About ten days later we received a call. The charm had been burned outside the land office on the day it was received. The following day, at noon, a family came by and looked at the house. It is very difficult to sell homes in Yugoslavia, but the next week, the family returned and offered to pay the full asking price for the house in cash.

My student was soon able to pay his debts and to pay for the remainder of his training. He had been waiting eight years to sell his house; with the help if the charm, the house sold practically over night, despite highlighter, copy machine and overnight mail!

When word got out about this incident, I received many requests for my services, but I cannot serve in this way. I can only help someone in real need, not speculators who buy and sell for profit.

Let me cite another example: One of my patients was a hairdresser who was quite poor. He saw me eight times for medical concerns and then asked me about the direction of his life. I suggested he would be good at business and perhaps he could develop hair products to sell. He paid for his consultation and later presented me with the first bottles of shampoo and conditioner. He perfected his product formulas, set up his business and soon got very rich—his name is Paul Mitchell.

Recently, a woman who was crippled and in great pain came crawling into the clinic. I knew from her records that there was no medical answer for her condition. Her very concerned husband wanted to be in the treatment room with her, but I asked him to stay in the waiting room for just five minutes. After a few minutes I called him in, but his wife told him she wanted to sleep for a while, so he returned to the waiting room. Twenty minutes later, to the husband's utter amazement, his wife walked out of the treatment room unassisted. Days later, the couple returned to show me that she was still walking although she had never before responded to medical treatment. When she asked about her treatment I told her that I had not treated her a medical patient, but rather as a friend.

I could tell endless stories about how Tao works. I am grateful to have learned about Tao and be part of its divine power, to be able to act as a medium, to pass so much energy to people in need. Many times, I feel selfish. I should, as Master Huang said, pass this knowledge to one student so she or he can continue the teachings of Tao. I am, in fact, looking for this one student to pass on the teachings. I have taught much about Tao to many students, and I want to teach as many people as I can reach. But I am also looking for one particular student. Many times, a student looks for a good teacher, but a teacher sometimes looks for a good student.

I feel very fortunate and grateful to have received such a broad education and I am happy to pass on the teachings of Tao. May they be received with an open mind.

In China they call her **Zhang I Hsien.** Everyone in the West knows her as **Lily Siou.** For ten years during her youth, she received secret Taoist training from the heavenly master, Chang En Fu of Lung Fu Shan in Chiangsi province. She was taught mastership of Tao Te Ching healing, acupuncture, herbal medicine, Chi Kung, spiritual secret charms, the Tao of one's destiny, the scholarly information of the I Ching, and the white magic power to benefit her patients. Dr. Siou also graduated from a formal traditional Chinese medical school in 1966. Continuing her training in Taoist philosophy, she received her Ph.D. in from the University of Hong Kong. She has received numerous awards

PHOTO BY ROBERT MATSUNAGA

of recognition over the years. In 1974 she was appointed by the governor to Hawaii's first acupuncture board and in 1976 received the Outstanding Women of America Award. In 1984 she was given the prestigious State of Hawaii's Award, Chinese Living Treasure, by the state legislature, a lifetime title. In 1993 Yintan City Government in China honored her as community president of Lung Fu Shan Taoist Delegation.

Dr. Siou's greatest wish is to restore the Healing Temple in Lung Fu Shan, China, to provide treatment and healing for both Chinese and Western patients for immune system diseases.

Adonai Zeus Shekhinah Elim Ogun Kat Buddha
Wyame Hel Rama Mitra Odomankoma Jupiter Het
Heru Agni Cagn Thor Brahma Tangaroa Father
Lugaba Papang Diana Al-Rahman Cerridwen Ahone
Yoma' Tirawa Atius Ganesha El Munganngua
Quetzalcoatl Hamakom ... ddai
Atibruku Moma YH Bun ... aiwa
Saraswati Inanna Mirir ... aong
Tonantzin Yuskeha Bha ... Head
Olodumare Shyama Ekv ... Heru
Nurrundere Daramilun ... tzeir
Hecate Chi Musubi Hin ... suna
Nanderuvucu Erishkigal ... man
Tsui-goab Ometeotl Os ... chtli
Surya Elohim Nyankop ... Ilu
Woden Great Spirit Les ... goro
Poseidon Chineke Nhialic Aciek Kari Auset Tcuwut
Makai Wakantanka Inari Ha-Qadosh barukh hu'
Tara Krishna Avaloket-iswara Rabb Goryo Qat Oke
Nurunderi Indra Shang-ti Amaterasu Ohmikami
Kannon Quan Yin Ise Lakshmi Awonawilona Bast
Omecihuatl Ruhanga Kosane Sophia Dionysus Ixchel
Mawu Ra Ardanariswara Oluwa Deng Hanuman
uNkulunkulu Kanobo Ngai Shamayim Cybele Dakini
Nataraj Pachamama Susanoo Katonda Avlukpo Eloah
Isis Temaukel Eleda Gaia Laxmi Mahmanmu-rok
Odin El-al Herukhuti Viracocha Marduk Ashira Biral
Shaddai Dzingbe Djohu-ma-di-hutu Astarte Ndengei
Koyatu Baha'u'llah Marrigan Baiame Om Pelepelewa
Durga Orisha Nyame Techaronhiawakhon Chukwu
Uvolovu Brahman Nephtys Ha-Maqom Tehuti Maat
Digambara Val Tik Chaitanya Amana Kwoth Num
Colok Nabango Fumeripitsj Shiva Varuna Lukanga
Bala Atibluku Karu Allah Sing Nainuema Artemis
Kartikeya Kuanyin Yelafaz T'ien Baal Shakti
Athena Olorun Nemesis Sheela-na-Gig Bhavartarini
Jesus Horus Izanagi Sebek Waq Ishtar Ti Seker
BegoTanutanu Sat Nam Kali Mirirul Bhavatarini
Tsui-goab Hatzur Brahman Ubusuna Tonantzin
YHVH Apollo Nana God Almighty Hu Vishnu Om

God
is
Fire

**Sr. Patricia
McGowan**

The mountains beckon to the hiker this time of year: snow has melted and filled the creeks to torrential flows, trees and bushes are in leaf, green things pop up everywhere, wildflowers abound. Yesterday I got up to a vista high enough to look across to the heights of the neighboring peaks. I looked down on the tops of aspens clustered like green bouquets. These mountains—higher than 14,000 feet—loom over my monastery reminding me of my ideals, challenging me beyond the comfort zone into the ethereal heights, telling me of magnificence and glory.

In 1983, I moved with several other monks from our idyllic surroundings and climate in Sedona, Arizona, having been crowded out by civilization, to our desert-mountain home here in Colorado. The new monastery is situated at 7,000 feet about two miles from the base of the mountain trails where most of the small cedars and pines have given way to the vast open valley floor covered with sand, a few bushes, cacti, and some desert grasses. Desert openness and rugged, majestic mountains provide rich imagery for our monks and the retreatants we host.

Some might consider this a wasteland, but we have discovered in this stark desert stillness a pregnancy, a place of waiting for revelation, for mystery to unfold and fill our emptiness to overflowing. In the noonday sun of the desert, pretense and lies are exposed.

The Sangre de Cristo Mountains are dangerous and unpredictable; every year climbers lose their lives in them. To ascend them requires great energy, determination, preparation, know-how. For the monks of the Spiritual Life Institute[1] living in these vast wilds is crucial. The unpredictable, uncontainable God thunders and light-enings, thrusts us out of the ruts of our everydayness, woos us with the magic of a thousand-colored sunset cast across the span of a hundred miles. Here we can adore, which is humanity's highest calling. We can see ourselves in perspective: we are not the center of reality. Imagery abounds. Torrents of water sometimes become flash floods and cascade down the mountainsides, reminding us of torrents of merciful love available to each of us for the asking.

Creation is a sign of the divinity; it is an icon that points beyond itself to its creator, whom it resembles somewhat. So it is important to respect nature, to learn her laws, and be in harmony with them since those laws are of divine origin. We are meant to be in union with wildlife and storms, oceans, birds, wildflowers and trees, to enjoy and begin again with each sunrise with its new beginning, to breathe a sigh of relief and to rest with each sunset. A certain harmony prevails in nature because she does not resist the force of the Real.

Consuming Fire

Creation, however, is broken and bent as well. We sometimes call our environs a 'crucified paradise.' Humanity perpetrates disharmony. Humans deliberately pollute the water they drink, murder each other, steal each other's goods, lie and cheat for profit or pleasure. Something is wrong. Someone's perspective is distorted. For harmony to be restored, change must occur within the heart of reality, within the individual persons who make up our world. We call this process transformation. Fire is both the force that purifies as well as the final cause, the love-force in which one can participate ultimately, becoming fire.

> . . . Cleave the sky—the clouds bleed flame;
>   Fire through the rain.
> Cleave my heart and in its chambers,
>   Fire through my veins.
> Heart of the Fire burning inside . . .
>   From the ground beneath our feet,
>   to the reach of heaven's height;
> There is fire, there is heat,
>   yearning upward toward the light.
> . . . Tear the clouds around my soul,
>   and consume me with your flame
> In your burning make me whole;
>   I am branded with your name . . .
> And in the tempest of our time,
>   through the tumult of these days
> Be my life's blood as I climb
>   toward the summit of your blaze.
> Heart of the Fire burning inside . . .
> Firesong, burn on in me, till
>   your flame has set me free
> Blaze in all I touch and see
>   Firesong, burn on in me.[2]

Each morning in winter we light a fire in our wood stoves for warmth. Whenever possible we gather around a fire—to sing and laugh, drink and eat, tell stories and share our highest aspirations. Sometimes, in preparation for a great occasion, we keep a watchfire going throughout the night, each community member taking a turn.

Fire is a powerful image. The living flame, the one "that tenderly wounds my soul / in its deepest center"[3] symbolizes for me the passionate God-energy into which we are all called. We can skirt the fire and escape, even for a long time, but it will always be there beckoning, urging, sparking energies of my own to cooperate and enter the flame. The living flame from without attracts the heart, while at the same time it illuminates and ignites the depths of the soul from within.

> O lamps of fire
> In whose splendors
> The deep caverns of feeling
> Once obscure and blind,
> Now give forth so rarely, so exquisitely,
> Both warmth and light to their Beloved.[4]

This living flame is personal. Whoever catches fire is caught up in this Christ-life, love-life, the life-force that is beyond what is merely natural. What is of utmost importance is entering the fire, becoming transformed by it. As Christ said, "I have come to set fire to the earth, and how I wish it were ablaze already."[5]

Passionate Monasticism

Twenty-two years ago I came to Nada Contemplative Center in Sedona, Arizona, to deepen my desire and my ability to pray. On a conscious level, I did not know that I really wanted to become more passionate. But something about the pioneer community's vitality—the way they put their whole selves into cooking, shoveling, sitting down to a common meal of hearty food, conversation and joviality, their reverence and stillness in the kiva-like[6] prayer room—attracted me and lured me back to stay.

Only gradually did this pioneer community think of itself as monastic. Monasticism is the paradigm for all forms of transformation because monastic life has envisioned and enfleshed a path that is eminently conducive to ongoing conversion. Through practice, pioneers discovered the main ingredients: prayer, solitude, spiritual direction, and the vowed life. These ingredients are crucial for any-one who is serious about leading a truly passionate life, because these are the disciplines that summon and nurture the small passions into the one singular passion, the living flame of love.

Monastic life is geared toward transformation. The raw ma-terial is a person who recognizes his or her own need to be changed and is willing to take the sometimes difficult steps to achieve a radi-cal change of mind and heart. "Monastic life," says Father McNamara, "is a commitment to the task of making one's empiri-cal self coincide with one's real self," that is, of converting the pseudo-self we project and preen and are anxious about into the purified, chiseled, hollowed and hallowed true self. Ultimately the person cannot achieve anything; she can only prepare to be trans-formed. But if the heart is true, the desire real, and she perseveres unto the end, transformation does occur.

We all have a hidden monk inside us. But we are often unwilling to go beyond the level of survival and basic functioning to understand our own patterns of behavior and then beyond again to the deeper level of longing for the transcendent. We all crave atten-tion and are restless looking for it; we fill our appetites for food, drink, sex, power, and importance in this search. Nothing, however, can satisfy this hunger except the transcendent. We were created to be loved by the Holy Other and to become divine. If we are in touch with this insistent desire, in touch with the inner monk, then one thing is necessary: adoration. Transformation prepares us for adoration—adoration of the Godhead.

A monk, however, should not be stodgy. Only a passionate person can be transformed, fully transformed, because only such a one lives to full capacity. Like a plane that has all its engines run-ning and ready for take-off, energy is not repressed or diverted, but is used in pursuit of one central goal: being in love with the Divine. Passion is good when it is directed outwards toward a worthy goal; trouble arises only when passions are too small.

> May a singular passion sweep over me like a tidal wave, quickening every fiber of my body, stirring my soul to the depths, bringing together and to a boil all my emotional energy, and marshaling all the forces of my erotic being into an intellectual act of uncon-ditional and universal love of God. May nothing of me or the scabrously raw matter of my being-in-the-

world be left out of this vast and undivided love. Amen.[7]

The passion of God longs to embrace the passion of each unique person. This divine embrace is the very thing our hearts long for, the ecstasy we are created to enjoy. Some few mystics, giants of humanity, have experienced this passion full-force. St. John of the Cross cries out:

"O living flame of love
That tenderly wounds my soul
In its deepest center! . . .
Now Consummate! if it be your will:
Tear through the veil of this sweet encounter!"[8]

St. Teresa of Avila experienced a seraphic arrow piercing her heart, leaving her in pain-filled ecstasy. More importantly, she expressed her passionate love by traveling the roads of Spain in heat and cold, illness and weariness, founding her monastic communities because her love—Christ—asked this unstinting service of her, and because she longed to express her love for him. These mystics show us the higher reaches of becoming fire.

Prayer

Prayer kindles the heart and sets it ablaze with love, after it first sears the soul with the light of truth. Prayer can be occupational or spousal. Occupational prayer is everything that makes up the work and play of my life. I should do everything as an offering of love, service, and adoration: washing laundry or dishes or floors; building a hermitage; planting, weeding, harvesting a garden; felling, splitting, delivering and stacking wood for winter fires; swimming or canoeing in the lake; skiing or hiking in the mountains; writing letters; balancing the books; hosting and counseling retreatants; playing a hilarious game of volleyball or baseball.

Spousal prayer is intimate converse between God and the soul. I pray when I am in touch with my deepest self, who cries out to the Holy Other with love. I pray when I moan as one who is incomplete looking for completion, as one who is empty hoping to be filled. Daily—hour by hour, year by year—I place myself in this presence listening; sometimes in the darkness groping for a small glimmer of light so I'll know I'm not alone; sometimes in dryness when I sense no tangible evidence of a companion; sometimes in the searing light of truth I'd rather not know about myself and what I should do; sometimes in a quiet rapture, being held in the embrace of Someone; later I know new strength and new virtue has permeated my soul as a result of this embrace. As years pass this rendezvous place becomes larger, more real, compelling and ineffable.

O lamps of fire . . . show myself to me. You are the Way, the Truth, and the Life. You are the Christ, the God-man who has illumined my way, taught me what is true and what is the highest quality life. You have called me into intimate life with your Father. You have allured me, led me into the desert where truly you have spoken to my heart. You who have promised to come and make your home in me have indeed come as my divine companion.

Solitude

Like my fellow monks, I have made solitude a priority in my life. One week of each month I spend in solitude; two days of each week are solitary days. What has solitude to say to the late 20th century?

In a world controlled by the economy, politics, the media and Hollywood, replete with illusions and mendacity, how can we escape? We must get out of the mainstream and examine what is really going on in this world. Prolonged times of solitude, preferably in the wilderness, give our soul space to breathe out what is superficial, irrelevant or phony, and to breathe in what is real, substantial and nourishing.

Today I am ensconced alone in a hogan on acres of wild desert along the San Isabel Creek. I can smell the low-growing cedars and pines of the foothills. The only sounds are the creek's roar, the wind's occasional howl, and the happy chatter of birds. I watch the storms build up across the desert and wait for a thunderous downpour; I note with my whole being the light change from morning to evening. I see and embrace the full moon rise over the mountains illuminating the night and casting shadows. I'll spend three days of my retreat here. I am becoming relaxed after a very intense three weeks of hard manual labor, hosting the overflow summer crowd of retreatants and guests, scurrying to meet editorial deadlines and answer correspondence, to select and edit taped conferences.

Here now, I can become relaxed. When I'm relaxed I can begin to re-integrate the levels of my being and move to the deepest core of my personality. Then I no longer feel estranged from myself or others. Instead I feel at one, having a clear sense of purpose. Here I can gather together all the passion of my being in preparation for the fire. The fuel of my life becomes dry and clear, ready to burn. Solitude's spaciousness aerates the fuel and with the heat of my increased longing the conflagration is rekindled.

I need solitude in order to know what to do—to listen to the deeper harmonies of my being and of the universe. The artist listens for inspiration and so do I. Of all the possible voices I hear, which is most true? I can only know when I listen from the deepest level of my being where the grace of Christ is at work prompting and guiding me. I can't be sure I'm doing God's will unless I can first hear the inner prompting which directs my thoughts and actions and connects me to all that is. One test of knowing the voice I listen to is true is whether or not its message makes me more human, caring, lighthearted, and unified with everyone and everything.

We were created to live together and in communion with each other. Solitude is always a means to deeper communion. The whole point is love, deeper love of God and others—all peoples of the earth and the earth itself. If we go apart for awhile, it is for two reasons: to be more totally with God and in God, and to be more completely with one another.

Spiritual Direction

As we go about our life of lovingly caring for each other, our garden, flowers, dogs and cats, in awe of starry sky and luscious lake, we ask: How far can we trust ourselves? We need to be listening for the deepest truth within, while testing what we hear by letting a trusted guide or teacher respond to our inner promptings, our dilemmas and tentative conclusions, the new directions we decide to take. The key here is having a guide or soul friend who has gone further than I, whose life manifests wisdom, knowledge, charity, compassion, and who has a gift for listening to and guiding others. This is the spiritual father/mother model of spiritual direction in the monastic life. I should be willing to reveal my whole soul to that person without hiding any secrets.

We all need help uncovering our deepest motivations. My very motive for wanting to be a better lover can be tainted by vanity or self-interest, for example. Just as King David needed the prophet Nathan to advise him, we need the prophet or confessor, the person who is pure of heart, for advice. The point of spiritual direction is to become more and more authentic. Socrates uses an appropriate analogy of the charioteer driving two horses, one talented, spirited and well trained, the other unruly, unreliable and dissipated. Part of us is noble and strives toward other-centeredness and divinity, while another part is lazy, selfish and arrogant, always looking out for the self. To become real, the more noble horse must take the lead and help the unruly partner integrate his dissipated energy for the sake of moving the chariot more quickly toward its goal. All the character armor, the attention-seeking, the little rebellions, and the jealousies must go.

By mid-life we discover that despite our athletic efforts we often run up against blocks in our behavior that are inexplicable. We may be obsessive or compulsive; we may over-react, rage, or project our feelings onto others. The spiritual person has to go through the arduous work of untangling this behavior, and getting to its roots if she is to become free. Sin is prone to entwine itself around psychologically complicated areas so that the problem gets exaggerated. But if we delve deep enough, we can discern the name of our permanent wounds and come to terms with our brokenness. All this comes about through the light of prayer, spiritual direction and/or counseling. The more authentic I can be before God and others the more real I am, the more personal I will be in relating, and the more energy or passion I will bring to all of my life. What is critical here is to go through the whole process and not stop halfway. Naming the psychological blocks, even at 'taproot' level is not enough. In nakedness we must bring those injuries into the divine arena to be exposed and embraced. We cannot bear that degree of exposure except in an aura of fearless love, trusting that we are esteemed highly by our divine Beloved and that a soul friend, too, trusts us.

Once we have experienced the lightness that comes from authenticity and contrition, then we can cry with John of the Cross:

> O sweet Cautery,
> O delightful wound! O gentle hand! O delicate touch
> That tastes of eternal life . . .
> In killing you changed my death to life.[9]

Discipline of the Vowed Life

Finally I come to the vows, the solemn public promises which are the backbone of monastic life—the vows that strip us, hone us, prepare us and dispose us for the grand conflagration of love: poverty, obedience, and chastity. They are essential for transformation.

As I gaze outside my large south-facing windows situated to catch most of the day's sun, I see the expansive desert, home to herds of deer and families of rabbits who regularly stop nearby to browse on grasses. I feel so rich. I am utterly grateful for what I am given. No fuss, no clutter, is how monks describe poverty. I must not crave or cling to anything (or any one) that might become an idol, taking the place of God. I have only what I need and a few amenities. I honor, appreciate and celebrate the things of the earth because they express and illuminate the nature of the Godhead.

Wabi is a Japanese term for frugality, simplicity, humility expressed in beautiful order. The *wabi*, for example, of a simple and beautiful room says much about the notion of poverty. Clutter obscures. Fuss craves. Attachment grasps. *Wabi* is detached, simple, waiting. In poverty I wait for completion. If I am too busy and too filled with 'stuff,' I cannot be open to receiving the gift. Receiving is our chief occupation as human beings, receiving the gift of life and the treasures of a day, be they fair or foul. Each is the material I have been given to create my character and my world. I should receive and return—transfigured—what I receive. So I am poor when I delight in the expanse of desert, the visits of deer and rabbits, the breathtaking purples of sunsets, the look and feel of well-made pottery, or even a well-made machine! I receive the gift and return it through my appreciation.

The key vow for transformation—for total surrender to the Holy Other—is obedience. When monks promise obedience to a community through its leaders, they intend to open their minds as wide as possible to be able to listen to the deepest truth as manifest in that community. "Where two or three are gathered together, there am I in their midst." That truth, I believe, is the will of God. Our society needs persons dedicated to this degree of listening to the deepest, truest harmonies of the universe for the sake of the common good. This listening requires egoless, selfless purity of heart, emptiness or poverty of spirit, and pure gratuitous love—detachment from 'my' opinions, 'my' projects, 'my' way of doing things, the way 'my' endeavors turn out.

Obedience is really about love. How is it possible for a disparate group of individuals, not necessarily attracted to each other, to become a family acting and thinking with one mind and one heart while at the same time cultivating their individual talents? Religious communities, like other communities, form around a common vision with common values, interests and standards. If all goes well and each member is faithful to the commitment, common understanding takes hold. Because we're flawed, however, someone must represent to us the common values, interests and standards and be responsible for evoking those from us so that our vision will indeed be enfleshed. This community leader is ultimately responsible for arbitrating differences so that all the members know for sure what the 'common' mind is and can act accordingly.

Nothing is as humbling as having to conform one's judgment to the community's preference. Good practice in ego diminishment! What makes all this possible is one motive: love of God to whom we long to surrender and love of those in our community. This discipline produces more 'selfed' individuals because they are not operating out of the surface self, but rather the true core, real, transparent self. They therefore become more highly individuated and interesting, a brand new expression of the God-life on earth. And the more authentically themselves they are, the more they are capable of real love.

Chastity is also about love, a love that reaches beyond nature. This love is vulnerable, ready to expose its own weaknesses. It is love without competition, love that is inclusive rather than exclusive, that loves for the sake of honoring and letting the other be, not for its own gratification. This quality of love requires purity of heart: no lust, no looking for rewards. Our community of both men and women face all the temptations of being romantically attracted to one another one might expect. We corral these energies into real friendship; our disciplined wildness is warm and natural. We discover that sublimated energy becomes wonderfully and wildly mystical, 'sexier' than lust! Mystical friendship becomes possible when people take seriously their desire to be pure and poor, chaste and obedient, when they have died to their own need for gratification and instead live and receive grace for the common good, the grace that radiates tenderness and caring beyond what one deserves. Then there is understanding and compassion which evokes the other's best self.

The secret of this love is its source. It doesn't come from the self. When the living flame of love burns deeply enough within one's heart, one's own power of loving gains a new source as if plugged into an infinite reservoir, and the soul cries out:

How gently and lovingly
You wake in my heart,
Where in secret You dwell alone;
And in Your sweet breathing
Filled with good and glory,
How tenderly You swell my heart with love.[10]

The vows, of course, are applicable to every person's life. Everyone can and should practice some form of *wabi*. Every family and community must, if it is to be virtuous and harmonious and joyful, practice true listening and looking to the common good. Every person who wants to reach beyond natural likes and dislikes to embrace the whole human family must begin to draw on divine love.

Transformation, Adoration

The most powerful image of divinity for me is fire—the fiery love spoken of in the Song of Songs—depicting the passionate love God has for me. Fire is love Itself! If I am responsive and am willing to be transformed, I, too, become fire. The fire of love is utterly personal, yet with no designs on anyone. It rejoices in the other's mystery, in the other's unique personhood, only glad that he exists because he exists, because she manifests some rare quality of the Creator who has given himself utterly to each one and to the entire cosmos. In the Song of Songs, God summons me:

Come then, my love,
   my lovely one come.

And I respond:

Let him kiss me with the kisses of his mouth!

More delightful is your love than wine.
My lover belongs to me and I to him.[11]

By my very life and breath I become adoration, gratitude for the gift given, celebrating that gift and returning it through praise, that is, adoration emanating in service and care for all the others. Until this process is consummated in me, I sing:

Firesong, burn on in me, till
your flame has set me free.
Burn in all I touch and see,
Firesong burn on in me.

Sister Patricia McGowan is
a Carmelite monk and founding
member of the Spiritual Life
Institute in Crestone, Colorado.
Born in Chicago, Illinois, she
received her B.A. from Sienna
Heights College, Adrian, Michigan
and her M.A. in Theology from St.
John's Univer-sity in Collegeville,
Minnesota. She established a
career in teaching, writing, and
religious education until joining
the Spiritual Life Institute. As a
member, Sister Patricia oversees
the spiritual direction and care of
retreatants, directs the Institute's
lay group, and edits both the
Institute's newsletter and tape-of-
the-month *Desert Express.* As a writer,
McGowan has published in *Desert
Call Quarterly Magazine* and *Nada
Network Newsletter.*

Adonai Zeus Shekhinah Elim Ogun Kat Buddha
Wyame Hel Rama Mitra Odomankoma Jupiter Het
Heru Agni Cagn Thor Brahma Tangaroa Father
Lugaba Papang Diana Al-Rahman Cerridwen Ahone
Yoma' Tirawa Atius G̲a̲n̲e̲s̲h̲a̲ E̲l̲ M̲u̲n̲g̲a̲n̲-ngua
Quetzalcoatl Hamakom 　　　　　　　　　ddai
Atibruku Moma YH Bunj　　　　　　　　aiwa
Saraswati Inanna Miriru　　　　　　　ong

A
Glimpse
of
Allah

Nargis Naqvi

Tonantzin Yuskeha Bha　　　　　　　lead
Olodumare Shyama Ekv　　　　　　　Jeru
Nurrundere Daramilun 　　　　　　　tzeir
Hecate Chi Musubi Hin　　　　　　　una
Nanderuvucu Erishkigal　　　　　　　man
Tsul-goab Ometeotl Os　　　　　　　htli
Surya Elohim Nyankop　　　　　　　Ilu
Woden Great Spirit Les　　　　　　goro
Poseidon Chineke Nhialic 　　　　　　wut
Makal Wakantanka Inari Ha-Qadosh barukh hu'
Tara Krishna Avaloket-iswara Rabb Goryo Qat Oke
Nurunderi Indra Shang-ti Amaterasu Ohmikami
Kannon Quan Yin Ise Lakshmi Awonawilona Bast
Omecihuatl Ruhanga Kosane Sophia Dionysus Ixchel
Mawu Ra Ardanariswara Oluwa Deng Hanuman
uNkulunkulu Kanobo Ngai Shamayim Cybele Dakini
Nataraj Pachamama Susanoo Katonda Avlukpo Eloah
Isis Temaukel Eleda Gaia Laxmi Mahmanmu-rok
Odin El-al Herukhuti Viracocha Marduk Ashira Biral
Shaddai Dzingbe Djohu-ma-di-hutu Astarte Ndengei
Koyatu Baha'u'llah Marrigan Baiame Om Pelepelewa
Durga Orisha Nyame Techaronhiawakhon Chukwu
Uvolovu Brahman Nephtys Ha-Maqom Tehuti Maat
Digambara Val Tik Chaitanya Amana Kwoth Num
Colok Nabango Fumeripitsj Shiva Varuna Lukanga
Bala Atibluku Karu Allah Sing Nainuema Artemis
Kartikeya Kuanyin Yelafaz T'ien Baal Shakti
Athena Olorun Nemesis Sheela-na-Gig Bhavartarini
Jesus Horus Izanagi Sebek Waq Ishtar Ti Seker
BegoTanutanu Sat Nam Kali Mirirul Bhavatarini
Tsui-goab Hatzur Brahman Ubusuna Tonantzin
YHVH Apollo Nana God Almighty Hu Vishnu Om

On the 27th of December, 1970, I was born in Belfast, Ireland. Forty days after my birth my father took a job in Riyadh, Saudi Arabia, leaving his teaching job in Ireland. So although my family is originally from Pakistan, I grew up in Riyadh, attending Arabic, American, and Pakistani schools. For three years we also lived in Jeddah, the port city, and I loved it.

I have traveled with my family to many different countries in Europe, America, Canada and Asia. Of all the places I have visited, I love London for its clothes and atmosphere; Lahore in Pakistan for the life, fashion, and culture which goes through it; Switzerland for its beauty; and Saudi Arabia because it is home and I have many lovely memories attached to it.

My family is Muslim, and I was raised in that belief. I don't remember if I ever thought of God as having a form. I know there were times when I tried to picture God, but when one believes that the divine is all around, then it is very hard to imagine that. Eventually, I figured out that the Supreme Being can listen to me, but I just cannot see him.

I've always thought of God as looking at the whole world and being able to see everyone and hear everything, even the smallest particle, and know what everyone is doing, hearing everything, even that which is not spoken aloud. When I started becoming aware that God can hear my thoughts as well, I began to be very cautious in what I thought. If I ever had a bad thought about something or someone, I always also got embarrassed that God might not like it. So I ended up trying to avoid anything which God would not like. It was funny how I'd have to change my opinion about someone if I tried to look at the person the way God would look at me.

When I was younger I followed what everyone in my family followed. I had no doubts about the existence of God, or Allah as he is called in Arabic and in my mind. But there were questions that I thought about like, Where did Allah come from? I came up with only one answer. It is just like living with a person who spoke a different language and that person never taught you his language. You would never know what that person was talking about. In that same way, Allah has given us a brain that can seek and know many answers, but it is limited in understanding where Allah came from because that is something he chose not to disclose.

When I turned 18, I started to understand the Qur'an a little better. I realized that it was the word of Allah and so I thought I should at least take a shot at studying it. I learned from the Qur'an how to go through life and how to deal with life's problems. I started to think through my problems and find ways to solve them. My restless personality became a little more stable. In the scriptures Allah spoke to me in such beautiful words that they made me cry. He became more and more real to me and I started to pray more often until it became a natural habit for me to do the prescribed prayer five times daily. Now I have become so aware of Allah's existence that no matter what I do, I always feel he is watching me. I no longer feel alone, and, in a way, that also keeps me from doing things that he wouldn't like.

In my religion there are so many things that are required but I still am not strong enough to follow all of them. There are things I do which should not be done. Things like back-biting and lying that one unconsciously does. I always try to stop as soon as the realization dawns on me that I am in the wrong, but being a human being, (and who said humans were perfect?) I always tend to make these mistakes. This world is so full of temptations that it really becomes hard to be able to keep up with one's beliefs. It's just like chocolate. We know chocolate is harmful to our bodies in the long run, but once in a while temptation gets the better of us and we indulge in chocolate, always thinking that tomorrow we will leave it alone. But tomorrow hardly ever comes!

Despite all this, I believe that Allah is all-forgiving and under-standing. He knows that I have good intentions and that I am try-ing, so he will help me on the right path as long as I really want to be there.

I find it hard to associate Allah with any form that can also be associated with a human being. I know I talk to Allah as if he were a friend, a friend who not only hears me but also understands me, but he is also more than a friend. He created me and so he knows all about me. He knows what I mean when I say something. He knows what I want to do. He is also the one that I seek help from.

Over the years I have stopped getting disappointed at things. Now my patience leads me to believe that something good will always happen. Allah has taught me to trust him with my life and that's exactly what I do. No matter how small a thing is that I want, it is to Allah that I turn.

The inspiration for my strong belief in one God came from my father. Islam basically teaches us to believe in one God and worship no one else, but my father, being a scientist, always required proof. He demands proof for whatever he believes. My respect for him grew and grew over the years and inspired me to start my own research. Since I like to paint as a hobby, looking at things around me with an eye for detail has become second nature to me.

When I came to the United States in 1991, everything was beautiful and green. I had seen this kind of green and brown nature all my life as I traveled with my family. But during that Fall, I saw for the first time the red and orange of the trees and in the winter the pure white of the snow. It was breathtaking. Every time I went anywhere I would just stop and gaze and praise God's work endlessly. I would get a lump in my throat just seeing his enormous existence all around me. Because of his orders the seasons change, the winds blow, the leaves fall. His existence seemed to hit me with a very strong force. As I watch the same routine followed year by year, I need no proof for the oneness and greatness of God. I always think that if there was more than one God, then this routine that the world has known since time began would not have such harmony. The other gods would have a say in the matter and would apply their powers to the world as well!

So I glimpse Allah all around me, listening to me and guiding me. I know he has given me everything one could ask for. I know he will always answer my prayer one way or the other. I have learned that if what I ask for is not good for me, then it's usually for the best that I don't get it. Just like parents stop kids from certain things. When we are the child in question, we think our parents are mean, but as we grow older, we realize their wise decision and are grateful for it.

Sometimes I wonder if I could be wrong in my thoughts about God. I don't think so, but who knows? Whatever the case, actions are judged by intentions and God knows mine clearly. So it is between him and me. At the age of 23 I realize I could be too young to think certain thoughts. Perhaps over the years I will learn more and will have more to say wisely and justly. But for now a verse from the Qur'an epitomizes my thoughts about Allah:

In the name of God, most gracious, most merciful,

Say: He is God, the one and only
God the eternal, absolute.

He begetteth not, nor is he begotten
And there is none like unto him. (Qur'an 30, 112)

I hope Allah will always be there for me as he is now. I see so many people lost and uncertain and unsatisfied among my generation, and I want somehow to help them. All I can do is to say that as my relationship with God grows stronger, all knots in life seem to untie by themselves.

Nargis Naqvi is a Pakistani from Saudi Arabia. She is currently a student of real estate finance and interior design at Mankato State University. She hopes to earn a master's degree from a larger U.S. university and then return to Saudi Arabia.

When not studying and traveling, she enjoys hobbies of playing the keyboard, reading, swimming, oil painting, horse riding, billiards, and "so many more that I can fill up at least another page with only that!" Nargis has two younger brothers and three younger sisters.

Adonai Zeus Shekhinah Elim Ogun Kat Buddha
Wyame Hel Rama Mitra Odomankoma Jupiter Het
Heru Agni Cagn Thor Brahma Tangaroa Father
Lugaba Papang Diana Al-Rahman Cerridwen Ahone
Yoma' Tirawa Atius _____ Eh_ M_____ ngua
Quetzalcoatl Hamakom _____ ddai
Atibruku Moma YH Bun_____ aiwa
Saraswati Inanna Mirir_____ uong
Tonantzin Yuskeha Bha_____ Head
Olodumare Shyama Ekv_____ Heru
Nurrundere Daramilun _____ tzeir
Hecate Chi Musubi Hin_____ suna
Nanderuvucu Erishkigal_____ man
Tsui-goab Ometeotl Os_____ chtli
Surya Elohim Nyankop_____ Ilu
Woden Great Spirit Lesa Boyjerh El Dan Gongoro
Poseidon Chineke Nhialic Aciek Kari Auset Tcuwut
Makai Wakantanka Inari Ha-Qadosh barukh hu'
Tara Krishna Avaloket-iswara Rabb Goryo Qat Oke
Nurunderi Indra Shang-ti Amaterasu Ohmikami
Kannon Quan Yin Ise Lakshmi Awonawilona Bast
Omecihuatl Ruhanga Kosane Sophia Dionysus Ixchel
Mawu Ra Ardanariswara Oluwa Deng Hanuman
uNkulunkulu Kanobo Ngai Shamayim Cybele Dakini
Nataraj Pachamama Susanoo Katonda Avlukpo Eloah
Isis Temaukel Eleda Gaia Laxmi Mahmanmu-rok
Odin El-al Herukhuti Viracocha Marduk Ashira Biral
Shaddai Dzingbe Djohu-ma-di-hutu Astarte Ndengei
Koyatu Baha'u'llah Marrigan Baiame Om Pelepelewa
Durga Orisha Nyame Techaronhiawakhon Chukwu
Uvolovu Brahman Nephtys Ha-Maqom Tehuti Maat
Digambara Val Tik Chaitanya Amana Kwoth Num
Colok Nabango Fumeripitsj Shiva Varuna Lukanga
Bala Atibluku Karu Allah Sing Nainuema Artemis
Kartikeya Kuanyin Yelafaz T'ien Baal Shakti
Athena Olorun Nemesis Sheela-na-Gig Bhavartarini
Jesus Horus Izanagi Sebek Waq Ishtar Ti Seker
BegoTanutanu Sat Nam Kali Mirirul Bhavatarini
Tsui-goab Hatzur Brahman Ubusuna Tonantzin
YHVH Apollo Nana God Almighty Hu Vishnu Om

The Goddess in Me

Antiga

The Goddess in you touched the Goddess in me
A rock broke loose and a brook ran free
And I started to write
I started to sing my songs. . .

CHARLOTTE KASL

S tarhawk once said: "The moment I heard the word *Goddess,* I felt differently about myself." That, too, was my experience.

I am a woman seeking to know, love, and trust female wisdom and strength within me and others. I need a female image of divinity to connect with the deep waters of my own spirit. It was my discovery of the Goddess that led me into a spirituality that has become increasingly powerful and meaningful in my life. This feminist spirituality that I practice is called witchcraft.

The word "witchcraft" often scares people. Part of the fright comes from being given information about witchcraft deliberately calculated to vilify the craft (another name for witchcraft). These vicious, misleading lies came from men who wanted to destroy witches and their craft, which included healing. It is as accurate as if the Nazis had been able to exterminate every Jew alive and then set about telling others what Jews believed and how they practiced their religion.

So, I'd like to begin with some definitions. What is witchcraft as it is defined by witches? What is feminism? What is spirituality?

Witchcraft is a pre-Christian religion that honors earth cycles and that images divinity in a female form—the Goddess who brings the world to life. The wicca God, the male aspect of the Goddess, is very different from the patriarchal God. Witches do not "have dominion" over all creatures. People are not seen as superior beings. All life is sacred; each creature plays a role in keeping life going and each creature is valued for what it contributes. Witchcraft is based on flowing with life cycles instead of trying to control them. A witch's life is based on these guidelines:

1. Harm no one (including yourself).

2. Whatever energy one puts into the world returns to her threefold.

Following these guidelines led me on a journey deep into myself—a search for soul, for the essence of myself, for the Goddess within. As a witch, I seek to balance inner and outer worlds, to connect and integrate, to become more fully aware of the impact of my actions on others. I define witchcraft as a religion while being aware that the word "religion" has unpleasant associations for many women. One reason for the painful experience inside of patriarchal religion is that it has not nurtured women. It has not empowered us. Lack of respect for female divinity, the Goddess, results in lack of respect for women. Religion is a forum for keeping alive that which connects us with the divine. When it leaves out over half of the human race in its imagery, then it does not give those left out as deep a connection with the divine as many of us have come to know we need.

I call myself a Dianic witch. Feminism is the philosophical basis for most Dianic witchcraft, which is witchcraft where women practice together. Feminism is a set of beliefs that recognize the often overlooked female contributions to society as necessary for the well being of all. It values female perspective as an essential part of the human experience, and affirms that every woman's story is worth listening to. Feminism provides a non-judgmental, witnessing type of listening for women willing to risk talking about their lives. Feminism empowers women. It gives us permission to be actors in the world rather than simply reactors to definitions given us from outside. It encourages defining who we are ourselves, and naming our experience: What does it mean to be a woman? What are women's ways? Our essence as well as our spirituality has been defined from outside of us by men for so long that many women believe that what men say about women is the way we are. Women often fail to ask ourselves what *we* know. Feminism is about having and creating choices, about trusting what we know. Feminism is learning to love, respect, and trust women exactly as we are.

Spirituality is the experience of connecting with the divine. It is difficult to speak about spirituality because it has to be felt to be known. My experience of the Goddess is both internal and external. I draw up energy from the earth into my body every day. I feel her in the trees, the rainbow, the warmth of friends. The Goddess can be anything I want her to be and I can have as many different images of her as I choose. My images don't have to be the same as someone else's for both to be meaningful and useful. There is no 'one right way' of envisioning and approaching the Goddess. One of the things I love about witchcraft and feminism is the both/and approach. We don't have to choose between my images and yours. We get to have both. What I expect my spirituality to give me is an ever-increasing ability to get my ego out of the way and let Goddess energy flow through.

When my children were almost grown, I began to explore the

question: What would spirituality be like if it were based on women's experience? I realized that a feminist spirituality would respect women and feminine qualities. It would honor all stages of a woman's life. Patriarchal society is especially cruel in its treatment of older women and disrespectful of children. Feminist spirituality would treat children as if they mattered, as if their words were worth hearing. It would give honor to elder women.

During my search for a spirituality that met my needs, I found the Triple Goddess, a trinity that predates patriarchal religions by millennia. The old understanding of the Goddess reflects a very different view of women's lives than the patriarchal one. It includes reverence for things female. The Goddess was seen as the original female who brought life into the world. Her trinity is Maiden, Mother, and Crone. In this trinity, I found honor for the female self that I need in order to grow and flourish. My discovery of the Goddess allowed me to see my life in a new light. I'd like to describe the images of the Triple Goddess so that every woman can explore what She might mean in her life.

The Maiden conveys an image of independence and self-sufficiency. The Maiden begins things. She is often associated with the ancient meaning of virgin: she who is one-in-herself, owned by no one else. She is not a woman without sexual experience. On the contrary, it is she who chooses with whom and when to be sexual. The ancient virgin was freely sexual. Sex was acknowledged to be a sacred act. Think for a moment what impact that belief, combined with a true respect for women, could have on current society. If sex is sacred, then rape, incest, battering, sexual abuse would be unthinkable. Any sexual act for which there is not true consent would simply not happen. The Maiden is usually seen as a young woman. She may be the warrior or the Amazon. She is also the child: the young, the innocent, the playful one. She reminds us that we are never too old to frolic and to play. And, she reminds us to take care of our younger selves. She reminds us that the life of all children is sacred and that harm to children harms the whole society.

The Mother, she who is in the fullness of her creative powers, conveys an image of abundance and of nurturing—others and herself. The Mother expresses her creativity through producing children, works of art, or any other sort of work that she chooses. Mother energy is about accomplishing and getting things done. When Goddess worship was widespread, creativity and procreativity had not yet been torn apart, nor were women relegated to bearing children as the only acceptable means of being creative. Women's creativity was honored in whatever form it took. Physical mother-hood was supported and honored in a way that does not happen in patriarchy. Women were given the support from the whole culture to raise and nurture children in a way that respected both mother and child.

The Crone, she who is old and wise, has left the active stage of life and is free to be more contemplative, as well as more outra-geous. She says what she thinks without regard for what others may think. She's ready to share the wisdom and strength gained from living. She is the teacher, the counselor, the model for accepting life as it is. The crone is the one who ends things. If there are things in your life that need to be ended, you can call on crone energy.

Of the three aspects of the Goddess, the Crone is the one most often overlooked. One of the reasons for this is that the Crone deals with death, the end of life. In patriarchal society, death is denied, so it makes sense that crone energy is likewise denied. The Crone is the "midwife for death." Death is seen as a passage, a transition to something else. Deathing is a process just like birthing. When I die, I want someone there to help me with it. Another reason for ignor-ing the Crone is that women are primarily viewed as sexual objects. Patriarchal thinking assumes that when a woman is older she is no longer sexually attractive. It is thought that she could not possibly be sexually active. She is no longer useful as a sex object. Therefore she doesn't exist. Even within witchcraft itself, the Crone is given less attention than the Maiden or Mother. This could be because the modern rebirth of the craft is quite recent. The craft may not have reached its crone stage and doesn't really know what crone energy within the craft might be like.

Knowing that there were times and places where older women were honored, respected, and valued is comforting to me as I go into my older years. It gives me the strength to ask for and receive the respect that I, as an older woman, deserve. It helps me ask for help when my aging body no longer functions like it used to. Based on a positive image of the crone, I have spoken about becoming older as a joyful event. Younger women hearing me have been sur-prised and pleased. One younger woman said to me: "I had never even considered that growing older might have a positive side." Most women have so internalized the negative image of older women, that this is a novel thought. There are many positive things about being older: I have only myself to be responsible for now. I need not be so concerned about what others may think of me. I have very little to lose by being myself. I like the gray streaks in my hair. I enjoy the character that wrinkles give my face. I no longer need base my actions on what others want. I am freer now than I have ever been. My crone years also have difficulties: health problems, financial problems, death of loved ones, slowing down—it takes so much longer to get things done. I find that the image of the crone helps me accept and embrace all of what it means to be older in a society that gives old age no honor at all.

Many societies which worshipped the Goddess had a respect for living women which people under patriarchy can barely imagine. My discovery of the Triple Goddess brought me face to face with the pain caused by lack of the Divine Female in my upbringing. When I first noticed the pain, I hardly knew what it was about, only that it hurt deeply. I was desperately searching for something, not knowing exactly what it was. The search took many years. At last, I realized that I sought a female divinity. I began to discover her in many places: in the earth, the water, the air, the fire, in ancient stories, in statues from pre-historic times, in animals, in plants, in the art and songs created by feminists, and most important, inside myself. Knowing the goddess inside me lets me know that the female body, the female psyche and the female spirit are sacred. Finding the Goddess brought me home to myself. Honoring the Goddess in my life encourages me to feel whole and valuable as a woman.

The act of defining divinity for myself brought the responsibility for my own life back to me. I felt helpless for many years in the face of the sexism and cruelty to women which is an accepted norm in our society. Knowing that my life is sacred has given me the courage to say "No" to the abuse I previously accepted, not knowing it could be any other way. The Goddess has brought me an awareness that I do have choices and that my life does matter.

Goddess-centered religion affirms that there are many paths to spirituality. I alone get to determine what path is right for me just as someone else gets to determine the path that is right for her. Contrary to what most of us have been taught, the spiritual truths of different people do not have to be the same to be valid.

I recently heard a woman say, "Up until now, I've had a hard time seeing my differences as something positive." It occurred to me that patriarchal monotheism (i.e., there is one God and one way to come to him) discourages us from seeing diversity as enriching. It encourages comparison that results in us putting ourselves and others down. The concept of the Goddess helps me see that differences are beautiful.

My discovery of the Goddess also brought me to a group of women who wanted female-centered spirituality. We began to find out how different it felt to worship the Goddess, and what female divinity could mean in our lives. We found that these "new" images were in fact quite ancient. Following ancient women's knowledge and tradition, our group met on the new moon. We celebrated the cycles of the moon, the turning of the seasons, the return of light and dark each year. Light is not seen as always good and dark as only bad. Dark and light are understood to be part of the cycle of life. Both are needed to sustain life on this planet. Our celebrations took the form of ritual, connecting us with the earth, her creatures and plants, with each other. These connections allowed us to feel strong. We created additional rituals to release despair and empower ourselves, to help us get through difficult times. This group eventually became a coven: a group of thirteen or fewer members. These small groups are the way witches organize themselves. Each coven is self-sufficient and independent. No outside group has any authority over it.

Within my coven, I found the safety to explore, to discover rituals that healed me, that spoke to my female essence. Through research, I discovered that the new moon has always been a woman's festival. The connection between the 28-day lunar cycle and women's menstrual cycles was noticed and honored in ancient times. Women menstruated together and in time with the moon. Rest from everyday activity during menstruation allowed women to have this time for deeper spiritual development.

In my coven I found sisterhood, a love of what is female, honoring of women's wisdom, and empowerment, both individually and collectively. We helped each other through painful times; we celebrated joyful times. We played freely, chanting and dancing, drumming and making music together. We gave ourselves permission to be the beautiful females we truly are.

Male-centered spirituality differs from female-centered spirituality in both its form and its focus. Male-centered spirituality has the form of a pyramid with many people at the base and a few near the top, and God at the pinnacle in control. There is an assumption that those at the top are better or closer to God than those at the bottom. Women have always been placed at the bottom of the pyramid. Women are used to ground male religion while "men only" at the top leaves male spirituality unbalanced. Many women are getting tired of this structure which sees some people as better than others and which allows those on top to dictate to those below.

Many women find meeting in a circle more in tune with their needs. The circle symbolizes equality—each person is in the same relationship to others in the circle. Equality does not mean that each person has the same expertise, experience, learning, or ability. It means that each person's worth or essence is valued and that her story is heard. Individual differences in the circle are perceived as enriching rather than divisive. Because our unique selves complement each other we come together to co-operate. We can integrate our energy for work, for play, and for support of each other.

The focus of male-centered spirituality is outside oneself. A male God or guru is necessary to save a person. An outward-directed focus encourages obedience to what someone else says is right. The focus of female-centered spirituality is inside of each person. Everyone is encouraged to know her own truth and trust it. Since we have all been brought up in a white male system, it takes concentration and commitment to shift focus. In the process of shifting, the focus may go from clear to murky (Dare I trust myself?) and back to clear or murky again. Progress for me is when I stay more and more centered and focused on my own truth.

As women move from pyramid-style religion to circle spirituality, we find it difficult to leave better/worse thinking behind us. To achieve equality takes continued awareness of the many behaviors detrimental to our well being that are firmly embedded in our consciousness. It takes alertness and willingness to change thinking, behavior, and point of view. Changing a point of view can be frightening. Our point of view—what we believe—is part of our identity. A challenge to change may feel like an invasion of our very essence. But when the forms given to us do not fit us, changing ultimately leaves us freer. Freedom, too, can be frightening. As women, we have been taught to live by what others tell us rather than to think for ourselves. Freedom brings all sorts of new challenges.

How do I find my own truth in the face of many people telling me that their truth ought to be mine? Discovering my own truth starts with my own experience. For example, what has been my experience of spirituality? I was brought up in a Southern Presbyterian church and taken to church religiously each Sunday. What I liked in church was the singing. When I sang, I felt connected with the Goddess (though this isn't what I called her then), in tune with the fullest use of my own body. When I walked the mountains, saw the wildflowers, and picked blackberries, I felt connected with the Goddess. My connection with the earth, especially the mountains where I was born, felt divine. I felt alive and excited to be alive. As a young child I had no way to express what I felt. I was not allowed to know that spirituality could exist outside formal religion, and spirituality was discouraged rather than encouraged inside the church.

It was not until I was an adult and began thinking about the question "What would spirituality be like if it were based on women's experience?" that I understood the difference between spirituality and religion. Religion is a form, a set of practices designed to transmit and sustain spirituality. Spirituality is the connection with divine energy. The religion that I was given was based on male experience and on revulsion for the female body. No wonder it did not fit my experience. It often invalidated my experience, telling me that what I felt wasn't real or wasn't right. No wonder I was confused. No wonder I thought that spirituality itself was at fault.

It was the women's movement that brought me to a place of being able to know that my own experience was true and valid, that my story was worth telling and being heard. Feminism was the stepping stone that led me to what I most wanted: a female-centered spirituality that holds female values in high esteem and encourages every woman to use all her talents and gifts to the fullest. As a young child, I was taught not to do things better than the boys—not to win races or overpower boys in tests of strength. I was encouraged to lie to myself and others about what I could do. Honesty was given lip service and was discouraged in actual practice. It was in the women's movement that honesty about what I felt, who I was, and what I could do was encouraged. It was in women's consciousness-raising groups that I could tell my story and be heard. Before, when I'd said what was true for me, it was denied or called a lie. It was when I began to tell the truth about my life to those who listened without judgment that I began to trust my own truth. I now know my truth by how I feel. Knowing my truth requires a level of awareness about how I feel that had never been encouraged. When I feel centered, when I like myself and other women, when I cease to blame others for the way I feel, when I accept me exactly as I am and know that I don't have to change to be O.K., when I feel in tune with the universe, then I know I have found my own truth.

Before male religion was thrust upon everyone, there was a Goddess, divinity in female form. She was worshipped for millennia. She was one, yet she had many aspects. She was called She-of-a-Thousand-Names. It was recognized that different people saw her differently. She was seen in whatever form a person or people felt inspired by and could feel close to. The one-and-only-right-way-to-approach-God type of thinking became popular after male religion had driven Goddess worshipping people deep underground. It was necessary to force people into beliefs and behaviors that were not in their best interests in order to firmly establish religion controlled by men.

The beginning of the patriarchal system is recorded in Genesis. An important passage shows a betrayal of women's rights which had, in Goddess-worshipping times, been honored. In Genesis 3:15, God says to the snake: "I will put enmity between thee and the woman and between thy seed and her seed." Anyone living at the time when this was written would have known the snake as a symbol of the Goddess. This passage is designed to make enemies of woman and the Goddess (her divine self), to set woman against herself. Obliterating the Goddess paved the way for defining woman as sub-human and taking human rights away from her. It paved the way for defining female sexuality as a commodity to be bought and sold or given away by someone other than herself, usually someone of the male sex.

Later myths also tell about destroying the snake: Apollo killing the python at Delphi, knights killing dragons, St. Patrick driving the snakes out of Ireland. They all tell of killing Goddess power. It required brute force and had to be done again and again. Women did not give up their Goddess given rites (rights) easily.

Forcing an antagonistic relationship between woman and the Goddess was cruelly devastating to women. Because the Goddess represents female strength and autonomy, this decree of enmity required woman to alienate herself from her own strength, to give up her autonomy. It asked her to stop loving herself and other women. The Goddess clearly represented free and joyful sexuality so it also required her to separate herself from her sexuality.

If one were trying to subjugate a people, a very sensitive place to attack, an important thing to take away would be their spirituality, their unity with divinity. Once a people's spirit was broken, once an individual's soul was taken from her and put in the care of a male authority figure and her connection with her own divinity was severed, then control and abuse in other areas became much easier. And so it was. Women's ritual, women's music and dance, women's language were destroyed. Women healers were declared illegal, then killed. The care of women's bodies was taken away from them and given to men. Women were persuaded that they were evil and that it was bad to be close to other women.

Women did not give in easily. Nine million of them had to be killed before women's culture and women's wisdom were buried so deep that most women no longer knew about it. The cruelty, suppression, and violence against women did not stop when male religion, government, and the male-only medical profession were firmly established. Fear of women's power has persisted. The actions of men in power seem to be saying: "If women discover who they are, they will again know their divine selves and will no longer submit to our definitions of who they are or permit the disrespect and physical abuse that keeps the system going." Continued violence (physical, economic, and emotional) against women does drain our energy. We are so busy trying to stay alive that we have no time to find our souls.

Early in the current women's movement, there was a belief that women didn't have time to explore spirituality. Spirituality was thought to be frivolous; there were more important things to do. I let this sense of urgency, the belief that we first had to fight and defeat patriarchy before we could allow ourselves the luxury of finding out who we really are, stop me for a long time. Then, I gradually came to know that fighting patriarchy with its weapons and on its terms was killing me. I found that I didn't even want to try. I began to realize that becoming centered in respect for myself as a woman was essential before I could do more. Spiritual celebration with other women gave me that respect as well as the energy to go on living in a world hostile to my full development as a woman. Through my spirituality, I gained the power to be myself.

Power, as it's defined in male-centered thought, is power to control the lives and actions of others. Power is seen as being scarce; there is very little of it. Sonia Johnson states that we had to be persuaded that what we needed was scarce (food, love, etc.) before oppression could happen. If we believed that there was enough, there would have been no reason to submit to oppression. Scarcity may even have been created in order to oppress. According to the scarcity model, if one person has power, the other person doesn't. Power, as I define it, is something quite different. It is the ability to be fully who we are. It grows as it's shared. It includes the power to say "No" to those who wish to control us. It includes the power to accept intuition and psychic ability as parts of our being. So it is no surprise that this view of power threatens male defined power. Shekinah Mountainwater says: "Psychic liberation is the ultimate revolution, for people free in their souls cannot easily be controlled."

Feminist spirituality, of which witchcraft is one branch, does challenge the way things are. It asks for changes that create a very different way of living, one in which women and men are known to be equally valuable. It asks that we work for goals that consider what will be good for all and that respect each person's freedom to make her own choices.

In the patriarchal system, women have often not been respected for their way of doing things. I used to feel terribly hurt when my husband refused to respect my ways. I would demand his respect and, of course, not get it. Respect is crucial for my feeling of self-esteem. I had been divorced for years before I discovered that when I gave myself the respect that I deserved, I no longer needed to demand it from others. Self-respect gave me the wisdom to avoid those who could not respect me.

We need to clearly understand that what was done can be undone. We can refuse to allow our sexuality to be bought and sold and our rituals to be erased. When we reclaim control of our sexuality and reestablish sacred rituals to reconnect our strength in the Goddess, we will remove the foundation of patriarchy. That system will then no longer be able to control women for its own uses and will crumble. This may already be happening.

Our rites and our rights were taken away from us. We can give them back to ourselves. We can create a consciousness that is proud of and centered in being female, that nurtures the female qualities the world needs, that gives females everywhere the respect we need to live fully and joyfully.

I have found empowerment in witchcraft—a circle within which I am protected, within which I am encouraged to be all I can be. In witch rituals, there is a sentence often passed around the circle from one woman to the next until all have heard it spoken to her. It is a blessing as well as an affirmation. I want to leave each reader with this belief and blessing: "Thou art Goddess."

Antiga is a feminist witch, writer, singer, artist, workshop facilitator, and outrageous womoon. She is currently working on a book, Yin I Ching, and singing at every possible opportunity.

Born into a family of feminists, Antiga became active in the woman's movement in 1969 and has since then taken her feminism into the area of women's spirituality. He interest in women and words led her to get an M.A. in linguistics and to study the ways in which the English language supports the sexism in our culture.

Antiga's work led her to search for a spirituality in tune with her feminism. She found this in witchcraft, a spirituality that images the divine in a female form, the Goddess, and honors the divine in everyone.

Adonai Zeus Shekhinah Elim Ogun Kat Buddha
Wyame Hel Rama Mitra Odomankoma Jupiter Het
Heru Agni Cagn Thor Brahma Tangaroa Father
Lugaba Papang Diana Al-Rahman Cerridwen Ahone
Yoma' Tirawa Atius Canoaba El Mungan ngua
Quetzalcoatl Hamakom ddai
Atibruku Moma YH Bun aiwa
Saraswati Inanna Mirir aong
Tonantzin Yuskeha Bha Head
Olodumare Shyama Ekv Heru
Nurrundere Daramilun tzeir
Hecate Chi Musubi Hin suna
Nanderuvucu Erishkigal man
Tsui-goab Ometeotl Os chtli
Surya Elohim Nyankop Ilu
Woden Great Spirit Les goro
Poseidon Chineke Nhialic uwut

Bubble God
the Great
vs.
God of Earth
and Flesh

**Ranae Lenore
Hanson**

Makai Wakantanka Inari Ha-Qadosh barukh hu'
Tara Krishna Avaloket-iswara Rabb Goryo Qat Oke
Nurunderi Indra Shang-ti Amaterasu Ohmikami
Kannon Quan Yin Ise Lakshmi Awonawilona Bast
Omecihuatl Ruhanga Kosane Sophia Dionysus Ixchel
Mawu Ra Ardanariswara Oluwa Deng Hanuman
uNkulunkulu Kanobo Ngai Shamayim Cybele Dakini
Nataraj Pachamama Susanoo Katonda Avlukpo Eloah
Isis Temaukel Eleda Gaia Laxmi Mahmanmu-rok
Odin El-al Herukhuti Viracocha Marduk Ashira Biral
Shaddai Dzingbe Djohu-ma-di-hutu Astarte Ndengei
Koyatu Baha'u'llah Marrigan Baiame Om Pelepelewa
Durga Orisha Nyame Techaronhiawakhon Chukwu
Uvolovu Brahman Nephtys Ha-Maqom Tehuti Maat
Digambara Val Tik Chaitanya Amana Kwoth Num
Colok Nabango Fumeripitsj Shiva Varuna Lukanga
Bala Atibluku Karu Allah Sing Nainuema Artemis
Kartikeya Kuanyin Yelafaz T'ien Baal Shakti
Athena Olorun Nemesis Sheela-na-Gig Bhavartarini
Jesus Horus Izanagi Sebek Waq Ishtar Ti Seker
BegoTanutanu Sat Nam Kali Mirirul Bhavatarini
Tsui-goab Hatzur Brahman Ubusuna Tonantzin
YHVH Apollo Nana God Almighty Hu Vishnu Om

I was raised in a lively, independent Protestant clan surrounded by much talk of the bigness of God, ("for the Lord your God is great and greatly to be feared"), and of tribulation and atonement and faith. There was talk of resurrection ("for as in Adam all died, so also in Christ shall all be made alive") and of the thousand years reign ("for, lo, the heaven and the earth shall pass away, and all things shall become new"). I knew strong women in flowered hats who had loving bosoms that met their bellies over their belts and who would stand up during Sunday afternoon meetings to speak of the curtains in the tabernacle and of the calling of the redeemed out of the world.

And it was out of the world, away form the earth, that they called me. ("For the Lord, your God is a jealous God, and greatly to be feared." "Come out from among them and be ye separate.")

By the time I was four, I experienced God as sitting above my head in a rocking chair holding a bottle of bubble soap and a bubble blower. He had created everything in the world by blowing bubbles that would pop when they hit the ground, leaving among the soap splatter such creatures as a mother (mine, for example), a tree (that oak), a car (our Rambler), or a dog. Rocking-chair God created everything. It followed naturally that he could destroy everything ("and God sent a great flood"). When I loved the earthy realness of anything, he would reach out with the pointed end of his bubble-blower and pop it, showing me how foolish it was to love mere matter, reminding me that only the maker was to be loved ("thou shalt have no other gods").

So my dog, Twinkle, to whom I sang as he danced his tiny whiteness into a ball of joyous puppyhood, was run over by a truck and rolled clumsily toward me in a red, matted lump. God rocked gleefully in his chair and filled my head with laughter. Mom and Dad took the dog and put him in the ground.

In first grade I loved a boy—secretly, so as to ward off the punishment of God. But a friend sniffed out my love and called the boy "Ranae's boyfriend," and immediately God began laughing and caused a car accident in which the boy and his father and brother were badly hurt. I grew dizzy with the laughter of God and ceased to love the boy, who then lived.

The next year, God laughed in victory as nurses held down my arms and legs and clapped an ether rag over my mouth and nose; he laughed when I woke up later with gravel in my throat ("be not like onto those evil ones who give themselves over to the vanity of the flesh").

He was a God to hate, and I hated him thoroughly. But he was also the only being of whose existence I was sure. I could tell no one of him or he would wipe them out. As a teenaged babysittter, I waited in a house in the woods for the parents' return. I forced myself to stay awake listening to God calling me from above and slightly behind. I would not answer, not even by falling asleep. ("Then Samuel answered, 'Speak Lord, for thy servant heareth.'") I would not go into the swirl where he was leading me, though he whispered and whistled my name.

Instead I clung to another face of God. God was love, God was victorious, God was spirit, not a man with a white beard on a throne ("he is high and lifted up, and his train fills the temple"). But his temple was me. I was to please him. My body was his. My thoughts were known by him. He made everything. He was a jealous God. He had sent Jesus. I prayed daily; I desperately hoped that he was not the same as the God of the laugh.

At twenty I was first kissed—and not by the man I would marry, as I had anticipated. No, I was first kissed by a woman, a friend whom I adored. And the kiss stirred fire in my belly. A few days later, I sat on the carpet with the electric heater warming one side of my body, gazing on the sleeping form of my friend and wondering if I would ever dare let her kiss me again, if I would perhaps even someday kiss her. Then out of the silence, God spoke. "Stop," he said, firmly and loudly.

"No," I whispered back. And I kissed her that night.

Yet I knew he would destroy my life. His bubble-poker was poised. ("The reprobate I will give over to the lusts of their hearts.")

The remnants of my life were gathered into a basket by a whispering vision of God, by a hinted-at, other aspect of divinity. ("For, lo, I will speak gently, I will speak gently to Israel.")

As a young teenager, I attended a summer Bible camp with my parents on the shores of a northern lake. Our evening meetings were lively jam sessions of scriptural exhortation, testimony, chorus singing with clapping and swaying, speaking in tongues, moaning and harmonizing in spiritual chant, tambourine playing, and dancing for God. My parents were the most reserved of the lot. "A person does not have to talk in tongues to prove he is saved," they said. They favored virtuous living and Bible study. So mostly I stood with them, stern against the sway of emotion that surged through the small chapel.

One night an elder stood up and called into the air above our heads: "There is a spirit of repression at work among us! Set us free, oh Lord, from the spirit that seeks to bind us!" I knew he meant that the dancing and moaning and humming in tongues had not sufficient fervor, and I was hoping steadfastly that it never would. I hated those hours of bitter resistance against emotional abandon. But listening to him I decided that my desire for quiet was no reason that others should be deprived of ecstasy. I took that "spirit of repression" out of the building and left them to their joy. Once outside, I sat on the grass, trying to recognize myself as a work of the devil, having no part in the workings of God.

But then I looked up at the trees. A breeze was blowing through the leaves and then leaping from them to the surface of the lake, where it rippled the tight crust of sunset glow into a patterned silver sheen. Birds sang and bobbed at the edge of the water. In the east, the sky was turning a deep furry blue.

"I know God," I thought. "*This* is God; God is out here in these leaves, in this wind. They cannot keep God inside."

Throughout all my years of growing I had this other image of holiness. It was the holiness of the body and of all embodied being. It was the wonder of flesh that tingled and ears that heard. ("There are three things too wonderful for me, yea, four that I know not of: the way of an eagle in the air; the way of a serpent upon a rock; the way of a ship in the midst of the sea; and the way of a man with a maid.") It was amazing that the eyes in me could commune with a star, could notice its glow against the black of the sky with pines framing and blurring its light as the wind blew. I decided, while watching one star, that the purpose of life was simply to notice and adore all beings in the wonder of their presence.

So in the dark years after that kiss when I thought I had abandoned God, or been forsaken by him, I also knew somehow that God—more basic God, older and deeper, more silent and more raucous God—was the earth and was my body and was calling me in, into the most center of body and earth.

Slowly through the years, God of Earth began speaking to me, not audibly as had God the Maker of Things, who had told me to stop, but speaking persistently through each pushing fiddlehead fern. This God, this life embodied, spoke in the rough of tree bark, spoke in the patterns of clouds. Again and again, each time I was alone, they (I could not experience this God as one) told me what I must do. They asked me to bear them a child.

On the practical level, their call was not easily filled. I was not married, no one was asking for me, and I come from family-focused stock. But I was helping to raise the child of a friend; he agreed to have child with me.

In labor with that child, I found God in the air coming to my mouth, then transformed to a bud that emerged molecule by molecule, push by push, from my womb. When my son was born, the bud of God unfurled, a flower from my flesh.

Later God asked for another child through me, and when my daughter was born I saw the body of God.

So, God for me became flesh ("and dwelt among us"). God was my son asking at three, "Mom, I know I came from you and you came from grandma but where did the first person come from?"

"Some say God formed them from the dust of the earth," I said. (Some say, from the great primordial cunt, I thought.)

"Where do you think they came from?" I asked.

"I don't know, " he said.

"Neither do I," I said.

From the earth, I might have said, from God which is the earth. Of God, which they themselves are. (God will be all and in all.) "People can come from you," I said. "And from your baby sister."

"But the first ones, Mom," he asked, "did they come from God?"

Then you will ask where God comes from. Who can say where God came from? "God is not the maker of things," I said, "but the very beingness of things themselves. God is earth and more. God is me and you. And God is the ant on the path."

"Oh," he said. "I don't understand."

"Neither do I," I told him.

That summer the earth where we lived dried up. The trees dropped their leaves. The ozone hole widened above us. Birds panted with open beaks on our lawn. People were advised to go out of the house only with sunscreen and dark glasses. And what of the rabbits, I wondered. Were they wearing polarized lenses? What of the white skin of mice?

I knew the earth was dying, right when I had learned to live it. Once again Bubble God laughed. ("Thou shalt have no other gods. . .they love the creation more than the creator. . .and I will give them up. . .depart from me. . .and he hated the creation which his hand had created.")

But I was no longer six. For thirty years my parents had spoken to me of the poisoning of the earth by man; now I saw that the killing was done. All that remained were long hours of death. Bubble God was no longer above my head in a chair; I was in his chair and his poker was in my hand, wet with the blood of the earth.

I drive a car. The land I live on was given to my fathers by those who thought of themselves as my benefactors and who had killed the ones who lived on the land before us by giving them smallpox-infected blankets. True, I have done many good things, but DDT runs through my blood and I have passed it on to my children. ("Mom," he said, "I can't breathe. Mom, why do I have to have asthma? Mom, I can't breathe.")

Here I stand on Golgatha. God is dying, and I am of the tribe of the killers. With the death of this God, my light will go out and the lights of my children and yours. It would not be much were it only our lights, but this is the light of all life. Of all life as I know the term.

Ranae Hanson spent the first twenty years of her life in Northern Minnesota, and still returns there often. She lives now in St. Paul with her family and teaches humanities at Minneapolis Community College. Ranae is a member of the Minneapolis Friends Meeting (Quakers).

Adonai Zeus Shekhinah Elim Ogun Kat Buddha
Wyame Hel Rama Mitra Odomankoma Jupiter Het
Heru Agni Cagn Thor Brahma Tangaroa Father
Lugaba Papang Diana Al-Rahman Cerridwen Ahone
Yoma' Tirawa Atius Ganesha El Mungan-ngua
Quetzalcoatl Hamakom ddai
Atibruku Moma YH Bun aiwa

God
Awakening

Saraswati Inanna Miriru aong
Tonantzin Yuskeha Bha Head
Olodumare Shyama Ekv Heru
Nurrundere Daramilun tzeir
Hecate Chi Musubi Hin suna

Rabbi
Vicki Hollander

Nanderuvucu Erishkigal man
Tsui-goab Ometeotl Os chtli
Surya Elohim Nyankop Ilu
Woden Great Spirit Les goro
Poseidon Chineke Nhialic Aciek Kari Ausel Teuwut
Makai Wakantanka Inari Ha-Qadosh barukh hu'
Tara Krishna Avaloket-iswara Rabb Goryo Qat Oke
Nurunderi Indra Shang-ti Amaterasu Ohmikami
Kannon Quan Yin Ise Lakshmi Awonawilona Bast
Omecihuatl Ruhanga Kosane Sophia Dionysus Ixchel
Mawu Ra Ardanariswara Oluwa Deng Hanuman
uNkulunkulu Kanobo Ngai Shamayim Cybole Dakini
Nataraj Pachamama Susanoo Katonda Avlukpo Eloah
Isis Temaukel Eleda Gaia Laxmi Mahmanmu-rok
Odin El-al Herukhuti Viracocha Marduk Ashira Biral
Shaddai Dzingbe Djohu-ma-di-hutu Astarte Ndengei
Koyatu Baha'u'llah Marrigan Baiame Om Pelepelewa
Durga Orisha Nyame Techaronhiawakhon Chukwu
Uvolovu Brahman Nephtys Ha-Maqom Tehuti Maat
Digambara Val Tik Chaitanya Amana Kwoth Num
Colok Nabango Fumeripitsj Shiva Varuna Lukanga
Bala Atibluku Karu Allah Sing Nainuema Artemis
Kartikeya Kuanyin Yelafaz T'ien Baal Shakti
Athena Olorun Nemesis Sheela-na-Gig Bhavartarini
Jesus Horus Izanagi Sebek Waq Ishtar Ti Seker
BegoTanutanu Sat Nam Kali Mirirul Bhavatarini
Tsui-goab Hatzur Brahman Ubusuna Tonantzin
YHVH Apollo Nana God Almighty Hu Vishnu Om

I n my tradition, it is customary that the name of the Holy One is not completely written down. Commonly writers use 'G_d.' Yet when I try to speak of that One beyond and within us I have chosen to use 'G' to symbolize the wholeness, and completeness, the roundedness of our Source.

Trying to speak of G, of divine images, for me, is like standing before a towering stone wall. The stone, cold, hard, grey, impenetrable.

I needed to find another way to approach, through dreams, through poetry, through numbers and imagery, through the door where the conscious and the unconscious meet. Thus I invite you to join my reverie, my journey in process, of awakening and encountering G.

My language, vocabulary, and imagery emerges from the well of my tradition. So that you might walk with me, a glossary follows,[1] an invitation to drink and enter into my world and soul.

§

They say in my tradition
there are seventy names of G.

The world was created in seven days.
A life is mourned for seven days.
A minyan, prayer community, to speak of
G's holiness,
takes ten.

Seven times ten, G names.

One:
You are
uniting energies, elements, forms.
Before the before.
Before me, breathing,
waiting for company.

Two:
Number of witnesses to wed,
number of yuds in your name.
Time of knowing you,
before I knew.
When I was two I
watched you dress the universe each day
and fill it with wonders.

Three:
Number it takes to bless food and speak your name.
Number of angels telling Sarah when 90,
that despite nature and age,
she would birth.
My three saw you in the acorns I gathered,
in the honeysuckle round my back porch,
in snowflakes and spiderwebs.

Four:
Four questions at freedom time.
Four kinds of children.
Four cups of wine.
Four letters in your personal name.
Four worlds, ways of knowing you.
Four years old and time of percolating,
asking of you.
Not getting answers that fit
what I knew
in my body
already.

Five:
At five, in our tradition,
boys start to study Torah.
I was playing in patches of sun
learning your names
by tracing leaves.

Seven:
Seven days of the universe unfolding.
Seven weeks before the binding at Sinai.
Seven days of celebrating a marriage.

Seven days of shivah.
Seven when meeting you more formally.
In shul and siddur you were
Adonai, Elohim, Father, and King.
You were bigger than me, teamed up with the grown-ups.
The Grown-up of grown-ups.
I knew how you looked
sitting up there on your cloud-throne:
white hair, a long white beard, white robes, white skin,
smoke surrounding you.
A big Man.
Even though they told us we couldn't see you
and you were everywhere
bigger than "man,"
we knew.
They taught me
in religious school
that you were very close to us.
That you cared about us.
I could feel that.
It was something I knew.
I sat in the tawny wooden paneled synagogue
staring at the windows glowing with color.
You always seemed so close to me.
At times I would feel you touch me
to let me know you were there,
goosebumps on my arms,
warmth around my body, as if embraced.
You were always for me.
Always present.

Ten:
Ten men would make a minyan.
Sometimes a boy holding sefer Torah and nine men would work,
so those gathering could speak of your holiness in prayer.
Ten makes a community.
At ten boys would study Mishna.
Ten words given at Sinai, ways to walk,
blueprints, maps with navigational charts on how to weather
 the life storms ahead.

When I was ten
I knew my grandfather left Russia when eleven, my
grandmother, when she was twelve.
They were all by themselves
walking by foot through countries,
coins sewn into their pockets,
long stolen before reaching their destinations.
At ten I knew but for their trip,
I would not be here.
Portions of the family were killed in the Shoah.

I saw film footage of the camps.
My body knows my life is a gift
as surely as sun rises each day, and
that life is not to be taken lightly.
Walking with my father, an agnostic, at twilight,
he asks,
Where was G during all this?
I, your defender, his comforter,
find wind rushing in my mouth as in a cavern,
empty space,
questions ringing through me like a bell at dinnertime.

Thirteen:
Boys become bar mitzvah, called to Torah,
beholden to enact mitzvot,
adults in the Jewish community.
Not traditionally for me, a Jewish girl.

In my family, women were short, round, and strong.
Women outnumbered the men in every generation.
In my schul, I was told girls were equal to boys.
Women were welcomed.
I believed them.
I saw a recruitment film about the rabbinate.
Afterwards, approaching the rabbi to speak of my interest
he looked at me and said,
"Girls can't be rabbis."
I thought he was wrong.
It didn't make sense.
I figured it was his problem.
And planted that inside, seedlike for later.

I learned in religious school
that your sparks were sprinkled throughout
the universe
held sometimes in the tiniest most common seeming thing
which served as a container for holiness.
I, like the writer of Proverbs,
watched ants,
aware that they too held sparks.
I still walk around them carefully.
A time of seeing Elijah reflected in each passerby.
The possibility of miracles everywhere
if I could open my eyes to catch them at the right moment.
Be awake to them.

Fifteen:

At fifteen tradition says,
boys begin to study the Talmud.
I entered youth organizations
learning to sing the Hebrew songs by melody and sound
because I couldn't read Hebrew.
I found you in song, and dance,
in t'fillah out of doors,
in argumentation, in study, in embrace of companions.

Out of doors in prayer
you filled me powerfully,
plucked my soulstrings.
I, resonating, sought places without walls,
places where you and I could have the room and freedom to
stretch and meet,
converse and wrestle.

I remember the Chanukah candles alight, and
my anger.
It seemed so phony to me
of all things to mark at home,
this and nothing else.

I went to services by myself.
In that quiet wooden room, I found stillness inside.
We would meet there and other places.
You and I.

Eighteen:
Letters adding up to equal the word 'life.'
Eighteen opened a new door,
swinging two ways, departure and entry both.
The era inflamed with excavation,
searching out the depths and recesses of the human well.
I saw in the waters
my reflection as a woman
and following her,
saw that of a Jewish woman.

I sat in rooms of prayer.
Not knowing how to read the holy language,
pierced my soul through, red hot needle.
I wanted to speak to you with the ancient words.
I wanted them to be my own.
I walked through mazes of the aleph-bet,
slowly, slowly speaking,
like walking through thornbushes.
I struggled to keep up with the siddurs pages,
they, racing ahead like a new born colt
as soon as I would get close, breaking away at a gallop,
leaving me, behind, behind.
I wanted to come closer to you.

Like a blind one,
I edged forward.
Learning by myself, one mitzvah, one mitzvah.
In the forest, seeking you
calling your name,
trying to come home.

I claimed being a Jewish woman.
As traditionally outsiders to public ritual observance,
expounding Torah, textual traditions,
I bore an untold legacy.
I carried a freshness to add to Jewish life.
I felt that you and I had things to share,
things maybe the way
they could be,
offering light to some paths that had been darkened.

Twenty:
Twenty calls to seek a livelihood according to Mishnah.
I decided to enter Seminary.   ·
I needed to learn more of the tradition that spoke of you.
I needed a place to wrestle with you and my father's
questions, to wrestle with the Shoah and you.
I needed to come of age, as a knowledgeable Jewish
woman, to stand as adult within my community,
before you.

I had left the images of you
as elderly man.
I knew you as a feeling inside,
as a Being without.
Yet I needed names to call you
names from my heart, echoing earth, echoing what I know
and what I don't know.

As the numbers grew quieter,
as tradition left the numbers to living and
had less to say,
they left a space in which to meet.
A deserted space,
a wilderness,
a place of encounter.
And so I immersed in traditional texts,
the teaching, my balm.

I learned you had seventy names.
Slowly, like notes curling from wooden flute,
I met Ha-Kadosh Boruch Hu,
Ribbono Shel Olam, names from different centuries
each reflecting a different light
like a crystal catching suns rays.
I began to see you through others eyes,
traveling through history, the texts my magic carpets,
hearing men speak of you,
as Lover, Intimate, Friend.
I, listening, watching, marking,
understanding that closeness,
which at times I knew as a woman
in a different way.

I called upon you
as I walked in the lonely wilderness of seminary
as desolate as the parched earth of the Sinai,
wind whistling around the curves in my soul
trying to find my way.
The texts, the occasional wadi.
I walked, the stranger,
trying, trying to just
arrive at the edge of a fruitful land.
The journey, so harsh,
it was years before my dried out lips
could open to speak of it.
Daily, hourly, I questioned this road.
And you held me in Your hands,
my tears, your mikvah water.

I searched for more of your names
in the wells
of siddur and Torah,
in Talmud, and Midrash,
tucked in the byways of the texts.
Seeking names to call you,
I traveled back to the very beginning,
the first Adam, seer of sparks, bestower of names.
I wanted ways to speak with you,
places to meet you, encounter you, feel you,
touch.

Thirty:
At thirty, tradition says
one knows full strength.
I gave birth to my child,
life pulled from within me to without,
womb filled and emptied
like seed pulled from squash
clinging, yet ready to leave, separating yet
attached.
I understood through the chords of my body
your name,
HaRahaman.

And just as I birthed my daughter
and myself
mother,
I understood more of what
you might feel towards your beings,
internal scarlet thread looping around
heartbeats, rocks, earth, trees,
connecting all as precious, beloved.
Meeting you,
HaYotzeir.

As more of me unfolded
I found more of you.
As I grew into my skin
so did you meet me.

The thirties for full strength.
Thirty-six,
double chai, twice of life.

At thirty-three I was a single mother
with a three year old child.
At thirty-four my home was sold.
At thirty-six I was pulled into court,
a contest for custody, to try and give my daughter
a Jewish education.
At thirty-seven I finished retraining
to enable me to stay in the city my daughter was born
and survive financially.
At thirty-eight I found a beginning job.
Full strength.
It was you who towed me through my days.
I awoke, and looked for your postcards
in the sky of each morning,
messages that life would indeed brighten again.

I learned more about you.
I knew the inky blue depths of pain,
traveled in darkest tunnels
and when all seemed shorn away
and I stood, a female Job,
I felt you with me

somehow.
My comfort.
When the lights were out at night,
and my daughter, turned cherub,
breath as sweet as honeysuckle,
body rising and falling
as steadily as the sea,
you were there
by my side.

As I was born
another layer of skin shed.
As I become stronger
and clearer,
so did you.
My voice changed.
I moved from silence
to speaking.
I left what I should be
and began the exploration
of what makes me up now
and how I wish to be.
You were my coach.
Silent when I was confused.
Clear when I came closer.
My Guide, Moor, Beacon.

It was when I tried to sing to you
when I left the printed page
and tried to call to you
with poem to celebrate
the new moon, birthing the new month,
that your names rose to my lips
rolled around my tongue
like warmed fragrant soup,
seeping deep inside of me
and touching me
in brand new ways.

It was when I disentangled myself from fear,
moved into stories,
and let myself sing with them,

saw them as
gateways
to finding you,
that I met you in new ways.

It was when I remembered that long ago Jewish women
used song, and dance, and story and
firelight to touch spirit.
Sleeping close to earth,
they knew wisdoms.
It was when I started filling in the spaces of Torah
with what the women might have said
or dreamed
or spoken.
It was when I allowed myself to remember the
wisdoms of my grandmothers
and let them be guides
to knowing Torah, to finding you
in ways that women know,
that we have met in new ways.

It was when I imaged Israelites, men and women,
whose tents rested on earth,
heads cushioned by soil,
who marked their day by sun's rays
and their months by moon's glow,
whose sandals knew firmness in the land
and who drew circles to coax out precious water,
whose feet still knew how to dance
and whose bodies knew how to celebrate,
eyes knew how to laugh and souls knew humility;
these helped me hear
heartbeats:
mine, the earth's, the air's, my daughter's.
These drew me closer to your side.

And now
as I move, and write,
when I swim, and when I pray,
when I sit before someone, listening to their heart,
and when I walk alone beside the lake,
when I hold my daughter at night,

and when I sing and daven,
you are there.

I believe you have been waiting for us
to discover ourselves,
waiting there to show more of yourself.

As I unfold, you meet me.
As I see life's complexities, intricacies, mysteries,
I see more clearly your wonder.
As I ripen, I learn yet another of your 70 names,
Hatzur, Hamakom.

Rabbi Vicki Hollander was ordained in 1979 from the Hebrew Union College of the Jewish Institute of Religion. She has served reform, conservative, Chavurot, and traditional egalitarian minyans in the United States and Canada. Currently Rabbi Hollander resides in Seattle, Washington, and is the bereavement and volunteer coordinator at Hospice of Seattle. She serves a newly forming community, Eitz Or, and has a private practice in marriage and family therapy.

A poet, writer, and ritual maker, she is crafting new spiritual directions while delighting in asking questions.

Adonai Zeus Shekhinah Elim Ogun Kat Buddha
Wyame Hel Rama Mitra Odomankoma Jupiter Het
Heru Agni Cagn Thor Brahma Tangaroa Father
Lugaba Papang Diana Al-Rahman Cerridwen Ahone
Yoma' Tirawa Atius Ganesha El Mungan ngua
Quetzalcoatl Hamakom ddai
Atibruku Moma YH Bun aiwa
Saraswati Inanna Mirir aong
Tonantzin Yuskeha Bha Head
Olodumare Shyama Ekv Heru
Nurrundere Daramilun tzeir
Hecate Chi Musubi Hin suna
Nanderuvucu Erishkigal man
Tsui-goab Ometeotl Os chtli
Surya Elohim Nyankop Ilu
Woden Great Spirit Les goro
Poseidon Chineke Nhialic uwut

Our
Grandfather
The
Great Spirit

Wawokiya Win

Makai Wakantanka Inari Ha-Qadosh barukh hu'
Tara Krishna Avaloket-iswara Rabb Goryo Qat Oke
Nurunderi Indra Shang-ti Amaterasu Ohmikami
Kannon Quan Yin Ise Lakshmi Awonawilona Bast
Omecihuatl Ruhanga Kosane Sophia Dionysus Ixchel
Mawu Ra Ardanariswara Oluwa Deng Hanuman
uNkulunkulu Kanobo Ngai Shamayim Cybele Dakini
Nataraj Pachamama Susanoo Katonda Avlukpo Eloah
Isis Temaukel Éleda Gaia Laxmi Mahmanmu-rok
Odin El-al Herukhuti Viracocha Marduk Ashira Biral
Shaddai Dzingbe Djohu-ma-di-hutu Astarte Ndengei
Koyatu Baha'u'llah Marrigan Baiame Om Pelepelewa
Durga Orisha Nyame Techaronhiawakhon Chukwu
Uvolovu Brahman Nephtys Ha-Maqom Tehuti Maat
Digambara Val Tik Chaitanya Amana Kwoth Num
Colok Nabango Fumeripitsj Shiva Varuna Lukanga
Bala Atibluku Karu Allah Sing Nainuema Artemis
Kartikeya Kuanyin Yelafaz T'ien Baal Shakti
Athena Olorun Nemesis Sheela-na-Gig Bhavartarini
Jesus Horus Izanagi Sebek Waq Ishtar Ti Seker
BegoTanutanu Sat Nam Kali Mirirul Bhavatarini
Tsui-goab Hatzur Brahman Ubusuna Tonantzin
YHVH Apollo Nana God Almighty Hu Vishnu Om

I am a Lakota woman. My name, Wawokiya Win, means "Helpful Woman." I come from a little community on a South Dakota reservation. We are called the Cheyenne River Sioux Tribe. (Sioux, meaning "cutthroat" or "snake in the grass" is the word the French gave to the Lakota people). I grew up in a one-room shack with no running water, no electricity, no indoor plumbing. I was raised in the traditional Lakota environment, speaking our language and learning about my rich spiritual heritage.

To my people, God is the Creator, our Grandfather, the Great Spirit, and we see him everywhere in all his creation. For us, walking a spiritual path is not something to be taken lightly. Unlike a one-day-out-of-a-week ritual, every day is a day of worship for us. We walk a path in which we observe the Creator in our everyday existence. From the time we wake up with the morning sun *(Ata-Father)* and pray to a new day until the sun goes down, we give thanks to the Creator for life.

Our tradition has respect for all because everything on earth is considered natural, put here as a part of God, as a part of the Great Creator. God is that entity so powerful, so wonderful, which created all: the trees, the rocks, flowers, the four-leggeds, the two-leggeds, all things that crawl and the winged ones. The Lakota consider the breath of life given to each race and species as a wondrous part of the Great Spirit himself. We see God in everything that was put on this planet.

In this way also we recognize the earth as a female creation of God. The trees are the hair on her body, the rivers and streams are her blood veins, and all that is inside the earth are her vital organs. Like a woman, she nurtures and gives life to all her children. She provides food in a cycle called the "Circle of Life." It is a never-ending circle, an eternal cycle, each species depending on the next in order to survive. This earth we walk on, then, is sacred and accorded respect. We call her "Grandmother Earth" *(Unci Maka)*.

The Lakota people considered America a Garden of Eden before the *wasicu,* the white man, came. In the days of my people, before the coming of the *wasicu,* the Lakota considered themselves to be the care takers of the land; they earned for themselves the title "Landlords of the Plains."

Although they were fearless warriors and skilled hunters, the Lakota had great respect for their people, the land, the animals. They always prayed for the animal they killed by asking forgiveness of the animal for taking its life, and giving thanks for the sacrifice of its life in order that the people may survive. The warriors provided not only for their own families but also for others less fortunate in the band or camp. They cared for all those in the camp and never went into battle when their women and children were around.

The Lakota way was to praise each other a lot. There was great respect for the elders, women, and children. They bathed every day, even in winter time, and were well-groomed, and industrious. Welfare was a nightmare yet to come. Abuse, molestation, prostitution, and rape were unheard of. So was lying, and back stabbing, treachery, and cowardice.

Children were considered sacred, and were well cared for. They were not taken lightly; when a woman became with child the whole camp looked forward to the birth. It was always a joyous occasion for the whole community when a baby was born. Children were well taken care of by the whole *tiospiye* (clan). Nobody ever needed baby-sitters, because children went where they pleased; they always had a watchful eye over them. They were never scolded or spanked, but only praised. Early on, children were taught skills of survival and learned to respect themselves and others.

When a young girl reached womanhood, an honor ceremony was given on her behalf. Women were considered sacred, especially when they were on their time. Then they stayed in a lodge away from camp because it was their time of power. They were waited upon, and mothers, aunts, and grandmas came to visit and tell stories about women's ways. They were treated special until their time was over and they had to go back to camp. Then they were washed with a particular cleansing herb.

To us the *cunnunpa*, the "Pipe" is sacred. (The white people called it a "Peace Pipe.") It was given to us by the Great Spirit as a gift. To us, the *cunnunpa* is like the Bible is to Christians. There are natural laws attached to this pipe very much like the ten commandments of the Christians. Our dances and our ceremonies are also sacred. Our language itself is sacred.

The Lakota call themselves the *Ikci-wicasa*, the "common people" or "natural people." Thus we have natural laws which we follow. These are honesty, courage, fortitude, generosity, piety, respect, and humbleness. It is a hard road to walk, this red road, this *cunku luta.*

We look upon honor not as an external virtue, but as being part of the person. There is no sense in being half-way about it. Honor has to be an ongoing, day-to-day existence. Every man and woman must carry pride and honor in order to say he or she is a decent person. It takes a lot of discipline to walk the path of beauty and enlightenment, but it must be done. We Lakota humble ourselves and make personal sacrifices such as fasting, to honor the Great Spirit, but there is no devil or hell in the Lakota way of life. There is only the Great Spirit, and the Happy Hunting Ground. We do have *Iktomi,* the trickster, who tempts us, but there is no such thing as "sin" in Lakota life, because the people were of one mind and one spirit, and had a high standard of living. Ours was the way of the *Wolakota,* "peace or friendship."

The white men came to this country looking for freedom and escape from religious persecution. Yet they viewed the natives of this country as pagans and heathens, as savages. Using the Bible, guns, disease, and dishonesty, they created mayhem and destruction for the original inhabitants of this country. Indians were slaughtered and put on reservations, concentration camps without walls. Considered incompetent, they were oppressed by white society and persecuted for their refusal to sell their land. But our religion and our land were never for sale, because one cannot sell God. So in the 1800's our ceremonies and our forms of prayer were banned by the American government. It would not be until 1978, with the passage of the "1978 Freedom of Religion Act," that we were able to practice our way of life.

Now, after years of oppression and genocide, the Lakota are looked upon today as a focus of world attention because of our spiritual beliefs—the same beliefs we once were persecuted for having.

Family is important to us. The Lakota today remain close knit as large clans consisting of mothers, fathers, grandmothers, grandfathers, aunts, uncles, cousins, and extended family members. We all must get along in order to survive as a group or a band. The mother's and father's brother and sisters are considered second parents to the children. First cousins are considered brothers and sisters; therefore one individual can have many brothers and sisters depending on how many first cousins there are.

Respect for all is the Lakota way. Being selfish, self-centered and materialistic are not ways of the Lakota. We all need each other in order to survive. The only way to build a bond of trust and security for all is to respect one another and help one another.

We believe Grandmother Earth needs protection from all the abuse that is happening to her. We consider technology as a giant cancer which took over the land. Now we all must work together in order to preserve Grandmother Earth for future generations.

When people have sick minds, it creates an unhealthy environment for all of us. Because we all must coexist, we must be co-creative together in order to be healthy in mind and spirit. When we help one another to be healthy, we are also helping ourselves. Knowledge and wisdom are great virtues. With these, many people may understand that there is a reason for everybody to exist. To balance our life we need to depend on faith in our Grandfather, the Great Spirit.

Wawokiya Win is a full-blood Lakota from the Cheyenne River Reservation in South Dakota. She is the mother of three young children and a helper to her people, as her name implies. She is a very family-oriented person and prefers to remain reclusive, but as an emerging writer has written many articles about Native American rights in America. She wishes to bring awareness to the plight of her people and the history of their co-existence in America. This is related in her first book, soon to be published. Her articles appear in *The Lakota Times*, the *Native American Press*, and *Incomindios*, an international newsletter.

Adonai Zeus Shekhinah Elim Ogun Kat Buddha
Wyame Hel Rama Mitra Odomankoma Jupiter Het
Heru Agni Cagn Thor Brahma Tangaroa Father
Lugaba Papang Diana Al-Rahman Cerridwen Ahone
Yoma' Tirawa Atius Ganesha El Mungan ngua
Quetzalcoatl Hamakom ddai
Atibruku Moma YH Bun aiwa
Saraswati Inanna Miriru aong

The
Shadow
of the
Goddess

Linda Johnsen

Tonantzin Yuskeha Bha Head
Olodumare Shyama Ekv Heru
Nurrundere Daramilun otzeir
Hecate Chi Musubi Hin suna
Nanderuvucu Erishkigal man
Tsui-goab Ometeotl Os chtli
Surya Elohim Nyankop Ilu
Woden Great Spirit Lese goro
Poseidon Chineke Nhialic uwut
Makai Wakantanka Inari Ha-Qadosh barukh hu'
Tara Krishna Avaloket-iswara Rabb Goryo Qat Oke
Nurunderi Indra Shang-ti Amaterasu Ohmikami
Kannon Quan Yin Ise Lakshmi Awonawilona Bast
Omecihuatl Ruhanga Kosane Sophia Dionysus Ixchel
Mawu Ra Ardanariswara Oluwa Deng Hanuman
uNkulunkulu Kanobo Ngal Shamaytm Cybele Daktnf
Nataraj Pachamama Susanoo Katonda Avlukpo Eloah
Isis Temaukel Eleda Gaia Laxmi Mahmanmu-rok
Odin El-al Herukhuti Viracocha Marduk Ashira Biral
Shaddai Dzingbe Djohu-ma-di-hutu Astarte Ndengei
Koyatu Baha'u'llah Marrigan Baiame Om Pelepelewa
Durga Orisha Nyame Techaronhiawakhon Chukwu
Uvolovu Brahman Nephtys Ha-Maqom Tehuti Maat
Digambara Val Tik Chaitanya Amana Kwoth Num
Colok Nabango Fumeripitsj Shiva Varuna Lukanga
Bala Atibluku Karu Allah Sing Nainuema Artemis
Kartikeya Kuanyin Yelafaz T'ien Baal Shakti
Athena Olorun Nemesis Sheela-na-Gig Bhavartarini
Jesus Horus Izanagi Sebek Waq Ishtar Ti Seker
BegoTanutanu Sat Nam Kali Mirirul Bhavatarini
Tsui-goab Hatzur Brahman Ubusuna Tonantzin
YHVH Apollo Nana God Almighty Hu Vishnu Om

I t's 1989, another balmy October afternoon in the South Bay, and I'm planning supper as I leave my office at Stanford. I am pulling away from the campus when my bicycle wrenches away from me; it becomes a living thing, bucking in one direction, then lurching in another. I leap off the bike but cannot catch my balance. All around me veering cars are slamming to a halt, occupants bursting out, surprise and alarm clutching their faces as they struggle, like me, to remain upright. Behind us every shelf in Green Library is toppling onto the next as tens of thousands of books spill onto the floor. In the building I just left, chalk boards are shaking off walls and slabs of masonry are splintering free from the ceiling. There is a staccato of explosions: Memorial Church has just collapsed.

I ride the earth precariously as all around me science and art and religion come tumbling down.

§

The first earthquake I experienced occurred 21 years earlier in Chicago; it happened to me, not to the city. I was alone at home, walking through the dining room. One moment I was the familiar fatuous 14 year old, precocious, religious, utterly conventional. The next I was everything. What I am describing is not a metaphor—it was not as *if* I became everything—in that split second between raising my right foot and placing it back on the floor the part of me that is conscious swelled beyond the boundaries of my skin and suffused the air around me, the furniture, the walls. Every molecule in that room was thrilling with bliss—it was all alive, all completely conscious. In that fragment of time, I experienced God, the universe, myself, and there was no difference.

"What's happening to me?" some shard of myself that had not exploded in ecstasy shrieked. In that moment I imploded back into my body, and the shock of limited consciousness was staggering. I literally staggered. I am still staggering.

§

The fervor of the search while the fever is fresh, before intellectual smugness substitutes itself for personal experience, leads. I run from guide to guide, expecting that since I have a question, someone has an answer.

I describe the experience to my pastor, telling him I read about it in a book. (I am no fool; if I tell him what happened, he will think I am on drugs). He patiently explains, "The person who wrote that was lying. Such experiences don't exist."

"But isn't it possible that heaven is a state rather than a place, and that in some sense we are one with God?"

"No." He writes out a list of Biblical references for me to study and sends me away.

The next Sunday I try a Methodist minister. He is young and kind. The following week, a Baptist preacher. Experiences like I describe are created by the Devil to seduce souls away from God. I approach a Catholic priest. He doesn't have time for Lutheran teenagers.

The Spiritualist minister looks like Tyrone Power; he talks to dead people. He is very sincere but he doesn't hear a word I say. The Christian Scientists hold mind over matter; in their huge Grecian temple I sense piety and prayer but no trace of transcendence.

"God," I am crying, "You came and went. You didn't leave a clue."

§

I am sixteen. Swami Nikhilananda's abridged translation of the major Upanishads has been sitting on my bookshelf unopened for months. I bought it because I felt I should have at least one volume representing Hinduism in my growing personal library of religious thought—though what a culture that has not mastered the flush toilet might offer Westerners, I cannot imagine. One Saturday afternoon I am actually bored enough to pick it up, flip to the introduction. "The *Atman*, our own inner essence of consciousness, is identical with *Brahman*, the all pervading supreme consciousness," the writer is saying. "We only imagine that we and all other objects exist as separate entities. In reality, there is only one being, which is consciousness and bliss."

My hands tremble so violently I drop the book.

§

I blast through college, fending off Jesuits every step of the way. The library at Loyola University has one entire floor devoted to medieval Catholic theology alone; the section on all of East and South Asian religion is nine inches wide. Somehow I manage to educate myself in Indian philosophy. The Jesuits throw Aquinas at me; I heave Shankara back on them. It is fun—we all enjoy it.

Now I have found a real swami! Educated in the cave monasteries of Uttar Pradesh, he has started a yoga center near Chicago. I doubt he has any American students as well versed in classical Indian thought as I, and stop by to see what I can offer him.

The swami has my number. "The world is *maya*, an illusion," I explain to a hapless yoga student impressionable enough to listen.

"Wrong!" the swami shouts. "Maya is the power and glory of God!"

"According to the *Yoga Sutras*, the individual soul must merge back into the absolute . . ." I start to explain on a similar occasion.

"Wrong! That is Vedanta, not yoga! Don't confuse the systems!"

The swami never misses an opportunity to humiliate me, and the larger the audience, the better. I put up with it because I still hope one day he will stop dodging my questions and give me some straight answers: Where did we come from? How can we get back?

The swami is not interested in intellectual discourse. He is interested in life. His goal is giving me some perspective on my attitudes and behavior, not addressing burning issues like whether Shankara was a closet Buddhist or whether Madhava was influenced by Christianity. As for experiencing pure consciousness, all he can advise me to do is sit quietly and breathe. I am in despair. Where can I find a teacher who will provide real instruction?

One day the swami discovers that, although I study meditational systems avidly, I do not practice any. He is furious. He calls me into his office. I am going to be initiated. He gives me a mantra but he doesn't say it with his mouth; he speaks it with his entire body, the way waterfalls and winds and thunder speak. It is the most beautiful sound I have ever heard. His fingers twitch and I feel an odd swirling in my chest, as if a vortex is uncurling there. It is such an eerily tangible sensation that I debate with myself for days afterward whether I had somehow been hypnotized. Nevertheless, I dutifully read the traditional literature which claims that the mantra and the supreme consciousness in the form of one's personal deity are somehow "one" and begin the tedious discipline of repeating the mantra.

§

I am flailing about for a topic for a paper in Sanskrit Philosophical Literature. A voice in my mind suggests, "The Goddess." I have read the *Ramayana* and Vaishnava devotional poetry and I can acknowledge Rama as an apt metaphor for God, that handsome and kind hearted prince who drove away the demons. I have read the *Gita* and the *Bhagavatam* and the *Mahabharata* and I can even see the charming and enigmatic and occasionally downright machiavellian Krishna as symbol for the supreme being. But "the Divine Mother"? The image sits uneasily with me, too reminiscent of my conflicted relationship with my own mother. Besides, the Indian Goddess is a horror, girdled with hacked limbs, lapping blood from a broken human skull. How could Ramakrishna, the gentle and sublime saint of 19th century Calcutta, have worshipped this encrustation of everything abominable?

The late philosopher-sage Aurobindo tries to explain, "The figure of Kali which is so terrible to European eyes is, as we know, the Mother of the universe who accepts this fierce aspect of destruction in order to slay the *asuras*, the powers of evil in man and the world." Hindus, he says, "do not deny the evil side of the world; they take that also, and adorn the Mother on the one hand with evil, murder, plague, and the most horrible things, while on the other hand, they represent her as overflowing with blessings." Among the worshippers of the Divine Mother, he says, are "both men and women, who in time of distress face danger bravely, and pray to her with unflinching faith and whole-hearted love, recognizing her grandeur and divine power even behind misfortune and calamity."

It strikes me that in the West good and evil are strictly dichotomized. Our God, untouched by the vagaries of this world, reigns from heaven; Satan is consigned to the sulfurous ghetto of hell. The ambivalent aspects of the Christian deity are never dwelt upon: why Yahweh prefers to keep Adam and Eve in ignorance, expelling them from Paradise when they threaten his supremacy; why he orders the Israelites to massacre the innocent Canaanites; why he demands the grisly blood sacrifice of Jesus. Ignoring the demonic qualities of divinity as well as the revelatory function of Lucifer, the Western mind compartmentalizes "God" and the "Devil," seeing them as two opposing forces ceaselessly at war. In the Universal Mother this duality is breached. There can be no force other than divine force, the Goddess tradition intimates. There is no devil, there is not even any "I" apart from divine reality.

The course instructor, a Hindu pandit, likes my paper. He has been thinking of translating several esoteric Goddess texts from the Sanskrit, but he needs a graduate student to help him with his English. He asks if I would be willing to assist.

§

The swami and I are at odds again. He has instructed me to meditate at my heart center; I am trying to explain that he is wrong. I actually had tried to do so but focusing beneath the chin was too difficult an exercise, and besides, when I could manage to bring my attention to my heart it felt like a clogged toilet, swirling sluggishly with anger, bitterness and self preoccupation. "I am a mental person," I wave toward my brain, "so I meditate in the head."

"That" he points to my head, "belongs to you. This" he points to my heart, "belongs to God."

Once more I am impressed by how poorly he understands me.

§

I am spending months at the pandit's home, sitting on the floor, learning to eat yogurt and rice with my fingers, taking dictation from Sanskrit.

In the ancient Shakta texts the Goddess introduces herself: "I am the perfect undifferentiated intelligence out of which the universe emerges, in which it flourishes, and into which it vanishes, as if it were merely a reflection on the surface of my awareness. The ignorant know me as the universe; the wise recognize me as their own being, glowing as the light of consciousness in their hearts."

When Panditji speaks of the Goddess his whole body glows. I am astonished that such a brilliant man, fully versed in the impersonal philosophy of Shankara, worships such a personal form of God. He must know that anthropomorphic images of divinity are only figments of humanity's imagination.

He quotes the Goddess speaking in the *Tripura Rahasya*: "My nondual form of pure awareness is very difficult to attain. If you cannot conceive of my absolute formless being, then think of me in whatever form most strongly appeals to you. In whatever form you visualize me, in that very form I will come to you." Panditji continues to quote the text: "The entirety of all the galaxies is a fraction of her energy, and yet she is fully present in the atom. Her grace is so vast that whenever even the least significant of us remembers her with love, she will certainly appear." His eyes are so bright it is as if he is looking directly at her; involuntarily I turn my head, and feel a flash of disappointment that she isn't there—in that split second before my mind interjects, "Of course she isn't!"

§

Today I am going to have a past-life regression. I feel skeptical, yet I determine to remain open to the experience for its entertainment value.

The hypnotist sends me deep into the past and asks what I see. Of course I see nothing; "This isn't working," I tell her. Then I realize I don't see anything because my eyes are closed. I open them and discover I am a Brahmin boy sitting in a quiet valley surrounded by low hills. I have been meditating on the sun. I look up into the sky and discover something extraordinary: the sun is alive, it actually hears my prayers, it responds subtly but definitively.

The hypnotist leads me to the boy's home. The older man he lives with is not his father but his teacher; he is living with a group of other children in this man's house in an atmosphere of great happiness and purity. The hypnotist asks me to meet the person who will have the most profound impact on this lifetime, and I am outside again, looking up into the hills. A dark, semi-naked figure with long, unkempt hair is wending his way down a steep path. He approaches me; I look more closely and discover it is actually a middle-aged woman with eyes infinitely aware. A yogini.

I want to speak with her but the hypnotist yanks me away. I am in my early twenties, performing the *pujas*, the Vedic rituals, required of a Brahmin priest. Many villagers are coming to me, thin dark people wanting children, wanting cattle, wanting revenge on irritating neighbors. I am deeply unhappy. The life I had felt in these rites is completely gone; I am going through the rituals mechanically—the gods I pretend to invoke are not present. I am sick of the petty concerns of the villagers. I want only to flee to the mountains and plunge into meditation, to touch the feet of God in *samadhi*, and to merge inextricably in all-pervading being.

"Why don't you go?" the hypnotist asks. I see myself surrounded by my family: beautiful, laughing children throwing their small bodies at my legs. I am heaving them in the air, catching them in my strong hands. If I leave, my family will starve. There is no one else to support them. I love these children. I love them almost more than God . . .

"How do you die?" the hypnotist asks gently. I am freezing. I have abandoned my family. I have fled into the mountains to practice yoga but I do not know how to maintain myself in this climate. I am pummeled by gusts of icy wind and blinded by driving hail. I know I cannot survive and my heart is shrieking in anguish, "Another life, and I have not realized God! Another life, and God is still as far from me as the stars from their reflections in the sea!" But a final unconsciousness is overpowering me and I know I must focus my mind. With the last of my strength I recall all my awareness into my brain and consciously enter the emptiness.

The hypnotist asks with a shaking voice, "What is your experience immediately after death?"

It is completely dark.

Something shimmers.

The flickering light is moving closer. Oh my God, it is Surya, the sun god of my youth! He smiles, he raises his hand in blessing, he steps aside. It is Indra, the king of heaven! He smiles, he blesses me. Then she stands there, the beautiful, effulgent Goddess. She smiles . . .

The hypnotist senses that something is wrong. "You are back in the present, you are calm, you are relaxed." Her voice is urgent.

I am doubled up on the floor. Someone is twisting my heart from my body. The pain is unbelievable. I have been longing for God forever. He still has not come. Lifetime after lifetime I have called. We are still separate.

I am freezing.

"You are back in the present. You are calm, you are relaxed."

§

I finally walk out of a painful and unfulfilling relationship. Several weeks later I am still aching, continually fighting back tears. I cannot sleep so I pick up a copy of the *Chandi*, India's most highly venerated Goddess text. A merchant and a king have lost everything they owned, betrayed by the people they loved. They seek out the sage Medhas and ask, "Why is it that although these people have hurt us so badly, we still care for them?"

"Ah," sighs Medhas, "it is all *Maya*—the illusory power of the Lord, the Great Goddess who deludes us all, and even God himself."

"Tell us about this Goddess," the king and the merchant plead.

"Well," Medhas sighs, "I'll tell you one of her adventures. Once there was a terrible demon named Nisumbha who had conquered the entire earth. He was so powerful he even managed to throw the gods out of heaven, and he stole all the most precious items in the three worlds."

"The gods realized that in this emergency there was only one being strong enough to help them, and that was the Mother of the Universe. So they called out to the supreme primordial energy, 'Hail to the eternally auspicious Goddess, the essence of energy and of matter, Who is both exceedingly gentle and exceedingly terrible, the horrifying night of delusion, the clarity of pure understanding, consciousness, intelligence, tranquillity, activity, our Mother, our death, hail to you! Ruler of all, before whom we lie prostrate with devotion, at this very moment you destroy all our misfortunes!'

"Now Nisumbha's demon minions were walking through the Himalayas that same day when they spotted the most beautiful woman in the world sitting alone on a mountain peak. They reported this to Nisumbha who sent them back with a message for the mysterious lady. 'I am the lord of the three worlds, and all you see is mine. Marry me, beautiful one, and I will make the universe yours!'

"'Oh that's an attractive offer,' the woman coyly replied. 'But I've taken a vow that I will only marry the man who conquers me in battle.'

"Nisumbha was infuriated at this impudent reply and sent his henchmen to bring her back by force. As they approached, however, they noticed that the enchanting maiden seemed taller than they remembered, and the closer they came, the larger she grew. The rock on which she was seated uncurled itself; it was actually a ferocious lion. The woman turned toward the demons and they were surprised to find she had many arms, and in each hand a deadly weapon."

Medhas goes on to graphically describe the ensuing battle in which the Mother of the Universe destroys Nisumbha's armies, his generals, and finally the king of demons himself. Some she strikes with her baton or trident, many she grinds between her teeth, others succumb to the millions of goddesses she effortlessly projects from her own being. Kali, the fiercest of all goddesses, the embodiment of divine retribution, erupts from the Mother's forehead.

When the terrible demon perished, order was restored to the universe and harmony returned to nature. Indra and the other gods thanked the Goddess but they had one more request: that whenever any devotee sincerely cries to her from the midst of sorrow and despair she reappear. The supreme universal power graciously accedes.

I wake up the following morning expecting the familiar pool of grief to engulf me and am amazed to discover that it has totally evaporated. I feel absolutely fine; the conflicts and sense of loss around leaving the relationship have completely resolved.

I handle the *Chandi* with new respect. Somehow the Goddess fought a battle for me last night. And somehow the peace she bequeathed the world has nestled in my heart.

§

I am sitting alone in the meditation room; the others have sensibly slipped off to bed hours earlier. I am so frustrated I could burst. I have been living in this ashram for three years but feel no closer to the divine than ever. My life is a mockery; I have been dancing around the dinner table since I was fourteen years old, but have yet to taste the fare.

I move my awareness to my heart. Then I remember Panditji's face as he remembers the Goddess. I feel my heart begin to crack. "Mother . . ."

In that moment ecstasy so intense it feels like it is lifting me toward the ceiling sweeps through my body, rushing up, exploding. It doesn't stop. It surges and surges and surges like waves of exquisite bliss. She is here. I feel Her as palpably as if I could see her. She is all around. She is breathing in my body. She has thrown open my eyes in giddy astonishment at Her own exultant being! She laughs out loud—she is remembering who she is!

§

Life is a playful charade built around eager pilgrimages to the meditation room. Everyone is remarking how much I've changed. "You look great!" "It's such a pleasure being around you!" I smile as if I am flattered but I know it's not me. It's her.

How effortlessly I enter that ecstasy now. How wonderful that each day it lingers with me a little longer. And like music it has octaves: in the lower registers I remember her promises of love and reassurance in the scriptures, I picture her face, I recall the fantastic stories of her play with devotees throughout history, and tears of joy stream down my cheeks. In the mid range a flood of bliss swells through my body, carrying me miles beyond myself. In the higher octaves all emotive content falls away, and I experience a peace and silence so deep it is like death—except it is absolute, perfect life. These are her moods. I am so, so deeply grateful that she is sharing them with me.

§

"I don't meditate," confides a friend who has lived in the ashram for ten years. "I wish I could feel more enthusiastic about it. It's so—dry." She reminds me so much of myself until a few months ago that I could cry.

"How can you sit for so long?" she asks me earnestly. "While you're sitting for meditation, you're absolutely glowing."

I try to explain that meditating is like a tryst with a lover. It's full of delight. It pulsates with love. My friend walks away, incredulous.

I want to shout to everyone that we have just won the lottery, all of us, we have all won millions and millions of dollars. Why then, when the postman comes to deliver the check, do we protest, "No wait, I have to pay off my credit cards first! Let me take care of my mortgage payments, then I'll deposit the check. After I retire, when the doctor tells me I have six more months to live, at the moment before death, then I'll accept the prize."

The very air around us is glimmering with grace. Why believe we'll realize God years from now, after many years of spiritual practice, after many more lifetimes of practice? She's right here, right now! We don't have to wait another second.

I am spinning with the reality of her. Every breath is a miracle. Every moment is a revelation. The Great One is in us already. We are billionaires!

§

Here, in this old Sanskrit text, I gasp when I find my mantra. The swami never told me what it meant—that it is her name—the name of the very aspect of the Goddess I have been worshipping. All those years, repeating this mantra, without even realizing it, I had been calling her name. The mantra and the deity are one. All along, I was invoking her. All along, she was coming. All along, she was here.

§

Only one thing is stronger than spiritual sublimity, and that is common sense. I am now experiencing a powerful resurgence of common sense. I have been looking into the neurophysiological literature on brain states, especially intrigued by endorphins. Exercising, art, meditation, many activities can release hormones triggering drug-like exaggerated states of well-being. Many mystical experiences, including out-of-body traveling, near-death visions and ecstatic trances, can be simulated by electronically stimulating the cortex.

I look at the lives of several well known contemporary meditation teachers. Preaching the most sublime philosophies, they live the most dissolute lives. If higher states of consciousness are real, why have so many masters given themselves over to promiscuous sex and alcohol?

I am completely deflated. I don't believe anything anymore—not even my own experience. There is no limit—no limit—to the power of self delusion. I smile ruefully as I recall the passage from the *Chandi* in which the sage Medhas admits that everything—God Himself—is overcome by the power of Maya, the greatest Goddess of them all.

§

I am having lunch with an engineering student. He mentions a newspaper account of a woman who believes she has seen a ghost. He laughs.

"You believe in ghosts," I venture.

I am met with a stare of incredulity and even hostility. "Think you can prove that?" he drawls.

"Sure I can. If I take you and lock you up, alone, at night, in the mortuary, surrounded by dead bodies, and switch of the light, I'll bet dollars to dimes that you'll catch yourself glancing nervously over your shoulder some time that night. In fact, I'll bet that if a cool breeze blew down your neck, you would shit in your pants."

The budding engineer laughs uncomfortably. He knows I am right, but he won't think about what it means, think about that part of our hearts that goes on believing even when our minds know it can't be true.

We are all haunted. Something from the dark is pursuing us. What is it? Who is it?

§

My husband is an India buff and he is eager to take me to Devi Mandir, a Goddess temple in northern California. Sri Ma lives there, cooking for guests, sewing clothing she gives to anyone who stops by, scrubbing the bathrooms after worshippers leave. I have heard of Sri Ma. She is from Kamakhya, the holiest of the Goddess centers in India, and is one of north India's most respected women saints.

We enter the Mandir just as the *kanya kumari puja* is beginning. In this ancient Tantric rite a young girl is worshipped with flowers and sandalwood paste and rose water and honey, as if she were actually Bala—the Goddess in form of a girl child. A two-year-old blond in a stunning green and gold sari has been selected for the role and my mind is objecting, "They can't possibly be serious! No self-respecting two-year-old will stand for this!"

I glance over at Sri Ma; she is so still she is almost invisible. The pujari begins the ceremony, chanting in Sanskrit and waving a yak tail fan. Remarkably, the two-year-old does not fidget. Her face has changed. Her eyes seem a thousand years old. She sits quietly for 45 minutes, accepting the pujari's gifts, raising her right hand in blessing each time he requests her to. She breaks away from her seat only once—to lay her hand in blessing first on her mother's head, then on her father's, and then she returns to the seat. The puja continues.

It is an hour-and-a-half ride home but neither Johnathan nor I say a word. We both have the uncanny sense that something sacred has occurred—that with our own physical eyes we have actually seen the Goddess.

§

And now I am on Holy Hill, Berkeley, California. I am in seminary, sifting through Greek and Hebrew texts, digging up the roots of my culture's religious heritage. The professor in my New Testament course has been particularly helpful. We pour over the New Testament and works of the early church fathers in painstaking detail, examining closely the extensive research into the culture and language of first-century Palestine. It creates a fascinating and sobering picture. Somewhere between the demolition of the temple in Jerusalem (and with it the fledgling Christian Jewish community, comprising the few remaining individuals who actually knew the radical rabbi from Galilee) and the rampant success of Paul's mission to the Gentiles, the historical Jesus was almost completely lost. Paul managed to train the new Christians' attention away from Jesus' emphatic social and ethical message to his own Hellenized version of a mythical "Christ," and this unauthorized version became the "truth" of countless following generations. We learn how the books of the New Testament were fabricated, and how the early Christians understood these works to be partially fictional; how in fact many of them rejected outright spiritual novels like the Biblical book of John.

It is refreshing to study Christianity with a professor who is not afraid to look historical reality in the eye. I am impressed enough to attend his Sunday sermon at the North Bay church where he is minister. It leaves me aghast: he is teaching Christ crucified as brazenly as any fundamentalist, even though he knows the faith he is teaching his congregation is false. Know the truth and the truth will make you freak. He has a family to support; the truth will not pay his salary.

§

This is a skeptical age. Physiologists, data in hand, show us that lights and sounds experienced in meditation are only flickers of neural impulses. Moral sense can be removed from the frontal lobes, memory with a swatch of tissue.

From Vedic times, the sages warned spiritual aspirants against the guys with the black hats: the Charvakas, the materialists, the ones who believe in death. But this is the first time in history that modern, scientific Charvakas have come gunning for us with live ammunition.

I am staring at the wall. In the seams of the plaster I see wizards and gorillas and a woman with a trident riding a lion. Everywhere the mind projects meaning. On the surface of the infinite, chaotic, violent and indifferent universe I project the face of a benevolent Mother. Does she exist only in my mind? Or, as the yogis claim, do I exist only in hers?

§

"Hey bitch!" It is my Chicago swami. He knows few things upset me more than a macho swagger.

This time I do not take the bait. "Yes sir?"

He raises an eyebrow in surprise. "You have overcome your anger. I am pleased." He turns to his train of votaries and praises me profusely. He is still trying to knock me off center. He wants to see if I will swell up with pride.

I claim my center. He cannot take it from me anymore. I smile as I walk away. He gave me my center. The guru! What a character!

He calls me back. Looking into his eyes is like looking into the core of a nuclear reactor. The power, the energy, is awesome.

"All of the body is in the mind," he spits into the gutter, "but not all of the mind is in the body."

I reel away as if he had struck me.

§

I am curious to meet Ammachi, a living saint my own age. She grew up in southwest India, the victim of shocking familial abuse, but rather than surrender to bitterness and despair she surrendered to the Divine Mother and lived every moment in remembrance of God. If she suddenly realized she had walked several feet without thinking of God, she would literally retrace her steps and walk them again, mind contritely fixed on the feet of the Lord. When she was in her early twenties the Divine Mother appeared to her as a mass of light, commanded her to serve others, and merged into her body.

Ammachi is now one of India's best loved saints. Though she has never read the scriptures—she left school during the fourth grade to serve her family—scholars from all over South Asia come to her for explanations of abstruse scriptural passages. Ancient Upanishadic truths, rituals and mantras that she never learned, she teaches others spontaneously. They pour out of her like milk.

Some devotees have persuaded her to visit America. She speaks no English so she sings for us, a pleasant enough evening but I am tired and eager to go home. My husband refuses to leave without receiving her blessing so we wait in line for two hours while she counsels and embraces each person in the crowd. Finally standing before her I offer politely, "I wish I could be like you."

She laughs and responds in bubbling Malalayam. An Indian translates, "Mother says she is only a crazy girl. If you want to become like her, you would have to be crazy too." This answer startles me so much I look back at her eyes and see there—madness. This woman is completely crazy for God. Nothing else exists for her. All my life I have been crazy for knowledge, for money, for men, for food. I will have to offer myself—and this time completely—to the madness of Divine love.

I spend weeks with Ammachi, watching her like a hawk. She is in *sahaj samadhi*, her devotees claim, the continual state of absorption in God. I am watching to see if she slips out of that state. I scan every facial expression, each encounter with strangers, with devotees, for any telltale trace of egotism. Uninterrupted compassion, equality of vision, total equanimity, untiring service (literally untiring—she does not sleep!), perfect and spontaneous wisdom, all the qualities the scriptures claim should be evident in a realized soul, this woman actually displays in her life. It is amazing. She never leaves the present. Each day she personally welcomes thousands of seekers, and She is completely present with each one. Her own body does not exist for her. She is only there to serve and inspire.

I see a remarkable woman, a genuine saint of the caliber of Ramana Maharshi or Anandamayi Ma. Her devotees, however, see a physical embodiment of the Goddess Herself, a human incarnation of the Mother of the Universe. Miracles swirl around her. Not all are so readily amenable to droll psychosomatic explanations.

Why do I hold back, I wonder. Why is it so hard to believe, to trust, when in my heart I do believe? The Mother of the Universe gathers me in her arms and strokes my back, whispering to me some of the few words of English she knows, "My daughter. My daughter."

My heart is breaking. I see You, Mother, but I don't feel what you are feeling. Once, when I was fourteen years old, the hem of your skirt grazed my being. But all these years later we are still separate. Mother, I have been calling you forever! It is not enough to look at you as if you are the Divine mother. When the boundaries of my limited being wash completely and permanently away, dissolved in the solvent of your grace, when your reality becomes my reality, then . . . then I will know you are my true Mother!

Can the absolute reality manifest itself as a five foot girl from a fishing village in India? It's crazy! Mother make me crazy like you!

We have plunged into the 1990's, and all around me the world is tumbling down. Great nations are fragmenting, the environment is wrecked, many of my friends are out of work. My husband and I don't know how long we can hang on to our jobs as the economy spirals downward. Our wretched materialistic culture is crumbling into sharp, tiny pieces.

She's still playing with me, that perverse girl who projected this universe out of/onto her own being. She is swathed in layer after layer of falsehood, mistaken beliefs, limited concepts, misperceptions. Or is it layer after layer of truth?

A pandit once told me that Maya is our friend; She gives us the means to overcome her: meditation, love, selfless service, the guru. A swami once told me that Maya is the power and glory of God, the splendor of our own being. She is our savior; she reveals to us the way to freedom—at her leisure.

I am learning to revel in change because change is the nature of unchanging being. I am learning to let go of my possessions before she snatches them away. I am living as if there really is a conscious, caring Goddess because maybe there is. If there is, she has certainly done everything she can to show me so. And if she doesn't exist, well then her power of delusion is even stronger than I imagined!

Where am I now? I don't know. Am I on track? I'm not sure. I feel like I'm standing in the shadow of the Goddess. Everything around me is dark. But it feels like someone is standing behind me, someone who casts a long shadow. Someone vast.

It is completely dark. In my heart, something is shimmering.

Linda Johnson, has been fascinated with India's spiritual tradition from childhood. Raised a Christian in Chicago, she managed to ferret out information about the psychology, cosmology, and the feminine nature of the divine in Indian texts. She studied with pandits, swamis, and yoginis, finally traveling to the subcontinent and South Asia for research.

Linda holds an English degree, *magna cum laude*, from Loyola University of Chicago and a Master of Science degree in Eastern Studies, *summa cum laude*, from the University of Scranton.

She has published several articles on women's spirituality and on South Asian myth and philosophy, as well as contributing essays on the Hindu understanding of the Goddess in *Uncoiling the Snake: Ancient Patterns in Contemporary Women's Lives* (Harper-Collins) and *Daughters of the Goddess: The Women Saints of India* (Yes International).

Adonai Zeus Shekhinah Elim Ogun Kat Buddha
Wyame Hel Rama Mitra Odomankoma Jupiter Het
Heru Agni Cagn Thor Brahma Tangaroa Father
Lugaba Papang Diana Al-Rahman Cerridwen Ahone
Yoma' Tirawa Atius G___ El M___ngua
Quetzalcoatl Hamakom ___ddai
Atibruku Moma YH Bunj___ ___iwa
Saraswati Inanna Miriru___ ___ong
Tonantzin Yuskeha Bha___ ___ead
Olodumare Shyama Ekve___ ___eru
Nurrundere Daramilun ___tzeir
Hecate Chi Musubi Hin___ ___suna
Nanderuvucu Erishkigal ___man
Tsui-goab Ometeotl Osi___ ___chtli
Surya Elohim Nyankop___ Ilu
Woden Great Spirit Lesa Boyjerh El Dan Gongoro
Poseidon Chineke Nhialic Aciek Kari Auset Tcuwut
Makai Wakantanka Inari Ha-Qadosh barukh hu'
Tara Krishna Avaloket-iswara Rabb Goryo Qat Oke
Nurunderi Indra Shang-ti Amaterasu Ohmikami
Kannon Quan Yin Ise Lakshmi Awonawilona Bast
Omecihuatl Ruhanga Kosane Sophia Dionysus Ixchel
Mawu Ra Ardanariswara Oluwa Deng Hanuman
uNkulunkulu Kanobo Ngai Shamayim Cybele Dakini
Nataraj Pachamama Susanoo Katonda Avlukpo Eloah
Isis Temaukel Eleda Gaia Laxmi Mahmanmu-rok
Odin El-al Herukhuti Viracocha Marduk Ashira Biral
Shaddai Dzingbe Djohu-ma-di-hutu Astarte Ndengei
Koyatu Baha'u'llah Marrigan Baiame Om Pelepelewa
Durga Orisha Nyame Techaronhiawakhon Chukwu
Uvolovu Brahman Nephtys Ha-Maqom Tehuti Maat
Digambara Val Tik Chaitanya Amana Kwoth Num
Colok Nabango Fumeripitsj Shiva Varuna Lukanga
Bala Atibluku Karu Allah Sing Nainuema Artemis
Kartikeya Kuanyin Yelafaz T'ien Baal Shakti
Athena Olorun Nemesis Sheela-na-Gig Bhavartarini
Jesus Horus Izanagi Sebek Waq Ishtar Ti Seker
BegoTanutanu Sat Nam Kali Mirirul Bhavatarini
Tsui-goab Hatzur Brahman Ubusuna Tonantzin
YHVH Apollo Nana God Almighty Hu Vishnu Om

Be Still and Know

Teijo Munnich

A four-year-old child wandered into a garden and walked along the path, smelling the air, feeling the breeze, looking at the earth. A family of chives beckoned to her. She stooped and picked a chive, ate it. Yum yum. Awareness of God.

A five-year-old child sat in church next to her mother. Church is a quiet place, a nice place. She felt warm and calm. As the celebrant spoke, her mother held her hand. She looked at the speaker's gentle eyes, noticed his kind voice. He wore a dress just like the one God wears in her Bible. This must be God.

A six-year-old child has reached the age of reason, according to the Catholic Church and, therefore, at that point can begin formal training in religion. This is what I was taught about God:

God is our Father who lives in heaven. God created heaven and earth and all its creatures. People were made in God's image. Our purpose is to love and honor God and to keep His laws. God loves us. God is male. God is almighty, omnipresent, all-knowing, all-powerful, all-merciful, all-just. When you write about God, always capitalize his name or any words that refer to him. We show our love for God by keeping the commandments which he dictated to a man named Moses, on Mount Sinai; if we don't obey these commandments, we could go to hell when we die. It is difficult to talk to God directly, so if you want to talk to God, the best way is to go through a priest; or possibly one of the saints could help you. My third-grade teacher added that if we ever doubted God's existence, we should say a prayer. I had no reason not to believe any of this. At that point, I didn't have any doubts.

When I was a teenager, I wondered, "If God is all-merciful, would he really send someone to hell?" I asked the priest. This priest was a modern thinker and he agreed with me that it is quite unlikely that God would send someone to hell. My mind rushed on. "Well, maybe there isn't even a hell at all?" He couldn't agree. For him, that meant there isn't a heaven, either. I didn't understand his logic, but it did get me thinking that maybe there isn't a heaven. I thanked him for his help and left.

Now I was wondering if there really were places such as heaven and hell. If God is everywhere and in everything, doesn't that mean God is in me and in all things in the world? If God lives in heaven, does that mean he just goes there to sleep, and at that time does he stop being everywhere else? How can God live in heaven and be everywhere at the same time?

My mind moved on. If God is in everything, that must mean that everything is God. I said a prayer; this was starting to seem heretical. It was becoming difficult for me to continue thinking like this. Even though I doubted the existence of a place called hell, what if I was wrong? Then something interesting happened. Whenever I tried to ask these questions, the people I asked became evasive. They neither answered them nor totally ignored them. What they did was tell me to go elsewhere for my answers. So, I went elsewhere, out of church and into a world where others were asking the same questions.

When I was a young child, I believed in God through direct experience, subjective understanding of a higher power based on my interface with life. In school I was given information about God that had been gleaned from experiences and ideas of other spiritual seekers—objective information that had become tradition. But finally I wanted to know God in my own way again. I began talking directly to God about this, not using words of formal prayers but my words, asking my questions, explaining my understandings. I looked for manifestations of God: I went to the woods, to the lakes, to the mountains. I listened, I watched. I learned how to meditate, sitting still, watching my breath.

Grandma died. She had always claimed to be a nonbeliever. As she struggled with her last breaths, I found myself telling her, "Don't worry, Grandma, you'll go to heaven." That night I felt Grandma's presence in my room, asking me, "What now?" I was afraid. I felt responsible, like I was obliged to help her. I looked up. "God, help me!" I prayed. There was no answer. What should I do? Grandma was waiting. I tried to be quiet, to be present. I sat like this for a minute, taking a few deep breaths. As I became quieter, I became slowly aware that God is in me. I stopped looking outside myself for help. I knew I could deal with this. "Grandma," I said, "You're on your own." She left.

"Be still, and know that I am God." (Ps. 46:10).

That's all there is. It's that simple. Last week, I was walking down the path toward the meditation hall. I looked down and saw a patch of chives. Turning to my friend, I smiled and said, "Chives!" She laughed. "It doesn't take much to make you happy!" I looked down again. The chives waved.

Zen teachers often explain the process of realization in this way: First, mountain is mountain; then, mountain is not mountain; finally, mountain is mountain. When you reach the last stage, your experience is essentially the same as in the first stage. But at this point, no one can confuse you with something different.

A tiny bird is perched outside my window. "Good morning, Teijo." I kiss the bird with my joy. God is alive and speaking to me again.

Teijo Munnich is a Buddhist priest of the Soto Zen tradition. In the summer of 1975, during a quest for a spiritual teacher, she met Dainin Katagiri Roshi of the Zen Meditaiton Center and became his student. Although her intention at that time was simply to learn meditation from Katagiri Roshi, she was ordained in 1981 and became one of his twelve dharma heirs in 1989. She continued to practice with him until his death in 1990.

Teijo received formal training at Tassajara Zen Mountain Center in Carmel Valley, California, and Hosshinji Sodo in Obama, Japan. She is presently living in Asheville, North Carolina.

Adonai Zeus Shekhinah Elim Ogun Kat Buddha
Wyame Hel Rama Mitra Odomankoma Jupiter Het
Heru Agni Cagn Thor Brahma Tangaroa Father
Lugaba Papang Diana Al-Rahman Cerridwen Ahone
Yoma' Tirawa Atius _____ El M_____ngua
Quetzalcoatl Hamakom _____ ____ddai
Atibruku Moma YH Bur_____ aiwa
Saraswati Inanna Miriri_____ aong

Goddess Love

Oyo Fummilayo

Tonantzin Yuskeha Bha_____ Head
Olodumare Shyama Ekv_____ Heru
Nurrundere Daramilun _____ otzeir
Hecate Chi Musubi Hin_____ suna
Nanderuvucu Erishkigal_____ man
Tsui-goab Ometeotl Os_____ chtli
Surya Elohim Nyankop_____ Ilu
Woden Great Spirit Lesa Boyjern El Dan Gongoro
Poseidon Chineke Nhialic Aciek Kari Auset Tcuwut
Makai Wakantanka Inari Ha-Qadosh barukh hu'
Tara Krishna Avaloket-iswara Rabb Goryo Qat Oke
Nurunderi Indra Shang-ti Amaterasu Ohmikami
Kannon Quan Yin Ise Lakshmi Awonawilona Bast
Omecihuatl Ruhanga Kosane Sophia Dionysus Ixchel
Mawu Ra Ardanariswara Oluwa Deng Hanuman
uNkulunkulu Kanobo Ngai Shamayim Cybele Dakini
Nataraj Pachamama Susanoo Katonda Avlukpo Eloah
Isis Temaukel Eleda Gaia Laxmi Mahmanmu-rok
Odin El-al Herukhuti Viracocha Marduk Ashira Biral
Shaddai Dzingbe Djohu-ma-di-hutu Astarte Ndengei
Koyatu Baha'u'llah Marrigan Baiame Om Pelepelewa
Durga Orisha Nyame Techaronhiawakhon Chukwu
Uvolovu Brahman Nephtys Ha-Maqom Tehuti Maat
Digambara Val Tik Chaitanya Amana Kwoth Num
Colok Nabango Fumeripitsj Shiva Varuna Lukanga
Bala Atibluku Karu Allah Sing Nainuema Artemis
Kartikeya Kuanyin Yelafaz T'ien Baal Shakti
Athena Olorun Nemesis Sheela-na-Gig Bhavartarini
Jesus Horus Izanagi Sebek Waq Ishtar Ti Seker
BegoTanutanu Sat Nam Kali Mirirul Bhavatarini
Tsui-goab Hatzur Brahman Ubusuna Tonantzin
YHVH Apollo Nana God Almighty Hu Vishnu Om

For eons the Sky Spirit roamed the cosmos, alone and lonely. It is believed by some that when he viewed the planet earth and felt her warmth, he decided to rest there. Earth welcomed him and received him into her bosom to comfort him. He wept with joy at her beauty. Firm and round was she, and lush, with green leafy ferns for hair. As his tears of joy fell down upon the ground, green grass sprouted. And all species of flowering plants—brilliant yellows, hues of magenta, and deep blues—rooted themselves into the ground. Trees sprouted, pointing their nimble fingers in all directions.

For billions of years, this Owner of the Sky courted Mother Earth in grand fashion. He commanded comets and meteorites to set the sky ablaze with wondrous dancing light. He formed the milky way and all the starry constellations just for her amusement. The Sky Spirit loved. And the Goddess loved.

The Sky Spirit and Mother Earth decided to unite in harmony to live and rule together forever. The blessed mother became the bride of the holy father. Their movement in the dance of union molded the mountains and the valleys. The holy father filled the blessed mother with visions of all those who would inhabit earth. She received his seed of the future; the creatures would look much like the heavenly bodies, and share the same characteristics of those who guarded the heavens.

From their union came all creatures large and small, winged and finned. Some walked on two legs and others crawled on all fours. During the laborious birthing of the earth's creatures, Mother Nature moaned and writhed, giving birth in many diverse places. And as she gave birth, the consciousness of being was born in all creatures.

She instructed her children in language and in the dynamic laws of the universe. She taught about the interrelationship between all things in the universe animate or inanimate, casual or non casual, for all are made up of atoms. She taught them of intelligence, for every living thing possesses intelligence. She taught that no matter how humble any life form may be, it revolves around an inward growth of awareness and awakening. Even a vine in the dark will seek sunlight. All creatures leaned themselves forward to listen and to learn from the nurturer of all life as she taught.

"Intentions are the strongest motivations of conduct," she said. "No matter what activity one performs, no matter how difficult or tedious, no matter what sacrifices one makes to accomplish the tasks, it is the purpose and the way one goes about the activity that determines its whole meaning and end results." Finally she taught all creatures about the dynamic law of life and death and the laws of harmony and balance. How the blessed mother loved watching her children grow!

While the Owner of the Sky, the holy father, rested, the heavenly bodies stood guard. For what seemed like thousands of years to the mortal mind, the father slept only a twinkling of a nap. And when the he awakened, he summoned the sun for light so that he could see all the children that he and the blessed mother had produced. The creators of all things perfect and good stood smiling, overjoyed at their wondrous children. Every creature was distinctively different, yet, each one was the same. And the father and mother gave tender care to each one of their children.

Nurturing took an enormous amount of time, however, and the divine parents found that they could not spend much time together worshipping each other. How they longed for the union and the dance of one! So the creators of all decided to bring forth a helpmate. This one would possess the spiritual, mental, and emotional attributes of the great ones. This one would possess the mystery of the blessed mother. This one would possess the will of the holy father. This miracle would be called: World Ordered Macrocosmic Being (WOMB). This being would have the ability to create ideas and to put those ideas into form.

The heavenly bodies prepared the Sky Father for the night of union and the dance of one. The Keeper of the White Fire came forth to fashion a long and firm rod of fire as a gift for the blessed mother. The milky way formed an arch of stars around the head of the Owner of the Sky. The sun turned his back to allow the full face of the moon to shine down upon the path that the Sky Father would take to his bride. As the holy one moved across the vast face of the land, sparks of white fire emanated from the rod he held in his hands. His footsteps caused loud, rolling noises from the sky.

The blessed Mother readied the marriage bed for their union. Jasmine flowers, rose petals, lavender leaves, and branches from the wisteria trees were gathered. The small flying creatures came together to give beautiful song for the dance of one. As the Mother of All Nature smiled in anticipation, the wind rose up and rushed through her fern-like locks leaving whispers of love in her ears and upon her mind. Her breath came in gasps of excitement as the Sky Father drew nearer. When she exhaled, the trees shivered.

Face to face with each other the Father of the Sky presented the Blessed One with the rod of white fire. Each one holding the rod at opposite ends, the blessed Mother and the Sky Father began to dance. They were drunk with delight in each other's company. When they touched, sparks of white light jumped from their bodies and lightning was born. The holy Sky Spirit laughed from deep within the valleys of his great body and thunder was born. All creatures rejoiced in their union. And in the second coming of the holy ones, the Womb Goddess was brought forth. This Goddess would possess all the wonders of the universe and all the secret mysteries of the earth.

The Womb Goddess learned quickly and performed all her tasks with precision and speed. In the evening she would walk with the holy ones, and watch as they performed the union of oneness. Sometimes she longed for a companion for herself. One day, while walking with the holy ones, she communicated through the sound of one mind her desire for companionship. The father and mother took counsel and decided to bring forth a new creation. This creature would be the Macrocosmically Anointed New-Being (MAN).

In celebration at the decision, the Womb Goddess served the blessed ones the finest nectar that the fruit could sacrifice. And the blessed ones served the Goddess. The heavenly bodies stood guard, allowing all creatures great and small to attend the feast. So consumed with excitement was the Goddess that she fainted away into a deep sleep. Upon seeing this, the holy ones laughed, sending roars of thunder through the air. And work on the new being began.

The holy ones then spoke: "She is of us and of our spirit. Her mate will be made of earth and water. She possesses all the secrets and mysteries of the universe and nature. He will possess the gifts of reason and free will. And he will possess the seed that will bring forth fruit of its kind. She will bear the fruit in due season from her second womb where the rivers flow from the hollow valley of her body. We will live in their hearts and they will worship us." Then, as if with one mind, the holy ones scooped the earth from the ground, and they fashioned the dirt into Man.

When Man was completed, the creators placed his form in the position of oneness—face to face, and mouth to mouth—with the Womb Goddess. All creatures large and small, winged and finned, watched. The heavenly bodies watched as the two became one. In this position of oneness the Womb Goddess was transformed into the World Ordered Macrocosmically Anointed Newbeing (WOMAN). And into man she blew the first breath of life.

For the third time all the universe came into harmony and the creators smiled. The Earth Mother summoned the moon to cover the face of the sun for a little while longer and all the creatures found their way to slumber.

§

I'm not sure if I grew up with a mixture of religions or with mixed-up religions. It was very important for my mother that all of her children carry the same last name (though it didn't matter who your father was), wear clean underwear when you were going away from home, and be baptized before you were twelve years old. Until I was nine years old, I was brought up mainly in relatives' and friends' homes. I would come home on short visits to my mother's house. No one else in my family lived away from home. Just me.

My first bout with religion came when I was five, but my first experience with spirituality was when I was about three or four years old. I was virtually raised by my cousin, Anna. She was a madam, a bootlegger, and a part-time voodoo woman. I just thought that she was the greatest lady I had ever met. I lived with her and I did not want for anything. She and my "uncle Rueben" had no other children. I can remember the house always being fun, filled with people and laughter. They called her "Two-Headed," but I didn't find out that she was a spiritualist until she was dead and I was grown. Some of my mother's relatives thought I shouldn't be living with cousin Anna, but Mama never paid them any attention.

Cousin Anna took care of her father, who was my mother's uncle. Uncle Tom was the first to die. I came home to Louisville with Anna to his funeral. I was three years old. Uncle Tom was laid out in our family home in the living room. The day after his funeral, I was playing in the back room of the house when I noticed that the room had gotten extremely cold and dark. I tried to run, but I could not move, and before my eyes I saw the figure of a person sitting in what appeared to be a throne, with two figures standing beside it. The seated figure began to speak. It told me not to be afraid, for it did not come to harm me. It said that it had come to ask me if I wanted to go with it to another place. It told me to think carefully, and all I had to do was say yes and I would not have to live in this place. I told this figure that I wanted to stay. Three times it asked the same question, and three times I said that I wanted to stay.

Then the figure left as it had come, and the room returned to its normal state. I got up from the bed and went to my mother. I told her what had happened, but she said that I was just grieving over Uncle Tom's death, letting my imagination run away with me. No one believed me; my brothers made fun of me, and my sisters sneered at me. They put me to bed and that was that.

I was so glad to go back to Ohio with cousin Anna. There I didn't have the pressure of children bothering me. But that did not last for long. Shortly after Uncle Tom's death, cousin Anna got sick and died. It was back home for me.

Sometimes I would hear my mother talking about how afraid she was that cousin Anna had made voodoo spells on people and that her mysterious death was some sort of ritual sacrifice. But if it all was so bad, why did she let me go to live there? My mother took that answer to her grave; I am still confused.

I became a baptized Christian when I was six years old. We were always taught that if you did anything wrong before you turned twelve, then your parents would be punished for it. Well, my mother said that she would not die and go to hell for anybody except herself. Therefore, everyone in her house whose "behind pointed toward the ground" would become a Christian.

So we began to go to church almost every day. We were made to join the choir and other youth organizations. I hated going to church, and all that went with it except the music and the Lord's Supper. I didn't understand the sermons, and I did not understand how people could get all worked up about music but not the sermon words. And I didn't understand why you had to give money to God. God owned everything, so why did we have to pay him? I never saw Jesus come to church even though my Sunday School teacher said that he was alive and lived everywhere. And every Jesus I ever saw in books was white. The preacher said everyone was created in the image of God and that Jesus was God's son. And God was our Father in Heaven. So why was I not white? Where did I fit in?

I decided to search, for surely the answer was out there somewhere. My first inclination was to find a boyfriend who was not a Baptist. And I did. I found a boyfriend who was a Catholic. I liked the Catholic faith because they had short services. But they spoke a language that was foreign to me. My friend told me it was Latin. He taught me the words and their meanings but I thought it all lacked passion. The service was so mechanical that I became bored with it. Besides, not only was Jesus still white there, but the priest was too.

My mother was becoming disturbed with me. She did not understand why I could not be satisfied with the explanations the Sunday School teachers gave of the scriptures. I told her that we never learned anything new. "Every year we have the same lessons, and the pastor gives the same sermons year after year after year."

In my quest for the right religion, I was neglecting my spiritual path because I didn't know that I had a spiritual path. Not knowing did not make any difference, however, for I was still being visited by many beings in my sleep and in my quiet hours. By this time I was not discussing my visions with anyone, for I too believed that I was letting my imagination run away with me. I began to read many books on mythology and voodoo and satanic possession. Not good books, mind, but cheap novels.

I remember being visited one night by the figure who came to me when I was three. I knew this time that he was a man being. I called him He Who Sits on a Throne. He sat in front of my bed and told me I was to fight many battles. He said that I would bring light and healing when I passed through the stage of initiation after the battles. He said to remember that truth was the way and not to fear it. He said that through death we live. Now that really got my attention! He told me that suffering was not ordained sacred, but that trials made us strong. As he spoke, pictures of many places, people, and events both past and future flitted before my eyes. It was hard for me to keep up with all the images. Before he left me, there was cousin Anna telling me that if I listened, everything would be all right. She said for me to just call her when I needed her.

I was grown then, with children, and I began to go to church again. This time I went to a fundamental Baptist church, the "I believe everything in the Bible from cover to cover" kind of Baptist church. You could clap your hands, stomp your feet, and shout hallelujah! but if you were a woman, you could only cook, take care of the children, and pray in small women only groups. I saw trouble up the river!

I soon became a Saturday morning Bible-busting, door-knocking "Jesus Loves You and so do I" card-carrying neighborhood missionary for a predominantly White Baptist church. It was located in the suburbs of the city where many of their White members lived. This church could boast of a bus ministry of sometimes over a thousand young people from all over our city.

We brought them in. We brought them in from the highways and hedges. We brought them in to a white Jesus who did not come to church, and to God who owned everything but still made you pay to serve him. We brought them in until the gasoline crisis of the eighties hit our church.

There were twenty-one youth ministers. Since I was not a man, I could not be a minister in the church, but I was accepted as a ministry assistant and I could attend the Saturday prayer breakfast. The minister of the church began his talk at the breakfast by saying that God "lay something heavy on his heart." He continued, "The youth church has grown in leaps and bounds. And while the youth population has grown, the offering has not increased. The church has successful missions in the west side of the city (predominantly African American), but because of the high prices of fuel and bus maintenance and the low amount of offerings collected in those areas, God has told me that the little Black children are going to have to find other churches." By now he was crying real tears, and looking at me and the other two Black workers. I could not believe my ears. My family and I had gone to this church when services were held in the barn. We had paid for a load of bricks to help build the new edifice. Well, Jesus was still White, and I could not afford this God anymore.

But I must be very honest. I did learn new things about the Bible, and I did hear new sermons. I learned the difference between religion and spirituality, too. So I did not come away empty-handed nor did I leave empty-headed. I found out that in the small women's prayer groups, change took place. I learned that the women of that White male organization moved more spiritual energy than most of their counterparts. I learned that the women had an effect on the environment around them. I learned that I did not have to pay God in money. I learned that it did not matter what color Jesus was. I learned that what did matter is that we are all created in the image of God and that we all have the power of God "upon our lives." I also learned that these women felt that they were created in the images of men. And finally, I learned that these women had no clue as to how much personal spiritual power they possessed. They had no clue they had been participating in the sacred order of universal magic. And at the time I did not know either. But I did know that our prayers changed things, and that women's prayers had special effects.

So I left the church, and began to study on my own. I brought books on meditation and prayer and rethought everything I had been taught. Every morning I would get up and look into the mirror, and say to myself, "I will prosper everything I touch; and everything I touch will prosper me."

But everything that I touched did not prosper. I remembered in the past that I asked that my sight be taken away when I foresaw the death of a friend. And so it was. Then I did not know how to restore my vision. A friend took me to the high priestess in the Wiccan Order here. When the rushes of visions began, I felt like I was drunk. Images of people I had never seen before, pictures of places I had never been. Finally there was Cousin Anna telling me everything was going to be all right.

I studied books on spirituality, the Goddess, the Bible. I decided the world needed a new Bible where women would not be left out. And then Cousin Anna showed up, asking if I needed a boulder dropped on my head to know that everything that happened on earth happens in heaven. Like a lightning bolt I was struck: "Thy will be done on earth as it is in heaven." "As above, so below." There is no life unless the Goddess Loves. I found my osyter and pearl. The Goddess lives and loves in every woman. My belief is that through our Goddess/God powers, we control our lives and our environment. My celebration of life begins each day with the words: "Happy New Day!"

Oyo Fummilayo, author, actress professional storyteller, and singer, has performed locally, statewide in Kentucky, and nationally. As an author, Oyo has penned three books and two plays. As an actress, she has appeared on stage with Education Arts' in "Seeds from the Sun" and in a one-woman show as Harriet Tubman. As a professional storyteller, she has traveled throughout the United States to perpetuate the art of oral tradition through the African and African American folktale, the art of African rhythms, visual art, and African dance movement.

Ms. Fummilayo believes that "it is the responsibility of each African American to recapture the lost cultural heritage of our people, and to pass it on to our children in an educational and entertaining way."

Adonai Zeus Shekhinah Elim Ogun Kat Buddha
Wyame Hel Rama Mitra Odomankoma Jupiter Het
Heru   Agni   Cagn Thor Brahma Tangaroa Father
Lugaba Papang Diana Al-Rahman Cerridwen Ahone
Yoma' Tirawa Atius Gucumatz El Mungan ngua
Quetzalcoatl Hamakom   ddai
Atibruku Moma YH Bun   aiwa

Poems About the Divine Feminine

Cassia Berman

Saraswati Inanna   Miriru   aong
Tonantzin   Yuskeha   Bha   Head
Olodumare Shyama Ekv   Heru
Nurrundere   Daramilun   tzeir
Hecate Chi Musubi Hin   suna
Nanderuvucu   Erishkigal   man
Tsui-goab Ometeotl Os   chtli
Surya   Elohim   Nyankop   Ilu
Woden Great Spirit   Les   goro
Poseidon Chineke Nhialic Aciek Kari Auset   Tcuwut
Makai Wakantanka Inari Ha-Qadosh barukh hu'
Tara Krishna Avaloket-iswara Rabb Goryo Qat Oke
Nurunderi Indra   Shang-ti Amaterasu   Ohmikami
Kannon   Quan Yin   Ise Lakshmi Awonawilona Bast
Omecihuatl Ruhanga Kosane Sophia Dionysus Ixchel
Mawu Ra Ardanariswara   Oluwa Deng Hanuman
uNkulunkulu   Kanobo Ngai   Shamayim Cybele Dakini
Nataraj Pachamama Susanoo Katonda Avlukpo   Eloah
Isis Temaukel Eleda Gaia Laxmi Mahmanmu-rok
Odin El-al Herukhuti Viracocha Marduk Ashira Biral
Shaddai   Dzingbe Djohu-ma-di-hutu Astarte Ndengei
Koyatu Baha'u'llah Marrigan Baiame Om Pelepelewa
Durga   Orisha   Nyame   Techaronhiawakhon   Chukwu
Uvolovu Brahman Nephtys Ha-Maqom Tehuti Maat
Digambara Val Tik Chaitanya Amana Kwoth   Num
Colok Nabango Fumeripitsj Shiva Varuna Lukanga
Bala Atibluku Karu Allah Sing Nainuema Artemis
Kartikeya Kuanyin Yelafaz T'ien Baal   Shakti
Athena Olorun   Nemesis Sheela-na-Gig Bhavartarini
Jesus Horus Izanagi Sebek Waq Ishtar Ti Seker
BegoTanutanu   Sat Nam   Kali Mirirul   Bhavatarini
Tsui-goab Hatzur Brahman Ubusuna Tonantzin
YHVH Apollo Nana God Almighty Hu Vishnu   Om

Saraswati

She sits for eons in solitude
but since time is an illusion
She is also in eternal union with her Beloved.
That's why she's smiling
as her gifts emanate from her to the hearts of true devotees
and boons are granted to those who think they seek.

So do all my guides laugh at me
when I think I'm alone
and give me comfort
as if to a child
and pull me along now
to the place of eternal having of all I've been given for lifetimes
and all those I've loved merge into One
I can never lose or be parted from
so I can sit in wholeness of being
like her
and radiate, not wanting,
but union with the Source of All.

After Praying for Two Months to be Purified and Cleansed So I Can Serve Her, She Tells Me Not to Worry

Lucky little candleflames
dancing in blue glasses on Mary's altar.
Instead of burning down houses
or warming them
or cooking food or smelting iron
or doing any of the 10,000 useful things that fuel
   the never-ending needs of the world,
they are dancing for the Mother.

And I am doing nothing useful too.
Just shining and dancing and burning for You.

Reminder

With a love
      more tender than my mother's
God feeds me my lunch
            with my own hand

March Poem

As soon as I woke up early this morning, Gladootchkie was saying, "Oui, oui," telling me to take a walk with her, and as soon as I finished my coffee I did, in my nightgown, scarf and boots. And oh, she was right. She took me through the piled up leaves and dry weeds and bare trees, from some of whose branches icicles still hang. Isabella, her youngest daughter, was galloping through the weeds and running up trees, investigating whatever came in front of her nose, but Gladootchkie and I sat in a little hollow under a tree, and I looked at delicate white thread-like weeds tangled among the brown oak leaves that cover a few still-green blades of grass, small patches of snow, and rocks. I'm still civilized to the point that when I look at Nature's arrangements I think of the rooms of interior decoration schemes in department stores that I liked to imagine living in when I was a child. When you walk in the forest it's like walking from room to room, and when you sit in one place you can see even smaller rooms in the bumps and crevices of the earth.

We sat watching, so content in each other's presence, under a mottled grey sky, listening to the rushing waters of the creek, until my toes froze, and then I danced home without Gladootchkie (who chose to stay outside and meditate alone), over the mounds of leaves, some porous like mattresses, some frozen solid like mountains, and I stopped to thank God and the Mother and my guides and the devas for such a beautiful world, and ask that I be a messenger of joy in this world that needs it so much. I know how to suffer, but I would rather bring joy. And I asked the devas again, whom I still can't see except in sparkles in the air, that if there's anything I can do to help them, to heal the world or bring the spring or anything, please to show me.

The air sparkled, the sky breathed, the creek and tree branches sang, and at my feet I found an old paper cup imprinted with flowers and the message, "It's our pleasure to serve you." I wanted to object—"No, no it's not *you* who serve *me*"—but instead I accepted graciously and said, "And it is mine to serve Thee."

Cassia Berman was born in the Bronx in 1949. From an early age, she yearned to hear God's voice, which she thought would be booming, male, and Jewish. To her surprise, when she finally heard the voice of the divine in her late twenties, it was gentle, female, and in the imagings of all religions. Since that time, year after year, with grace and often a sense of humor, the divine Mother has shown her many of her faces and led her on a spiritual path that embraces all traditions.

A poet since childhood, Cassia received her B.A. from Sarah Lawrence College. In the 1970's she participated in the New York City poetry world, giving poetry readings and teaching workshops in

community organizations. In 1980 she moved to Woodstock in upstate New York where she now works as a freelance writer, editor, and literary assistant, teaching programs and leading meditations on the divine Mother, and participating in several of Woodstock's spiritual communities. A longtime student of the Chinese healing movement arts, she practices and teaches t-ai chi and qi gong. A student of the late spiritual teacher, Hilda Charlton, Cassia is a founding member and program director of the Vedantic Light, and the author of *Divine Mother Poems*.

Adonai Zeus Shekhinah Elim Ogun Kat Buddha
Wyame Hel Rama Mitra Odomankoma Jupiter Het
Heru Agni Cagn Thor Brahma Tangaroa Father
Lugaba Papang Diana Al-Rahman Cerridwen Ahone
Yoma' Tirawa Atius Gucumbo El Muyanyangua
Quetzalcoatl Hamakom ddai
Atibruku Moma YH Bun uiwa
Saraswati Inanna Miriru ong
Tonantzin Yuskeha Bha lead
Olodumare Shyama Ekv eru
Nurrundere Daramilun tzeir
Hecate Chi Musubi Hin una
Nanderuvucu Erishkigal man
Tsui-goab Ometeotl Os htli
Surya Elohim Nyankop Ilu
Woden Great Spirit Lese goro
Poseidon Chineke Nhialic Aciek Kari Auset Tcuwut
Makai Wakantanka Inari Ha-Qadosh barukh hu'
Tara Krishna Avaloket-iswara Rabb Goryo Qat Oke
Nurunderi Indra Shang-ti Amaterasu Ohmikami
Kannon Quan Yin Ise Lakshmi Awonawilona Bast
Omecihuatl Ruhanga Kosane Sophia Dionysus Ixchel
Mawu Ra Ardanariswara Oluwa Deng Hanuman
uNkulunkulu Kanobo Ngai Shamayim Cybele Dakini
Nataraj Pachamama Susanoo Katonda Avlukpo Eloah
Isis Temaukel Eleda Gaia Laxmi Mahmanmu-rok
Odin El-al Herukhuti Viracocha Marduk Ashira Biral
Shaddai Dzingbe Djohu-ma-di-hutu Astarte Ndengei
Koyatu Baha'u'llah Marrigan Baiame Om Pelepelewa
Durga Orisha Nyame Techaronhiawakhon Chukwu
Uvolovu Brahman Nephtys Ha-Maqom Tehuti Maat
Digambara Val Tik Chaitanya Amana Kwoth Num
Colok Nabango Fumeripitsj Shiva Varuna Lukanga
Bala Atibluku Karu Allah Sing Nainuema Artemis
Kartikeya Kuanyin Yelafaz T'ien Baal Shakti
Athena Olorun Nemesis Sheela-na-Gig Bhavartarini
Jesus Horus Izanagi Sebek Waq Ishtar Ti Seker
BegoTanutanu Sat Nam Kali Mirirul Bhavatarini
Tsui-goab Hatzur Brahman Ubusuna Tonantzin
YHVH Apollo Nana God Almighty Hu Vishnu Om

God Has Many Faces

Theresa King

W hen I was a very little girl growing up in metropolitan Chicago—Cicero to be exact—I used to follow my mother out to the alley at the call of the "Ragzanarn Man." For a long time I could not understand what he sang as he prodded his old horse to pull the dilapidated wagon through the alleys. Mom told me it was "rags and iron" he called out, inviting the housewives to bring their recyclables to him. Women brought out stacks of newspapers, old clothes, rags, broken bits of metal, rusty utensils, old pots. He paid them in cash. His gnarled hand would disappear into the crusted pocket of his sagging pants and pull out greasy bills and piles of coin, like some American Fagin, and carefully count out the trade.

I was afraid of the man. He had a long white beard and a wrinkled face. He was dirty and smelly, and his wagon was piled with the discards of households from all over the city. He sat up high on the driving shelf of the wagon holding a long stick with which he beat his poor, tired horse. Once I wanted to pet the horse, but he snarled a warning to keep me away, and from that day on I watched him fearfully from behind the garbage cans or between the slats of blinds at my bedroom window.

When I started kindergarten, Sister Miriam unfolded a large, bright picture of an old man with a long white beard, sitting high up on a big chair, holding a long golden stick. She said, "This, children, is God." I was horrified.

Later I learned that that awful man was our Father. The two concepts did not match. Father meant Daddy, and Daddy was kind and jovial, smelled good and hugged well, had a neat little mustache instead of a long beard, rolled down the hill with us at the park, baked us cherry pies and pancakes, sang beautifully on a stage. He was so far away from the old man with a long beard sitting up high that I dismissed that God image as one of the few mistakes Sister Miriam would ever make.

By the end of second grade I knew everything there was to know about God, especially about the God called Jesus. He was very handsome in spite of his long hair, spoke mostly in stories, and somehow lived behind the small golden door on the church altar. We were careful not to make him upset by being bad and secretly tried not to become involved with his Father in any way. We learned about the Holy Ghost, which was shown to be a white bird and made no sense at all, and about Mary, Jesus' mother, who was very kind and gentle, but also rather sad. We could tell her anything and she would understand. We were strictly cautioned that we could pray to her, but it had to be different from the way we prayed to Jesus because, after all, she was not God.

Years of theology and thousands of sermons later, the basis of God language did not appear to be much different from those early impressions. Much ado was made about the "one, true God" as opposed to the many "gods" of the "pagans." Yet all around me there was a multiplicity of "true" God images. There was devotion to the Trinity, Father, Son, and Holy Spirit. There was devotion to the Sacred Heart, the Infant of Prague, the Crucified Savior, the Good Shepherd, Christ the King, the Resurrected Lord, the Almighty Father, the Creator, the Holy Spirit, the merciful Judge. There were innumerable possibilities for devotion to Mary: the obedient young handmaiden, the Mother with the baby, the Queen of Heaven, the apparitions of Lourdes, Fatima, Guadalupe. There was devotion to the Holy Family, to Christ as Eucharistic Lord, Suffering Servant, Glorified Redeemer. The possibilities were endless. Each of these God images had its own devotion: retreats and novenas, statues and holy cards, pictures to hang on the wall, special prayers in the prayer books, churches and schools bearing their names.

I noticed that the image of God was directly related to the personality and lifestyle of the believer. I watched childless old nuns lovingly dress the statue of the Child Jesus in bejeweled silks and satins; cerebral college professors spend hours before the altar contemplating God as bread; celibate priests speak of the Virgin Mary with tears in their eyes and with words other men reserved for romance. A casual observer would be hard-pressed to recognize these images as representing the same God, much less the same religious tradition.

Being part of the tradition, however, it was natural to me to see God expressed in so many ways. It was not a problem to notice that a devotee who gently kissed the bleeding hand on the statue of the suffering Christ had no feelings, nor even patience, for the devotion to Christ the King. The Baby Jesus was not the same as The Final Judge; the Creator of Eden was not the Warlord of Israel.

Despite Church canons and religious doctrine, I realized that believers secretly imaged God in very personal ways. We all filled a need in our lives with the God we wanted. We all made God in our own image.

And since that was the case, then why were the images of one religion worthy, in fact solely true, while others were false gods? Who decided that? And on what basis?

Once the questions appeared, the answers had to be sought, and sought with a vengeance. God became a curiosity, a mystery to be solved.

In India my searches found a plethora of God images that pulled at my heart, or turned me away in revulsion. There were as many images as in Christianity, many of them similar, and some as difficult to understand. In Nepal and Tibet, the harsh landscape and struggling lives of the people manifested in the many violent images of the divine. In Mexico, familiar Christian God images were unselfconsciously combined with ancient Indian theology. In Eastern Europe the same images mixed with unnamed exotic overtones, and the face of the Black Madonna everywhere superseded that of Christ. In Japan *everything* seemed to be God—or at least deified—and over all sat the still, imposing image of Lord Buddha, used as a model or object of worship by millions.

It became obvious to me that our collective experience forms our image of God. The symbols of a particular place—whether desert or rain forest or Midwestern farm—together with group values and beliefs about the meaning of life and death, paint an image of divinity for each culture, every group within cultures. Variations are made according to the particular psychological needs of the group, and sometimes of the individual. These images are strengthened by emotion: the beauty of art and architecture, ritual and music. They make us loath to change any part of a belief system that ties us so keenly to family, childhood, friendship, holiday celebrations.

The freer individuals feel in the play of life, however, the freer they are to change the group's divinity for their own use. Our childish notions of God usually evolve to more sophisticated images as we mature. We learn more about scriptural exegesis and institutional power, or we discover thought patterns that no longer serve us, or perhaps we are enthralled by the beliefs of a culture other than our own. Then the task of sorting out God images begins in earnest. This does not happen easily, nor automatically. For some, the idea of questioning traditional beliefs, ideas, or images is too risky; it is easier to join the ranks of those who defend the status quo. But often it appears that the divine itself forces us to acknowledge that we need look again at what we think about God.

Years ago I worked in a large yoga institute as a staff member. Our spiritual teacher was also the chief administrator of the organization. Whenever staff members became complacent, either in the running of the office or in their spiritual development, our teacher would make an outrageous remark, or abruptly disturb the daily schedule, or move staff around at lightening speed. A friend in my office began to call our teacher The Cosmic Toilet Flusher, explaining that whenever everything is calm and quiet, he comes along and pushes a little handle casting all the peace into a maelstrom of activity and confusion to move us out of our complacency. I thought the term was also an apt image for God.

Belief in God is not an idle pastime. Our God image makes us *do* things. We may be compelled to serve the homeless, work in a hospice, send money to charity, march in a demonstration, write books, join a discussion group, raise a child. Our God image also makes us *think* things. It leads us to think about ourselves in particular ways, about our place in the cosmos, our delight or disappointment in our gender or our social role. It leads us to think about others in compassion and understanding or condemnation. It forms our judgment of wrongdoers, the breadth or narrowness of our vision for community. The way we think about God directly influences the way we think about ourselves and others. It is the fulcrum on which the community balances, the scale upon which actions are weighed.

That is why communities of God believers can kill members in his name; why "righteous" countries can go to war to claim land or secure raw materials, why women can be beaten by their husbands, why lawbreakers can be punished, why the sexual life of leaders can label them unfit for politics, why hard work is glorified, why workers among the poor are called saints by some and troublemakers by others, why some groups call an act sin and others call it a mistake, why death is feared or welcomed, why illness is a divine reckoning or a gift for self-knowledge, why tolerance and love of neighbor are automatic or one of the hardest struggles on the face of the earth.

In London, at the Museum of Mankind, I learned of a wonderful divine image that haunts me still. The Sea Goddess of various Eskimo groups tangles up the fish, seals, and walruses in her long, flowing hair, and holds them at the bottom of the sea as if in a net. When the people can find no food, they apologize to the Goddess for offending her and beg her to comb out her hair, thus freeing the animals for hunting.

The image of God performing such an everyday task as combing her long hair is a wonderful juxtaposition of intimacy and power, immanence and transcendence. It reminds us that God is far beyond us, but also very near, able to totally ignore us or able to hear our every word when we call. It touches on the question of the negative side of God. It speaks to me of what I call the "human quandary of the two Gods: the God We Want and the God That Is."

The God We Want is imaged in all the religions of the world, in the minds of millions of creatures attempting to know and name their creator. This God is called Mother, Father, Friend, Brother, Lover, Lord. This God knows our thoughts, keeps us from danger, sends grace to guide us. This God is as close as the next breath, as immanent as our own heartbeats.

The God That Is is not imaginable. It is the absolute totality of consciousness; the transcendent being beyond the ability of the mind to know; the thought beyond all thought; the image beyond all power to imagine; the form that does not exist; that Living Force which subequatorial Africans insist has no face, but whose power is everywhere; that Origin, the Tantrics tell us, which spins out universes in a constant creation and destruction beyond time and space; the incomprehensible ground of all being; the self-absorbent Source from which everything flows and into which everything will inevitably return.

Historically, human beings have named as God anything which was more than they. It may have been another human being, bigger, stronger, of a different skin color. To ancient natural cultures it may have been the soldier who appeared carrying a blazing gun. To fearful or superstitious cultures, it may have been a stranger who could accurately predict the future or cure the sick. We keep expanding our definition of God because we keep reclaiming more and more of what it means to be human. We are the gods of a thousands years ago.

Now that we and our neighbors are becoming a global community, claiming our individual differences and sharing more and more in modern technologies and trade products, what will the new collective experience name as the image of God? What will God look like to this multicultural group which will surely share earth values and human concerns as we travel deeper and deeper through the realms of space? And what will God look like after eons of planetary interaction?

That God image will certainly be many-sided. I am always

suspicious of people who are all kind, or spiritual leaders who are only sweet with no fire, or of a God that is one-sided! Life is a play of opposites. It is a constant balance of extremes. I think wisdom, like God, exists at the point where the two ends meet. Just as we struggle day after day to balance our known and unknown parts, our feminine and masculine traits, our good and evil sides, our openness and our fears, our past and our future, so we must struggle to understand the God We Want in light of the fact that it is not necessarily the God That Is.

If we are lucky, reality has a way of imposing itself upon us whenever we think we have life (and God) all figured out. Reality does violence to our simplistic naiveté, to our need for life to be a certain way, to the fear that sends us into hiding against risk. This reality is also God. It is called the Mother by cultures which have long realized that destruction is a holy and valid face of God. This Mother brings death as well as life. She destroys as well as creates. She is the bringer of both illusion and pure truth—our twin tools in the ceaseless task of remembering who we are and where we are going. She smashes our preconceived notions and makes us teeter on the edge of childishness and maturity, knowing and not knowing, until we can find the truth that exists within good and evil both. She forces us to grow up.

> When I was young
> I wrote sweet love poems
> to the Mother of the Universe
> singing ecstatic lyrics
> weaving garlands of joyous blossoms
> open, pure.
>
> But now She crouches beside me
> cackling at the pretty words
> tearing the perfumed pages
> and weighing each sweetness
> on the edge of her long, sharp nail
> red with blood.

Some day we will know God. We will not have to guess about the divine image, just as we will not have to wonder what else lies hidden in our unconscious minds. What thoughts will we think when we learn to use the 90% of our brains as yet untapped? What expansion will occur when we meet life forms superior to our own?

How will our lives change when we clearly remember everything that ever happened to us on our long journey through history and through life? What will God look like then?

In the meantime, we struggle under the task of finding meaning in our lives, preparing for a swiftly-changing future, and dealing with our historical patterns. God, of course, is with us; we know that. We just don't know what it means.

Perhaps the search for the face of God is a planned part of the evolution of humanity. Perhaps we move through time from image to image, learning about the God We Want, revering tradition, honoring revealed scripture, carrying out the terms of the holy covenants as we understand them, while we are being moved—sometimes imperceptively, sometimes quite drastically—to the next step of the plan towards the God That Is.

Every group does the same, sometimes overlapping findings, sometimes stepping into new concepts quite alone. We cannot do otherwise. We must be true to our own inner promptings, to that divine spark that pushes us to question, to grapple with the unknowable, to be curious about the forbidden. It is God itself that asks the questions because it is God itself that is the answer.

Perhaps eventually, after all the questions have been asked and all the secrets laid open to the light, the pairs of opposites—birth and death, good and evil, light and darkness, sin and goodness, love and war, ennui and ecstasy, creation and annihilation—will be found to be the same. Perhaps then the many faces of God will show us the God That Is.

Theresa King is a writer, publisher, and teacher of spirituality. Her work is the expression of a lifetime of study, practice, and worldwide travel. A religious from her teens, she left the convent to study theology in the Netherlands and England as well as explore other spiritualities in Nepal, India, Mexico, and Japan. She has spent 22 years with a Himalayan yoga master, seven as his assistant.

She holds a B.S. in Education, an M.A. in Human Development and Spirituality. Theresa currently lives in St. Paul, MN.

Notes

FEMININE ASPECTS OF DIVINITY, p. 1:

1 Beaseley, Norman. *Mary Baker Eddy*. (New York, 1963), p.304.
2 *Science and Health with Key to the Scriptures*, on Gen. 1:27.
3 Brinton, Howard. *The Mystic Will*. (New York, 1963), p.178f, 201.
4 Morgan, John H. "Eternal Father-Eternal Mother in Shaker Theology," *Inward Light*, Spring, 1973.
5 Zernov, Nicolas. *Three Russian Prophets*. (London, 1944), p.121.
6 Scholem, Gershom. *Major Trends in Jewish Mysticism*. (New York, 1961), p.229.
7 Patai, Raphael. *The Hebrew Goddess*. (New York, 1967), p.161ff.
8 Schloem, op. cit., p.249f, 279f.
9 Buber, Martin. *For the Sake of Heaven*. (New York, 1945), p.228ff.
10 Landstrom, Elsie. "A Lightning Flash of Living Love," *Inward Light*, Spring, 1972, p.27ff.

THE DIVINE DISTURBER, p. 21:

1 Alice Walker, *The Color Purple* (San Diego: Harcourt Brace Jovanovich, 1982), 166-67.
2 Joann Wolski Conn, "Women's Spirituality: Restriction and Reconstruction," in *Women's Spirituality: Resources for Christian Development* (New York: Paulist, 1986), 9.
3 Mary Collins, *Women at Prayer* (New York: Paulist Press, 1987), 13.
4 Rosemary Radford Ruether, ed. *Religion and Sexism: Images of Woman in the Jewish and Christian Traditions* (New York: Simon and Schuster, 1974), 9.
5 Rosemary Radford Ruether, "The Western Religious Tradition and Violence Against Women in the Home," in *Christianity, Patriarchy, & Abuse: A Feminist Critique*, Eds. Joanne Carlson Brown and Carole R. Bohn (New York: Pilgrim Press, 1989), 32.
6 Phyllis Trible, "Feminist Hermeneutics and Biblical Studies," in *The Christian Century*, 99 (Feb. 3-10, 1982) 116.
7 Sandra M. Schneiders, "The Effects of Women's Experience on their Spirituality," in *Women's Spirituality: Resources for Christian Development*, Ed. Joann Wolski Conn, 42.
8 Schneiders, *Women and the Word: The Gender of God in the New Testament and the Spirituality of Women* (New York: Paulist, 1986), 70-71.
9 Marjorie Procter-Smith, *In Her Own Rite: Constructing Feminist Liturgical Tradition* (Nashville: Abingdon, 1990), 37-38.
10 Sallie McFague, *Models for God: Theology for an Ecological, Nuclear Age* (Philadelphia: Fortress, 1987), ix.
11 Procter-Smith, *In Her Own Rite*, 91.
12 Carol Christ, "Why Women Need the Goddess: Phenomenological, Psychological, and Political Reflections," in *Womanspirit Rising: A Feminist Reader in Religion*, eds. Carol P. Christ and Judith Plaskow, (San Francisco: Harper & Row, 1979), 273-287.
13 Procter-Smith, op. cit., 92.
14 McFague, op. cit., 171.
15 Schüssler Fiorenza, *In Memory of Her*, 121.
16 Ruether, *Sexism and God Talk*, 71.

GOD IS A VERB, p. 49:

1 See *The Hebrew Goddess,* by Raphael Patai (KTAV Publishing House, 1967), for a discussion of the divine feminine in the spiritual history of Israel.

IMAGES OF GOD, CLOSENESS AND POWER, p. 87:

1 The above verse was the basis of a *dvar torah* (homily) delivered by Eva Brown at the Jewish Community of Amherst in September 1991. Some of the inspiration for this discussion is derived from her words.

2 Unpublished poem reprinted with the permission of the author, Ani Tuzman.

3 Poem published in *Kol HaNeshama,* the Reconstructionist Sabbath Eve Prayerbook.

4 There is a wonderful discussion of this verse in Lawrence Kushner's *God Was In This Place, And I, I Did Not Know.* Jewish Lights Publishing, Woodstock, Vermont, 1991.

GOD IS ALWAYS PREGNANT, p. 117:

1 Leon-Portilla, ed., *The Broken Spears: The Aztec Account of the Conquest of Mexico.* Boston: Beacon Press, 1962.

2 The Nahuatl refers to the language, values, and customs that are shared by a number of tribes which comprised the Aztec empire. The Aztecs were a demographic subgroup, a dominant one, of the Nahuatl people. See leon-Portilla, pp xxix-xxx.

3 Mirande, Alfredo and Enriquez, Evangelina. *La Chicana: The Mexican American Woman.* Chicago: University of Chicago Press, 1979.

4 Elizondo, Virgilio. *La Morenita.* Texas: Mexican American Cultural Center, 1978, p. 117.

5 Leon-Portilla p. 180.

6 Leon-Portilla p. 183.

7 Ricard, Robert. *The Spiritual Conquest of Mexico.* Berkeley: The University of California Press, 1966.

8 Elizondo, Virgilio. *Mestizaje: The Dialectic of Cultural Birth and the Gospel.* San Antonio, TX: Mexican American Cultural Center, 1978. This book provides much of the historical documentation about the image itself from the original texts.

9 Elizondo, p. 90.

10 Documents of Puebla: Conculsions of the Secretariat for Latin America. The National Conference of Catholic Bishops, Washington, D.C., 1979, No. 291.

11 Callahan, Philip. "The Tilma: Under Infra-red Radition," *CARA Studies in Popular Devotion, Vol. II: Guadalupan Studies, No. 3.* Washington D.C.: Center for Applied Research in the Apostolate, 1981, p. 15.

12 Diaz, Vicente. "New Revelations from the Cloak of Juan Diego," *Colombia,* 65: 12 (December) 1985, p. 8-15.

13 Smith, Jody Brant. *The Image of Guadalupe, Myth or Miracle?* New York: Doubleday and Co., Image Books, 1984.

14 When I went to the Guadalupan scholars of Mexico and asked how they would respond to the allegation that there had been some later additions to the image, they absolutely refuted the idea. The Nica Cahoe, the original document, records the elements of the image. The belt was described in that document, and so any later painting could only be touchups of the image rather than additions.

15 Elizondo, p. 3

16 Callahan, p. 10

254   *THE DIVINE MOSAIC*

[17] Kolhenschlag, Madonna. *Lost in the Land of Oz.* San Francisco: Harper & Row, 1988.

[18] Craighead, Meinrad and Giles, Mary. *The Feminist Mystique and Other Essays on Women and Spirituality.* New York: Crossroads, 1982.

THE DARK DEVI, p. 134:

[1] Ramprasad Sen, *Grace and Mercy in Her Wild Hair: Selected Poems to the Mother Goddess,* trans. Leonard Nathan and Clinton Seely (Boulder, Colorado: Great Eastern Book Company, 1982), p. 65.

[2] *Hymns to the Goddess and Hymn to Kali,* trans. John Woodroffe [Arthur Avalon] (Wilmot, Wisconsin: Lotus Light Publications, 1981), p. 278.

[3] Ramprasad Sen, *Grace and Mercy in Her Wild Hair,* p. 61.

[4] David R. Kinsley, *The Sword and the Flute: Kali and Krishna, Dark Visions of the Terrible and the Sublime in Hindu Mythology* (Berkeley: University of California Press, 1975), p. 84.

[5] Ibid., p. 155.

[6] Marie-Louise von Franz, in an interview in the film "C.G. Jung: A Matter of Heart," 1986.

[7] Mahendranath Gupta, compiled, *The Gospel of Sri Ramakrishna,* trans. Swami Nikhilananda (New York: Ramakrishna-Vivekananda Center, 1942), p. 336.

[8] Catherine Clementin-Ojha, "The Tradition of Female Gurus," *Manushi: A Journal About Women in Society* 6 (November-December, 1985): 8.

[9] Beloved.

[10] Ritual Worship.

[11] A Sanskrit term meaning "sight."

[12] Sister Nivedita, "Kali The Mother," Vol. 1 of *The Complete Works of Sister Nivedita* (Calcutta: Ramakrishna Sarada Mission, 1967), p. 461

GOD IS FIRE, p. 163

[1] The Spiritual Life Institute is a small monastic community of apostolic hermits founded for both men and women in 1960 by William McNamara O.C.D. with a mandate from the visionary Pope John XXIII. Tessa Bielecki, who joined the Institute as executive secretary in 1967, became its co-foundress. The institute is Roman Catholic in origin and universal in outreach, thinking globally and acting locally. The purpose of SLI is to foster contemplation in North America.

[2] Thomas Renaud. "Firesong" copyright 1992.

[3] "The Living Flame of Love" from *The Collected Words of St. John of the Cross,* trans. by Kieran Kavanaugh, O.C.D. and Otilio Rodriguez, O.C.D., c. 1979 by Washington, Province of Discalced Carmelites. ICS Publications, 2131 Lincoln Road, NE, Washington, D.C., 20002.

[4] Ibid.

[5] Luke, 12:49.

[6] A Native American underground sacred place.

[7] Prayer by William McNamara

[8] "The Living Flame of Love" op cit.

[9] Ibid.

[10] Ibid.

[11] Song of Solomon, 2:11; 1:1-3; 2:16.

GOD AWAKENING, p. 204:

1 Glossary:

Adam: The Hebrew name for the first human being; the Hebrew root being the same as for Adama or earth.

Adonai: The Hebrew word for Master.

Aleph-bet: Hebrew alphabet, e.g.: a,b,

Bar Mitzvah: A life turning point, where traditionally a boy of 13 becomes recognized in Jewish life as an adult. He can be a witness in a court of law, and is beholden to observe the mitzvot, or Jewish legal and ritual injunctions.

Chai: The Hebrew word "chai" when the values of each letter is added up, the number equals 18.

Chanuka: The Jewish holiday falling generally in December which marks a time when spiritual freedom was challenged, and when our observance was retained in the face of that challenge.

Circle-drawing: We've a tradition of Honi the circle-maker, who during times of draught, would draw circles and speak with G, coax, argue, engage in discussion, so that water would indeed flow, or cease flowing.

Double Chai: Again like Chai, another example of gematria. Chai, twice adds up to 36.

Elijah: In Jewish tradition Elijah is the harbinger of the Messiah. Jewish folk legend has it, that Elijah roams the earth in disguise. Sometimes he hides as a beggar, sometimes as the unknown stranger. Thus one is always on the lookout to honor the stranger, care for the one who needs, to hasten that time of peace.

Elohim: A Hebrew word for G. It is a difficult word as it is plural and connotes the G of gods.

Four: References to the Passover Seder in which the number four repeats. Passover is seen as the time of the freeing of the Israelites from the slavery of Pharaoh in Egypt. In the Hagada, the special book read during the seder, there are four cups of wine, as well as a passage that discusses four children's responses to hearing of the Exodus from Egypt.

Four Worlds: There is a notion in mystical thought, that there are four worlds or ways to know G, each higher than the next.

Gematria: In Jewish tradition each Hebrew letter has a numerical value. There is a whole tradition of gematria, which is the art of taking words and numbers and weaving stories and values.

Ha Kodosh Baruch Hu/ Ribbono Shel Olam: Both names are from rabbinical sources, and are intimate names. The Hebrew carries a sense of internal connection. The English translations sound hard and don't speak to the nuances of the names: The Holy One Blessed be (He), Master of the World.

Harahaman: derived from the root "rehem" which means womb. It also holds the Hebrew word "Ham," or warmth. Thus the English translation of "Merciful One" doesn't quite reach the sense of warmth, womb of the Hebrew. Thus I translate it "One of deep inside loving," trying to reach the warmth of loving connect that a mother feels towards her child.

Hatzur, Hamakom: Two traditional names of G. Hatzur connotes solidity, comfort, protection. In English it means the Rock. Hamakom, for me, speaks to a simultaneously internal-external experience, internally with and externally full. Hamakom, means the Place. Once again the English translation does not convey for me, the deeply emotional nuances of these terms.

Hayotzeir: Too is difficult in translation. The Hebrew contains the root "yatzar," or speaks to creative power. It also contains the word "Tzar," or narrow place. It contains the image of creating from narrowness to birthing into a larger space. Again the English translation sounds harsh, "Creator" not conveying the process of shaping, and carrying out into the world.

Jewish movements: My synagogue was a Reform synagogue. There are six or more movements within Jewish life. The Reform movement from its inception, philosophically pronounced the ritual equality of men and women, welcoming women to public ritual observance and public ritual spiritual roles on par with Jewish men.

Midrash: Texts which comment on the Torah, weaving story, legends, moral teachings, and pieces of legal commentary.

Mikvah: A ritual bath, with freshly flowing waters.

Minyan: A group of ten adult males according to Jewish tradition, is the number that one must have in order to pray all of the prayers publicly. In some communities when 10 men couldn't be found, a legal fiction of a young boy next to a Torah scroll would make up a 10th man.

Mishnah: A Hebrew compilation of some of the legal practices mentioned in the Torah.

Mitzvot: Literally, "commandments." There are 613 mitzvot consisting of positive and negative actions. Traditionally when a boy becomes a Jewish adult he is legally and morally responsible to respond to these observances.

Mitzvah: A Jewish action, observance.

Personal name: Yud, Hey, Vav, Hey was known as the personal intimate name of G, revealed to Moses at the burning bush.

Proverbs: A section of the Bible, Old Testament.

Rabbinate: The institutions that ordain rabbis: Jewish teachers—legal arbiters—leaders.

7 Days of Creation: The book of Genesis recounts the seven days of creation, which people love to debate, the problem, was time invented? What makes a day?

7 days of celebrating a wedding: It was a tradition after a marriage for the couple to stay within the community for 7 days of celebration.

7 weeks before binding: Between the holidays of Passover and Shavout, are 7 weeks. Shavout is seen as the holiday where the relationship between G and Israel was bound, Passover being the engagement, Shavout, being the wedding.

Sefer Torah: Refers to the Torah scroll. The Torah was hand calligraphered on parchments, sewn together and wrapped around a wooden holder.

Shivah: The period of seven days of mourning which follows burial.

Shoah: The Hebrew word for the Holocaust. It connotes devastating wipeout, destruction, annihilation.

Shul: A yiddish word for synagogue.

Siddur: A Hebrew word for prayerbook.

Sinai: The mountain where according to Torah, the ten commandments were given, and where the Israelites bound themselves, were "wedded" in relationship with G. The desert mountainous area south of Israel.

T'fillah: The Hebrew word for prayer.

Talmud: A multi-volume work which is a vast commentary on the Mishnah, enlarging and expounding it merges legal decision-making with folk tale. It uses complex legal argumentation modes, as well as philosophical forms of reasoning.

Ten words: A reference to the ten commandments given at Mount Sinai. tradition has it that there were ten utterances.

Torah: The first five books of the Bible, initial part of the Old Testament.

Wadi: An oasis in the desert.

Yud: A Hebrew letter. Two yuds together are a symbol of Adonai, one of G's names.

Bibliography

ANDERSON, Sherry Ruth and Hopkins, Patricia. *The Feminine Face of God: The Unfolding of the Sacred in Women.* New York: Bantam, 1991.

ANGELES, Peter. *Critiques of God.* Buffalo, NY: Prometheus Books, 1976.

ANTHONY, Dick, Ecker, Bruce and Wilber, Ken, eds. *Spiritual Choices: The Problem of Recognizing Authentic Paths to Inner Transformation.* New York: Paragon House Publishers, 1987.

BEYER, Stephan. *The Cult of Tara: Magic and Ritual in Tibet.* Berkeley, CA: University of California Press, 1978.

BUKKYO Dendo Kyokai. *The World of Shinto. The Teachings of Confucianism.* Tokyo: 1985.

CAMPBELL, Joseph and Muses, Charles, eds. *In All Her Names: Explorations of the Feminine in Divinity.* San Francisco: Harper San Francisco, 1990.

DANIELOU, Alain. *Hindu Polytheism.* New York: Pantheon Books, 1964.

DELORIA, Vine, Jr. *God is Red.* NY: Delta Books, 1973.

ELIADE, Mircea. *Essential Sacred Writings from Around the World.* San Francisco: Harper San Francisco, 1967.

ELLIOTT, Holly Bridges. *Beholding God in Many Faces.* Winona, MN: St. Mary's Press, 1993.

FOX, Matthew, ed. *Western Spirituality: Historical Roots, Ecumenical Routes.* Santa Fe, NM: Bear & Co., 1981.

GALLAND, China. *Longing for Darkness: Tara and the Black Madonna.* New York: Penguin Books, 1990.

GIMBUTAS, Marija. *The Goddesses and Gods of Old Europe: Myths and Cult Images.* Berkeley, CA: University of California Press, 1989.

HICK, John. *God Has Many Names.* Philadelphia: Westminster Press, 1980.

———. *The Myth of Christian Uniqueness.* Maryknoll NY: Orbis Books, 1989.

———. and Paul F. Knitter, eds. *The Myth of Christian Uniqueness.* London: SCM Press, Ltd., 1987.

HOUSTON, Jean. *Godseed.* Wheaton, IL: Quest, 1992.

JOHNSON, Elizabeth. *She Who Is: The Mystery of God in Feminist Theological Discourse.* New York: Crossroad, 1993.

JOHNSON, William. *The Mysticism of the Cloud of Unknowing: A Modern Interpretation.* St. Meinrad, IN: Abbey Press, 1967.

JOHNSON, Woodbridge O. *Other Christs.* New York: Pageant Press International Corp., 1971.

KADLONBOVSKY, E. and Palmer, G.E.H., trans. *Early Fathers from the Philokalia.* London, Faber and Faber, 1954.4

KADOWAKI, J.K. *Zen and the Bible: A Priest's Experience.* London: Routledge & Kegan Paul, 1982.

KING, Theresa, ed. *The Spiral Path: Explorations in Women's Spirituality.* St. Paul, MN: Yes International Publishers, 1992.

KINSLEY, David. *Hindu Goddesses: Visions of the Divine Feminine in the Hindu Religious Tradition.* Berkeley: University of California Press, 1986.

KNITTER, Paul F. *No Other Name? A Critical Survey of Christian Attitudes Toward the World Religions.* Maryknoll, NY: Orbis Books, 1985.

KÜNG, Hans. *Does God Exist?* NY: Vintage Books, 1981.

LEMEE, Jean, trans. *Hymns from the Rig Veda*. New York: Alfred A. Knopf, 1975.

LOY, David. *Pointing at the Moon*. Malaysia: Buddhist Digest, 1985.

MCFAGUE, Sallie. *Models of God*. Philadelphia: Fortress Press, 1987.

MCGAA, Ed. *Mother Earth Spirituality: Native American Paths to Healing Ourselves and Our World*. San Francisco: Harper Row, 1990.

MCVEIGH, Malcolm. *God in Africa*. Hartford, VT: Claude Stark, 1974.

MAITLAND, Sara. *A Map of the New Country: Women and Christianity*. London: Routledge and Kegan Paul, 1983.

MARKALE, Jean. *Women of the Celts*. Rochester, VT: Inner Traditions International, Ltd., 1972.

MEDICINE EAGLE, Brooke. *Buffalo Woman Comes Singing*. New York: Ballantine Books, 1991.

MURPHY, Joseph M. *Santeria: An African Religion in America*. Boston: Beacon Press, 1989.

NASAR, Seyyed Hossein, ed. *Islamic Spirituality: Foundations*. London: Routledge & Kegan Paul, 1987.

NATIONAL Geographic Society. *Great Religions of the World*. Washington, D.C.: 1971.

O'BRIEN, Justin. *Christianity and Yoga: A Meeting of Mystic Paths*. London: Arkana, 1989.

PANIKKAR, Raimundo. *The Vedic Experience Mantramañjari: An Anthology of the Vedas for Modern Man and Contemporary Celebration*. Berkeley, CA: University of California Press, 1977.

———. *Worship and Secular Man*. Maryknoll, NY: Orbis Books, 1973.

PARRINDER, Geoffrey. *Avatar and Incarnation: The Wild Lectures in Natural and Comparative Religion in the University of Oxford*. London: Faber & Faber, 1970.

PELIKAN, Jaroslav, ed. *The World Treasury of Modern Religious Thought*. Boston: Little, Brown and Co., 1990.

PEREIRA, José, ed. *Hindu Theology: A Reader*. Garden City, NY: Image Books, 1976.

PHILLIPS, J.B. *Your God is too Small*. New York: MacMillian Press, 1961.

PONCÉ, Charles. *Kabbalah: An Introduction and Illumination for the World Today*. Wheaton, IL: Theosophical Publishing House, 1973.

RAMA, Swami, et al. *Meditation in Christianity*. Honesdale, PA: The Himalayan Press, 1983.

RIMPOCHE, Sogyal. *The Tibetan Book of Living and Dying*. San Francisco: Harper San Francisco, 1992.

ROBERTS, Bernadette. *The Experience of No-Self: A Contemplative Journey*. Boulder, CO: Shambhala Publications, Inc., 1982.

ROBINSON, John A. *Exploration into God*. Stanford, CA: Stanford University Press, 1967.

ROBINSON, Richard H. and Johnson, Willard. *The Buddhist Religion: A Historical Introduction*. Belmont, CA: Wadsworth, 1982.

SHARMA, Arvind. ed. *Women in World Religions*. Albany, NY: State University of New York Press, 1987.

SHEA, John. *Stories of God: An Unauthorized Biography*. Chicago, IL: The Thomas More Press, 1978.

SCHÜSSLER Fiorenza, Elizabeth. *In Memory of Her: A Feminist Theological*

Reconstruction of Christian Origins. New York: Crossroad, 1987.
SINGH, Satya Prakash, Ph.D. *Sri Aurobindo and Whitehead on the Nature of God.* India: Vigyan Press, 1972.
SONTAG, Fredertick and Darrol Bryant. *God.* New York: The Rose of Sharon Press, 1982.
SPRETNAK, Charlene. *Lost Goddesses of Early Greece: A Collection of Pre-Hellenic Myths.* Boston: Beacon Press, 1978.
————. *States of Grace: The Recovery of Meaning in the Postmodern Age.* San Francisco: Harper San Francisco, 1991.
SPRING-WIND Buddhist Cultural Forum. *Women and Buddhism.* Canada: 1986.
STARHAWK. *The Spiral Dance: A Rebirth of the Ancient Religion of the Great Goddess.* San Francisco: Harper & Row, 1979.
STEUER, Axel, McClendon, James, eds. *Is God God?* Nashville, TN: Abiugdon, 1981.
TEISH, Luisah. *Jambalaya: The Natural Woman's Book of Personal Charms and Practical Rituals.* San Francisco: Harper, 1985.
THISTLETHWAITE, Susan Brooks. *Sex, Race, and God: Christian Feminism in Black and White.* New York: Crossroad, 1989.
UNDERHILL, Evelyn. *Mysticism.* NY: Meridian Press, 1955.
WARD, Keith. *The Concept of God.* New York: St. Martin's Press, 1974.
WORTHINGTON, Vivian. *A History of Yoga.* London: Arkana, 1982.
YUNGBLUT, John R. *Discovering God Within.* Philadelphia: Westminster Press, 1979.
ZUBIRI, Xavier. *Nature, History, God.* Lanhan, MD: University Press of America, 1981.

Adonai Zeus Shekhinah Elim Ogun Kat Buddha
Wyame Hel Rama Mitra Odomankoma Jupiter Het
Heru Agni Cagn Thor Brahma Tangaroa Father
Lugaba Papang Diana Al-Rahman Cerridwen Ahone
Yoma' Tirawa Atius Ganesha El Mungan-ngua
Quetzalcoatl Hamakom Ribbono shel-olam Shaddai
Atibruku Moma YH Bunjil Harahaman Watauinaiwa
Saraswati Inanna Mirirul Puluga Gicelamu'kaong
Tonantzin Yuskeha Bhavatarini Father White Head
Olodumare Shyama Ekvamkar Waq Hatzur Heru
Nurrundere Daramilun Adon Ca Vishnu HaYotzeir
Hecate Chi Musubi Hintubuhet Ausar Ti Ubusuna
Nanderuvucu Erishkigal Laxha Yahweh Brahman
Tsui-goab Ometeotl Osiris Aum Huitzilopochtli
Surya Elohim Nyankopon-Onyankopon Rudra Ilu
Woden Great Spirit Lesa Boyjerh El Dan Gongoro
Poseidon Chineke Nhialic Aciek Kari Auset Tcuwut
Makai Wakantanka Inari Ha-Qadosh barukh hu'
Tara Krishna Avaloket-iswara Rabb Goryo Qat Oke
Nurunderi Indra Shang-ti Amaterasu Ohmikami
Kannon Quan Yin Ise Lakshmi Awonawilona Bast
Omecihuatl Ruhanga Kosane Sophia Dionysus Ixchel
Mawu Ra Ardanariswara Oluwa Deng Hanuman
uNkulunkulu Kanobo Ngai Shamayim Cybele Dakini
Nataraj Pachamama Susanoo Katonda Avlukpo Eloah
Isis Temaukel Eleda Gaia Laxmi Mahmanmu-rok
Odin El-al Herukhuti Viracocha Marduk Ashira Biral
Shaddai Dzingbe Djohu-ma-di-hutu Astarte Ndengei
Koyatu Baha'u'llah Marrigan Baiame Om Pelepelewa
Durga Orisha Nyame Techaronhiawakhon Chukwu
Uvolovu Brahman Nephtys Ha-Maqom Tehuti Maat
Digambara Val Tik Chaitanya Amana Kwoth Num
Colok Nabango Fumeripitsj Shiva Varuna Lukanga
Bala Atibluku Karu Allah Sing Nainuema Artemis
Kartikeya Kuanyin Yelafaz T'ien Baal Shakti
Athena Olorun Nemesis Sheela-na-Gig Bhavartarini
Jesus Horus Izanagi Sebek Waq Ishtar Ti Seker
BegoTanutanu Sat Nam Kali Mirirul Bhavatarini
Tsui-goab Hatzur Brahman Ubusuna Tonantzin
YHVH Apollo Nana God Almighty Hu Vishnu Om